# Modernity's Wager

# Modernity's Wager

AUTHORITY, THE SELF,
AND TRANSCENDENCE

*Adam B. Seligman*

PRINCETON UNIVERSITY PRESS

PRINCETON AND OXFORD

Published by Princeton University Press, 41 William Street,
Princeton, New Jersey 08540
In the United Kingdom: Princeton University Press,
3 Market Place, Woodstock, Oxfordshire OX20 1SY

*Library of Congress Cataloging-in-Publication Data*

Seligman, A.
Modernity's wager: authority, the self, and transcendence.
p.   cm.
Includes bibliographical references and index.
ISBN 0-691-05061-9 (CL : alk.paper)
1. Authority.   2. Self.   3. Transcendence (Philosophy).
I.  Title.

HM1251 .S45 2000
303.3′6—dc21        00-027418

This book has been composed in Baskerville

The paper used in this publication meets the minimum requirements
of ANSI/NISO Z39.48-1992 (R1997) (*Permanence of Paper*)

www.pup.princeton.edu

Printed in the United States of America

1   3   5   7   9   10   8   6   4   2

I have not written this book to teach the reader anything new. Rather is it my aim to direct his attention to certain well known and generally accepted truths, for the very fact that they are well known and generally accepted is the cause of their being overlooked.

—Moses Hayyim Luzzatto, *Mesillat Yesharim*

# CONTENTS

## PREFACE AND ACKNOWLEDGMENTS

AUTHORITY and the need for authority are irrevocable aspects of self and of the human condition. This remains the case even after more than a century of belief in the secular, democratic message of modernity. The following is an attempt to come to terms with this truth as well as to explain the particular difficulties we moderns have with the idea of authority. In fact, the idea of authority is so inimicable to the assumptions of most secular Western intellectuals that we have lost our ability to understand its continuing force in so many parts of the world, including our own. Establishing the connection of authority to certain critical aspects of self-identity will, I hope, contribute to a greater understanding of authority and its continuing resonance in today's world.

There is a wonderful sentence at the very end of Martin Hollis's *Reason in Action* where he posits the "epistemological unity of mankind which involves recognizing that the actor's moral identity is at stake in every action." While I am not convinced that this is true of every action it could nevertheless be the guiding epigram for this book. For in making the argument for authority and for the need to take authority seriously in any account of the self, I am indeed invoking an "epistemological unity" to human experience. Modern, rational, calculative, and post-Cartesian individuals no less than traditional, communal, and collectively "constituted" individuals all rest their sense of self on an external, expressive, and authoritative set of assumptions and moral orientations. In *Sources of the Self*, Charles Taylor notes how selfhood and morality are "inextricably intertwined." Here, I stress the authority of the moral and how certain ideas of selfhood can in fact vitiate that authority and with it any idea of morality. In a word, the argument which follows is that, without a sacred locus of self, any attempt to account for action cannot rise beyond the purely calculative, power-orientated acts of utility maximization. If the self has a sacred locus, however, then it must be an authoritative one as well, for what is the sacred if not authoritative? Though the above sentences are no doubt tautological, that does not as such make them any less true, and to engage the debate over ends and means that inheres in all arguments over tautology would in fact be to beg the fundamental questions of the following chapters.

Originating from within the social sciences, the argument of these chapters necessarily goes beyond them, though just how far short of theology it falls I am not sure. From the writings of Marcel Gauchet in *The Disillusionment of the World* to a renewed interest in the works of Leo

Strauss, a new sensitivity or at the very least curiosity about issues of authority does seem to have returned to the workshops of the social scientists and other laborers in the smithy of the mind. Indeed, the contemporary debate over Strauss—was he a Jewish philosopher or a philosopher
who happened to be Jewish?—is one that Strauss himself would have
recognized as about the respective places of philosophy and revelation
and is itself an indication of these stirrings. Similarly, recent works such
as O'Donovan's attempt to create a modern Christian political theology
(in his *Desire of the Nations*) or the four-volume reader on rabbinic political thought that Michael Walzer and others are publishing (and whose
first volume is dedicated to the theme of *authority*) are, I believe, all indications of this trend.

Ultimately, I take these as indicators or illustrations of the thesis
worked out in the following pages, that a purely autonomous and atomistic view of the self is insufficient, not only on the prescriptive level, but
equally on the descriptive level, incapable finally of giving a proper account of human action in the world. For that we must return to that
concept we moderns so instinctively reject, to the idea of authority as an
essential aspect of life in the world. As noted by Philip Rieff, who was
exquisitely sensitive to the issues analyzed here, "From authority itself
there is no escape." And once having recognized that, we must begin the
laborious work of answering its call, but without retreating from the rule
of reason, without which we would be condemned to the most Goyaesque
of dreams.

My own understanding of these issues has been greatly influenced by
years of continual debate with my social choice nemesis, Mark Lichbach.
I am grateful for his ongoing critique. Both John Holmwood and
Shlomo Fischer found the time to read the text carefully and comment
on it sagaciously. My debt to them both only grows with the passage of
time. Paula Fredriksen has done her best to keep me from making too
many egregious mistakes in my interpretation of Paul, as Jonathan
Imber has in my presentation of social theory. It would be a poorer
effort but for their help. The importance of the problem of moral luck
and related issues to the concerns of authority and the self developed
from a series of most stimulating conversations with Luis Castro Leiva,
first in Caracas and then in Boston. His sudden and tragic passing this
past year leaves us all much diminished both as scholars and as citizens.
Shmuel Eisenstadt kindly found the time to read and comment on the
whole of the manuscript with his usual and extraordinary percipiency.
As in the past, my colleagues at the Institute for the Study of Economic
Culture at Boston University have continued to provide an environment

of both careful criticism and intellectual nourishment. Some of the arguments developed in chapter five first appeared in *Society* (36, no. 5 [1999]: 7–8). Finally, I would like to thank all the participants in the two "Toleration Project" workshops in Berlin and Vienna (where the issues dealt with in chapter five were hammered out), who provided the depth and grace necessary to begin rethinking our received wisdom on the issue of toleration.

It was eighteen years ago in Jerusalem that I began my work, essentially as an apprentice in sociology, with the old question of Werner Sombart: "Why is there no socialism in the U.S.A.?" In the early 1980s that question maintained the same resonances it had had from the beginning of the century. Today, by century's end, however, the very cognitive, moral, and social contexts within which the question was posed for nearly one hundred years no longer make sense. They simply do not exist. So complete was its failure that few even recall the dream.

It was, however, in an attempt to answer that question that I began my studies of Puritan thought, searching for the roots of an individualism that, from the perspective of Jerusalem and of the intractable conflict between Jews and Palestinians, appeared so salvific. From the Hebrew University campus on Mount Scopus every Friday in 1989, one could see the Old City enveloped in clouds of tear gas and hear the wail of the ambulances on their way to the hospitals. From such a "Cittie upon a Hill," Samuel Sewall's Plum Island in his *Phenomena quedom Apocalyptica* (1697) surely seemed "the Inheritance of the Saints of Light."

The stone streets of Jerusalem were, however, soon replaced by the asphalt freeways of Los Angeles and with them the challenge of understanding just what held such seemingly autonomous selves together at all. How from Puritan selves, albeit highly secular and post-modern ones, was a society nevertheless constituted? Grappling with this question sent me not only to eighteenth-century political economy but also to Budapest, which, as with many other Eastern European societies in 1990, was struggling with these questions with an urgency and vigor that had intimations of historical greatness (alas unfulfilled).

From these encounters came my work on civil society and with it the realization that the real philosophical problem of civil society is the problem of trust. And somehow I cannot disengage my pursuit of an understanding of trust from *The Autobiography of Henry Adams*. More than most, Adams understood the modern age and especially the apotheosis of modernity in the United States of America, as well as the transformation of American mores and morals that made modernity possible. Somewhere between the Virgin and the Dynamo the problem of trust emerged and with it the contradictions of individual freedom in the modern world.

For trust, I soon learned, had to do most of all with human agency, and agency stands but darkly between veils of either authority or power.

Hence the current project, an attempt to unravel the skeins of agency, which, in its unraveling, has laid bare as well the skeletal assumptions of the social sciences *tout court*. The phenomenology of agency has led beyond modernity, beyond the Puritans to assumptions of self and society that stand in inimicable relation to the whole epistemological edifice of modern social and political thought.

In a sense, then, I feel I am here closing a chapter, one that began eighteen years ago in Jerusalem. From the problem of Puritan individualism, I was forced to contemplate the possible forms of solidarity between such individuals (hence the early modern idea of civil society), from that to the problem of trust (within societies), and thence to the nature of said individuals, trusting or not. Each answer opened up new questions as a line of thought was (I wish I could say relentlessly) pursued. And while it is no doubt true that the issue of authority raised here brings in its wake the necessity to pursue the foundations of tolerance, some tentative closure has nevertheless been reached.

I was once asked what it was like to write a dissertation with Shmuel Noah Eisenstadt. I replied that he asked me a question. It took me four years to answer it, and that was my dissertation. Well, that was not quite correct. For it has taken more like fourteen years to answer, and even so the answer, spread over numerous books and articles, is provisional at best. It is an answer, though, ironically one arrived at here, by the Charles River where I had, so long ago and so foolishly, thought so many answers were to be found. I simply had the domain assumptions slightly askew.

The following is both a questioning and an attempt to reinterpret precisely those domain assumptions on the nature of the self and hence, of necessity, of the relations between selves.

*Newton, Massachusetts*

# Modernity's Wager

# INTRODUCTION

From ancient Babylon to contemporary Indonesia, from China to Canada, and from the Inuit to the Parisian, all peoples and societies have experienced power and its differential distribution. Defined by Max Weber as "the probability that one actor within a social relationship will be in a position to carry out his own will despite resistance," power has been a fact of social life from time out of mind.[1]

Like people everywhere and in all ages, most members of modern societies readily understand the workings of power. Power and power differentials are everywhere. We are schooled in its uses and abuses. We ascertain its trappings. We know who wields it and who does not. We are, in this country anyway, concerned about spreading it around more fairly, as can be seen by the pervasive rhetoric of empowerment.

One thing that sets modern society apart from most other peoples and places, however, is the difficulty its members have in appreciating and fully understanding one of power's cognate terms: *authority*. This book is about authority and the need to sensitize ourselves to its resonances despite our impulses to the contrary. It sets out and develops four major claims about authority and its relation to self-identities, as follows:

1. Modernity, whether in the form of liberal politics, capitalist exchange, or the epistemologies of the social sciences, is inherently hostile to the idea and experience of authority and as a result has difficulty understanding its persistence.
2. Despite this aversion of modern politics and society to authority, any account of the self that does not include an account of authority will ultimately fail to explain human action and experience in the world.
3. We ignore the phenomenon of authority at our peril, for by so doing we fail to recognize the import of the reemergence of ethnic, religious, and primordial identities in today's global culture.
4. By establishing the necessary connection of authority to ideas of selfhood through such phenomena as community and the sacred, this book hopes to resensitize us to this ineliminable aspect of our existence while at the same time maintaining commitments to democracy, pluralism, and tolerance.

The remainder of the introduction is devoted to a preliminary clarification of the above points.

The idea of authority is traditionally defined as legitimate power, that is, as power which is seen as fairly exercised or justly wielded. Authority, then, with its attendant association of legitimacy, stands in contradistinction to power *simpliciter*. It was Max Weber who offered a succinct and powerful formulation of the two possible foundations of legitimacy.

The first he terms *subjective* and the second *external*. Weber posits the three possible bases of the *subjective* as follows: "1) affectual: resulting from emotional surrender; or 2) value-rational: determined by the belief in the absolute validity of the order as the expression of ultimate values of an ethical or esthetic or of any other type; or 3) religious: determined by the belief that salvation depends upon obedience to the order." The *external* bases of legitimacy he defines as "guaranteed by the expectation of specific external effects, that is, by interest situations."[2]

To a great extent, modern, liberal societies have come to base their legitimacy on the second, *external* source, upon a politics of interest, as delineated in the writings of Hobbes and Hume. As a result, people living in these societies find it difficult to understand and empathize with the motives and motivations of people for whom the other set of justifying practices—those rooted in ultimate and more usually in sacred values—provides the foundations of legitimacy and hence of authority.

Motives and motivations are central here. For authority to exist, as opposed to power, the legitimacy of its actions must be registered in the subjective experience and consciousness of the actors. Whereas power rests solely on the coercion of the will, authority rests on what Weber has called the "inner justification" of dominion.[3] This inner, subjective experience is at the heart of the phenomenon of authority. In fact, if we can grasp the relevance of Weber's two modes of legitimacy in terms of this subjective experience, we are at least on the way to understanding why most secular liberal members of modern societies have such difficulty understanding authority in other social settings.

We in modern societies accept the existence of power differentials, accept the need to coerce our will, in order to fulfill certain needs or attain certain goals. In the language of social choice theory, we rein in our wills in order to maximize certain utilities. Hence, we obey the doctor's exhortations to refrain from smoking and limit our drinking; we abide the boring professor in order to complete the course and get a high grade; we do not tell our customer what we really think of her because we want her business; and we vote for a candidate whose behavior appalls us, because we believe our interests will be best served by this politician rather than that one. In the specific settings of "authority" relations then—with teachers, politicians, and even business colleagues—we bend our will to theirs not out of belief in the salvation of our souls or in a set of *ultimate values*. Nor do we accept their dictates out of the "disinterested motives" to which Weber referred in his first "affectual" category of subjective legitimacy.[4]

Quite the opposite. We accept the authority of those wielding power because over the long run it is in our interest to do so. Specific instances of such relations may be defined by the workings of pure power. But even when it is not power that is at play but rather some form of the legitimate nature of the exchange, the legitimacy is rooted in interests. Moreover, as Ralf Dahrendorf observed more than a generation ago, most people in modern societies are differentially distributed into different power groupings (what he termed "Imperatively Coordinated Associations," based on Weber's *Herrschaftsverbund*) so that in some groups we may be near the top of the power pyramid and in others near the bottom.[5] No cosmological significance is attributed to these differences, no weight in terms of ultimate and sacred values. The categories represent only competencies and their social valuation. We are better at some things that society rewards more or less highly, less successful at others, and the differences are mediated by different forms of exchange. Distinctions are, that is, about nothing more than utility functions. And such for most of us is the basis of the social order: not God's will, not the salvation of our souls, not the realization of ultimate values, but simply the satisfaction of interests.

This has been the traditional *economistic* reading of society and the social order, one that has made quite some headway in the social sciences in the form of social choice and rational choice theory. It is, as Brian Barry put it some thirty years ago, an essentially "Benthamite" understanding of society.

> Its most important assumptions are: that men tend to act rationally in the pursuit of their ends; that most men in all societies want power, status and economic goods; and that internalized restraints on the pursuit of these are less significant than sanctions which make use of them (public disapproval, legal punishments etc.). Its characteristic method of proceeding is to work out how men rationally pursuing power, status and economic goods would behave in a certain set-up, and then to suggest that men in the real word behave sufficiently similarly to make the conclusions applicable.[6]

In this understanding we are dealing therefore not with inner restraints but with external coercion of our will, either by the threat of sanctions or the need to fulfill interests. Its opposite number is that other, "innerly justified" disinterested acceptance of authority predicated not on external concerns but on internal ones. This is not a will coerced (from without) but a will subjugated (from within). One would hardly say of the observant Orthodox Jew who refused to eat pork and the observant Muslim who refused to drink wine that they were coerced from without. Rather one would say that they accepted the law's authority and subjugated themselves to it from within. It would in fact be difficult to describe their actions in terms of maximizing utilities or obtaining a set of discrete goods. They were simply being what they are, being themselves. An observant Jew or Muslim could not remain such and at the same time become an eater of pork. If they did, they would become something different. Now moving from being an observant Jew or Muslim to being a nonobservant one is something quite different from changing one's profession from electrician to tennis pro. What makes it different is precisely the acceptance of a certain authority as a critical component of self-identity.

The point here is simple, that ideas of authority and of self are inseparable, as certain understandings of self imply certain understandings of authority. The opposite is of course also the case. Hence when moderns adhere to certain Benthamite ideas of the self, implied as well are certain ideas about authority, as essentially predicated on the fulfillment of interests. Similarly, when we advance or advocate values and beliefs in a more equal distribution of power and eschew any idea of a more innerly justified authority, we also signal certain ideas of the self and of relations between selves. Most broadly put, this modern idea of the self is an autonomous, atomistic, and self-regulating moral agent endowed with rights. And relations between selves are seen in terms of an exchange based on the mutual interests of the contracting parties. These views are held so absolutely that they shackle our imagination and understanding of other notions of selves or of authority, specifically such as are innerly justified.

This state of affairs is unfortunate for at least two reasons. On the purely intellectual side, it makes it difficult for the social sciences and indeed for important parts of philosophy to explain human action in terms of anything but purely calculative, power-oriented acts of utility maximization and corresponding notions of negotiation and exchange. But what of such powerful motivations as shame and pride or collective guilt and responsibility, or even the attempt to rationalize and "tame" luck or *fortuna?* These, unfortunately, are left under-problematized and misunderstood.

On the more substantive level, the rational choice position leaves us without an explanation for a key cultural component of globalization— the reemergence of salient religious identities and commitments in many parts of the world. Indeed, we find in contemporary India, Israel, Algeria, Turkey, Egypt, the Balkans, Latin America, and Eastern Europe a renewed vigor in many different forms of (mostly) revealed religion that no one would have imagined a generation ago. Moreover, the areas where this revival occurs are also the sites of great conflict and often of war and terrorism. These contemporary developments force us to retreat from the "secularization thesis" of the 1960s, which held that modernization went hand in hand with secularization. Not surprisingly, too, this resurgence of religious identities has been noted in much scholarly literature—from the Fundamentalism Project at the University of Chicago to David Martin's work on evangelical Christianity in Latin America, to the influential works of Samuel Huntington and of Benjamin Barber.[7] These are but some of the more popular and widely disseminated works on the new religious consciousness. What is unquestionable is that one aspect of globalization is the rise of a new religious consciousness that cuts across existing modes of identity, commitment, and senses of national community.

At the same time increasing attention is being paid to issues of collective responsibility as we see in the Truth and Reconciliation Committee in South Africa, the War Crimes Tribunal in the Hague, the *lustration* process in the former Czechoslovakia, the ongoing concern with responsibility for the crimes of the Holocaust, even the struggle to extradite Pinochet to Spain to stand trial for events of the 1970s in Chile. This is perhaps the defining issue of life in Bosnia and Herzegovina today, though it is equally important in France in the myriad discussions and debates over French responsibility for both Vichy and Algeria. The current academic interest in the problem of evil captures aspects of this problem of individual and collective responsibility as well.

The confluence of all these issues undermines the liberal vision of community founded on the radical autonomy of the individual. Even in the United States the idea of the liberal self is under attack by a host of forces, from the Christian Coalition to the communitarian movement. What is the attraction of these forces in a world that, after all, is more and more identified with pluralistic societal structures, equalitarian ideas of individual rights, and market economies oriented to the choice and actions of individual economic actors? A more nuanced and sophisticated inquiry into the reemergent religious consciousness must thus be offered. Any simple equating of religion with fundamentalism just won't do. Such an inquiry can most usefully be achieved by analyzing the connection between authority and self-identity so commonly found in religion. However, this connection is so inimicable to our modernist, often social scientific understanding that we must begin by addressing the objections raised by that perspective. We must, as it were, clear the way before we can come to appreciate a mode of being and understanding ourselves that has become foreign to many of us.

Let us begin with those ideas of self that lie at the basis of social scientific inquiry, a mode of thought that developed together with modernist (and generally democratic) sensibilities in many parts of the world, for example, in the France of the Third Republic, the Chicago of the Progressive Era, or the Turkey of Ataturk. The debates that today define and shape the disciplines of the social sciences—over structure and agency, rational action, social choice models, and the structure/agency debate—all are refractions of the politics of democratic practice. They inform struggles over entitlements, affirmative action, distributive justice, and the state, as well as over local communities, identities, and commitments.

The assumptions of modern, democratic, and liberal political practice are integral to the social sciences. This is true of the more agent-orientated theoretical assumptions of Mancur Olson or Kenneth Arrow, as well as of the more collectivist and culturalist orientation rooted in the sociologies of Emile Durkheim and Talcott Parsons. In fact, in chapter one I argue that this congruence of political ideology and scientific practice can be found most saliently in the concept of social role. And that once social scientists make use of the concept of *social role*, which they must, to discuss *social structure* in any meaningful way, they become locked into a particular epistemology that prejudices their ability to understand the place of authority in constituting individual selves. Even differences between rational choice and more culturalist approaches pale in significance before their more fundamentally shared assumptions on personal identity and selfhood.

This is not to say that such approaches are inherently false. But their assumptions about the nature of the self and its relation with others, rooted as they are in the political assumptions of modernity, are seriously circumscribed and of only limited value when analyzing the "revolt against modernity" characterized by nonmodern modes of action and existence, including those motivated by religious commitments and ethnic, primordial identities. To fathom such identities we need to develop an empathy with a kind of self that is in its essence foreign to us, as citizens and as scholars.

Arising out of a skepticism toward the ethical systems of Aristotelian and neo-Thomistic thought, the modern idea of the self was given its best expression by Bernard de Mandeville at the beginning of the eighteenth century. He wrote:

> man centers every thing in himself, and neither loves nor hates, but for his own Sake. . . . Every individual is a little World by itself, and all Creatures, as far as their Understanding and Abilities will let them, endeavor to make that Self happy: This in all of them is the continual Labour, and seems to be the whole Design of Life. Hence it follows, that in the Choice of Things Men

must be determined by the Perception they have of Happiness; and no Person can commit or set about an Action, which at that then present time seems not [to] be the best to him.[8]

The social bonds existing between such agents were characterized not long afterward by Hume in this now famous quote:

Your corn is ripe today; mine will be so to-morrow. 'Tis profitable for us both, that I shou'd labour with you today, and that you shou'd aid me to-morrow. I have no kindness for you, and know you have as little for me.... Hence I learn to do a service to another, without bearing him any real kindness; because I foresee, that he will return my service, in expectation of another of the same kind, and in order to maintain the same correspondence of good offices with me or with others.[9]

This is a vision of a society regulated, not by any shared moral commitments nor by any Thomistic hierarchy of natural and divine law, but simply by the workings and pursuit of interest.

Finally, the adjudication of disputes between such self-regulating and autonomous agents was, in Adam Smith's words, achieved through appeal "to the eyes of the third party, that impartial spectator, the great inmate of the breast who judges impartially between conflicting interests." In Smith's terms:

We endeavor to examine our own conduct as we imagine any other fair and impartial spectator would examine it. If, upon placing ourselves in his situation, we thoroughly enter into all the passions and motives which influenced it, we approve of it, by sympathy with the approbation of this supposed equitable judge. If otherwise, we enter into his disapprobation and condemn it.[10]

Before we can make any proper comparison of opposing interests, we must change our position. We must view them from neither our own place nor yet from his, neither with our own eyes nor yet with his, but from the place and with the eyes of a third person, who has no particular connection with either, and who judges impartially between us.[11]

Mandeville, Hume, and Smith, taken together, allow us to "triangulate" the terms of modern politics as well as of the social sciences. Their perspective defines an orientation based on the autonomous, contracting individual engaged in exchange with other such individuals. They adjudicate their differences on the basis of negotiation.

We are so embedded in this world that a world of authority and a sacred locus beyond the realms of negotiation and exchange—the world of increasing numbers of our contemporaries—is one that many of us can grasp only with difficulty. Some idea of a self as constituted by goods internal to it, rather than simply as a maximizer of utility functions (i.e., goods) external to it, is therefore presented here as a necessary corrective to the prevalent overemphasis on the idea of the individual as morally autonomous and self-regulated. The hope is to get beyond the conventional dichotomies of authority and autonomy that have become the touchstones of a secular, Enlightenment conscience.

Authoritative, sacred values are, of course, linked to modes of communal identity, boundaries, commitments, and desiderata. In the broadest of terms, different forms of community can be parsed into those resting on *primordial, civic,* and *transcendent* identities and principles, respectively.[12] Different ideas of the sacred and of communal membership are represented as well in different principles of generalized exchange, which mediate the workings of market and negotiation.[13] Thus the principles of kinship solidarity "trump" the workings of market rationality in very different ways than do those of liberal individualism, which are, in turn, of a very different order from those predicated on transcendent values and Godly dictates. In slightly altered terms, potlatch is as different from child labor laws as both are from prohibitions against usury.

Matthew Arnold once defined righteousness as the "not ourselves." Although that "not ourselves" can take many forms, the most "not ourselves" that we can conceive is the transcendent. For transcendence is the most radical form of heteronomy, with heteronomy understood as subject to the authority of another, to an external law. Not surprisingly, then, the discovery of transcendence in the period that the philosopher Karl Jaspers termed the "Axial Age" (roughly between 500 B.C.E. and 600 C.E.) played a critical role in reframing and constituting our ideas of authority as well as of the self.[14] The contemporary return to modes of self-identity predicated on such a basis, as well as on more primordially defined forms of collectivity, is to be understood in terms of a reaction or revolt against modernity and those forms of liberal individualist community most associated with the project of modernity. In fact, one of the arguments presented here is that it is the very spread of modern principles of self and of community (that triangulated vision noted above) in the social and political realms that calls forth its own antithesis. Civic community, that is, engenders its own ghosts in the form of renewed ethnic and religious allegiances.

To understand just why this is so we must explore aspects of existence not given their due in modern, liberal visions of self and community. These are aspects that turn on emotions such as shame, pride, collective guilt, and collective responsibility—ideas that cannot be comfortably understood in terms of autonomy and self-regulation. It is an idea of ethical being at odds with the regnant Mandevillian and Humean assumptions, an idea of a constituted self that ties one to others in a way that is beyond the calculations of pure exchange. It is this vision of self that is at the core of the very contemporary "politics of identity," that is, of mutual recognition, which fully autonomous and self-regulating selves would, presumably, be able to do well without.

As children in the United States, we grew up with the phrase "sticks and stones may break my bones, but names will never harm me." In the Middle East, just the opposite saying holds: "Wounds heal, but words hurt forever." Different ideas of the self and of the self's relation with others are contained in these sayings. The one is autonomous, where all that can be hurt by others is the physical 'shell'. The core, what is inside and internal, remains forever inviolable. The other is open to the interlocutor. The 'inside' is in endless and often dangerous dialogue and confrontation with the external world. However, as we know from the often vociferous contemporary debates around multiculturalism and identity politics, it is not only in the Middle East that these modes of community and of selfhood hold sway, but, increasingly, in our own society as well. Just how different our attempts to ban certain forms of speech as hateful, disrespectful, and hurtful to groups in the polity are from the Maldive Islands' banning of the animated movie *The Prince of Egypt* as disrespectful of Moses (and hence of Muslims), I am not sure. Both, however, have everything to do with "names" rather than "sticks and stones." Ultimately, the inability of liberal models of self to adequately account for central components of social and individual life is an issue not only in explaining social action in the Indian Ocean, but in the Rocky Mountains as well.

One aspect of the dichotomy between the different orientations of the self lies in how they variously privilege the internal and the external in understanding moral action. The modernist Kantian privileging of intent over action was challenged some twenty years ago in the accounts of Bernard Williams and Thomas Nagel of "moral luck." In these justly famous philosophical essays they critique that account of morality turning on the internal state of the agent—on intent rather than on the action itself and the environments of action. And Williams has continued to criticize the more modernist reading of moral action, with its slighting of the act and indeed of those other forces beyond our own control that nevertheless influence our action. He gives primacy to the workings of *fortuna* and *tyche* as constitutive components of ethical action. His is an understanding of the human agent much closer to the view offered here. Indeed, the issues of shame and honor and their dependence on action over which we exert no control or only minimal control are at the core of those contingent phenomena that play such a role in framing issues of moral luck. Shame, then, relates both to control and *fortuna* and to relations between selves who are not defined as autonomous. Put otherwise, the politics of recognition and identity is not far from the calculus of shame and honor.

Our own concepts of self and society are deeply tied to an idea of the self as interior, as tied up with intent, control of our actions, moral autonomy, and individual states of conscience. To no small extent, this modern, secular, and Enlightenment view is rooted in the Christian salvational drama and the progressive institutionalization of Christianity as a major world religion. As much as Hobbes feared and despised the Puritan sectaries, his own vision of the individual owed much to a reading of the self developed by Paul, Augustine, Luther, Calvin, and their seventeenth century followers. The moral autonomy of the rights-bearing modern citizen derives from the two-thousand-year-old transformation of the Jewish redemptive vision and the interiorization of its soteriological drama: from the community to the individual, from the realm of external acts to that of internal states. Paul on the law is as good a guide to our contemporary understanding and sensibility as are the writings of most social scientists and psychologists. And the road to the prisoner's dilemma and social choice theory passes through the internalized conscience and introspective self of Augustine, Luther, and the pietistic sects of the Protestant Reformation.

Marcel Mauss, Louis Dumont, and Charles Taylor have all recognized this theme and developed it in suggestive ways.[15] The autonomous (internalized) self and ultimately the rights-bearing citizen was the unintended, unplanned, and somewhat ironic consequence of Reformed religiosity. But so was the secular, disenchanted, transcendentless world, a world without sacrality and, to return to the theme with which we began, without authority.

The centerless world of radical secularization—this fundamentalist doctrine of enlightened reason—has called into being its own nemesis in the form of an often fundamentalist religiosity. Both are in a sense the outcomes of what I term *modernity's wager*. Pascal's wager of the seventeenth century, of reason for faith, was replaced in the eighteenth century by a wager over the terms of sacrality. Modern culture and politics, I argue, staked its all on the ability to construct an authoritative locus of sacrality on a foundation of transcendental rather than transcendent dictates. We have eschewed any idea of the revealed truth of a transcendent Being in favor of "self-evident" truths, thought to be as amenable to reason as the principles of Euclidian geometry. Emile Durkheim recognized this well when he noted that "since each of us incarnates something of humanity, each individual consciousness contains something divine and thus finds itself marked with a character which renders it sacred and inviolable to others."[16] We have wagered our idea of the sacred on beliefs in individual rights, rooted in reason and serving as the "touchstone of [our] morality," partaking in "transcendental majesty."[17] This appeal to reason as the sacred remains at the base of contemporary democratic and liberal ideas of citizenship, political order, and individual identities.

Whether such as this can support the armature of the sacred has been for some time open to question (think of Max Weber's critique of modern positive law doctrine).[18] Indeed it is increasingly uncertain that it is a wager that we shall win. For as religious dictates are coming increasingly to reshape the personal, social, and public behavior of men and women in many parts of the world, so is there increasing concern that these newly emerging (or reemerging) religious identities will erect barriers to tolerance, understanding, and the ability to coexist in mutual respect and recognition.

After all, the development of pluralism, democracy, and toleration in the West has been marked by a retreat of religion from the public arena, its privatization, and the general growth of secularization as the defining context of public life. Pluralism as a value implies the ability to exist together with other, competing visions of society and of the cosmos. It implies tolerance, not solely of error (what can perhaps be termed tolerance with a small *t*) but also of alternative and competing civilizational worldviews (tolerance with a capital *T*), with their own claims to the public sphere and the organization of communal life.

As society secularized, religion retreated from the public domain, reduced its claims on the public sphere, and became more and more a matter of the congregant's internal value disposition—with the result of a concomitant growth in tolerance of other faiths. But pluralism and tolerance seem to hold only as long as religion is privatized. To us, any other accommodation seems almost inconceivable.

However, this is only one historical path, the path taken by Western Christianity as it secularized. But is this model necessarily the only one? We have no reason to believe that the path of privatization in Judaism or Islam would be similar to that of Christianity, because the very terms of communal membership and individual identity are so different in these religions from what they are in a secularized Christian polity. Realizing this situation, what is presented here are the beginnings of a very different type of argument for tolerance and for pluralism, based not on a privatized conscience but on a skeptical one, on arguments of an epistemological modesty and a sense of humility as providing a foundation for mutual recognition, sympathy, and what the moralists of the Scottish Enlightenment termed benevolence.

These, then, are the major contours of the argument. It begins with a discussion of how different social scientific approaches view the individual and the nature of individual action (or agency in the parlance of the social sciences). The first chapter explores the assumptions that underlie the different approaches of rational actor models of self. These are then compared with more Durkheimian and culturalist constructions of the world of acting human selves.

Chapter two argues for a fundamentally expressive and constituted understanding of selves as humans constitute themselves and their world over against the contingencies of chance or *fortuna*. It charts out the three major terms of such constitutive identities—primordial, transcendent, and civic—each entailing its own idea of authority and so of community as well as of self.

Chapter three continues this argument and uses the themes of "moral luck," collective responsibility, and the experience of shame to argue for an extended, not fully autonomous understanding of self. This provides a deeper comprehension of personhood than more liberal-individualistic and autonomous readings. Derived from all of this is the idea of authority as that through which (and only through which) the self can come to exist.

Chapter four traces a history of our particular Western (and perforce Christian) notions of self from their origins in Pauline messianism (and the critical ways in which Saul of Tarsus transformed Judaism) through Augustine, Luther, and the traditions of sectarian Protestantism to the establishment of what are essentially secularized liberal "Protestant" ideas of selfhood. These are embodied within an idea of the sacred that is internalized and ultimately voided of the transcendent referent. Here as elsewhere, the argument is that such autonomous views are inadequate; that the loss of heteronomy and the interiorization of the sacred (and hence of authority) within the self leads ultimately to the demise of all ideas of authority and thus of the particular view of the self which attends on it.

Chapter five concludes by taking up the challenge inherent in all previous chapters, that is, of how to return to an appreciation of authority without at the same time returning to those absolutist and repressive modes of action that have been the hallmarks of societies paying at least lip service to authority. A position of tolerance is hence posited, one predicated on a certain idea of epistemological modesty and rational skepticism, a hesitant faith in the claims of an authority that is nevertheless recognized as such.

## Chapter One

# THE SELF IN THE SOCIAL SCIENCES

ONE OF THE more intractable problems in the social sciences is the problem of explaining human agency, or what is often termed the structure/action debate. The problem seems to crop up anew with each generation of practitioners, who have generated a small library on this problem alone. The very triumph of sociology, anthropology, and political science as disciplinary specialties has, however, been marked by a loss of certain categories of thought and by an ever increasing difficulty in expressing human existence in the world in terms of words and concepts that had, in a presociological era, stood at the core of all attempts to represent human existence to ourselves.

Absent from many contemporary social science bibliographies is the concept of *will*, which would seem to be intrinsic to what we generally understand by agency. And by the time we reach mid-century American sociology, the term can be found only among discussions of those "forerunners of social thought," such as Hobbes and Rousseau, that are often included in the introductory chapters of textbooks. For more contemporary discussions of *will*, however, one must go down the hall to the psychology department or attend to the often unspoken assumptions of social choice theorists and economists.

"Economics" it is said "is all about why people make choices, and sociology is all about why people have no choices to make." We may parse this quote out in either of two ways. First, we may view it historically. Economics as the more modern of sciences reflects the economic autonomy of the particular property owner, autonomy that emerges with the advent of capitalism. In this reading, sociology is but the inheritor of an older tradition of moral inquiry and social philosophy that roots man's existence in shared communities of value (Durkheim's conscience collective) that define the self. Or second, one may view these differences analytically. Thus economics, that mode of inquiry which begins with the "methodological individualism" of utility maximization, invokes a hermeneutic that is essentially psychological in nature and one that privileges individual passions, interests, and desiderata over collective structures, identities, and constructs. By contrast, sociology can only be structural and therefore must slight individual decision making and agency in favor of the patterned play of expectations and reciprocity that constitute the institutions of social life. The result is that the epistemological assumptions of each of these disciplines do not sit well together.[1] As Karl Marx noted long ago, "Men make their own history, but they do not make it just as they please." We do, willfully and purposefully, attempt to make history, social institutions, rules, and culture, yet these, in turn, continually make and remake us in the process. Thus Philip Abrams has pointed out:

> Taking and selling prisoners becomes the institutions of slavery. Offering one's services to a soldier in return for his protection becomes feudalism. Organizing the control of an enlarged labour force on the basis of standardized rules becomes bureaucracy. And slavery, feudalism and bureaucracy become the fixed, eternal settings in which struggles for prosperity or survival or freedom are then pursued. By substituting cash payment for labour services the lord and peasant jointly embark on the dismantling of the feudal order their great grandparents had constructed.[2]

While both structure and action may define social existence, all theoretical programs ultimately come down on the side of one or the other. In practice there is no coherent and internally consistent theoretical program that unites both. Hence if economics is the theory of agency par excellence, the different models of sociological reasoning are no less the benchmark of all theories of structure.

The problem with the sociological mode of reasoning was expressed perhaps most succinctly by Ralf Dahrendorf close to forty years ago, in his discussion of "sociological role."[3] When stripped of all theoretical baggage and normative debate, social roles are in essence nothing more nor less than the fundamental unit of the division of labor upon which any form of sociological inquiry must rest, whether implicitly or explicitly. And it matters not if one adopts a Marxist vocabulary of class or a Weberian nomenclature of status or if one studies deviance, the family, collective movements, or religion in China—the foundations of all these analyses are the same. Without such a concept of social role it is simply impossible to discuss society in any coherent fashion. The explanatory value of the concept of role is certainly great and supports the entire edifice of structural-functional sociological and anthropological reasoning—but at a very high cost, the cost of transcendental freedom. For Dahrendorf the cost of sociology becoming a science is "losing sight of people as human beings."[4] As he continues:

> As long as sociologists interpret their task in moral terms, they must renounce the analysis of social reality; as soon as they strive for scientific insight, they must forgo their moral concern with the individual and his liberty. What makes the paradox of moral and alienated man so urgent is not that sociology has strayed from its proper task, but that it has become a true

science. The former process would be reversible, but the latter leads to an inescapable question. Is man a social being whose behavior, being predetermined, is calculable and controllable? Or is he an autonomous individual, with some irreducible measure of freedom to act as he chooses?[5]

To this central question, Dahrendorf offers the following answer:

> Although the free, integral individual is not accessible to empirical research and cannot be, we know about him in ourselves and in others. And although the constructed, conditioned exemplar is based on the systematic study of phenomena, all the study in the world cannot make it more than a construction of the mind. . . . Whenever we deal with human beings, we must consider not only pure knowledge but the practical realm of morality, and in this realm our paradox changes from a question of knowledge that can be examined (or evaded) into a problem that must be faced before any meaningful progress can be made.[6]

Dahrendorf puts his finger on *the* problem of sociological reasoning: its inability to accommodate agency or the willful activity of role incumbents, while at the same time maintaining the necessarily systemic framework of its theoretical edifice.

Assuming the category of role, it becomes difficult to discuss human agency as something other than "deviance," as stepping out of proper role performance. There have been myriad attempts to elude this rather unpalatable conclusion. Robert Merton's work on deviance and nonconformism, for example, is an attempt to chart out a number of possible forms of role compliance in terms of differing structural conditions of role performance, or what Arthur Stinchcombe called "socially structured alternatives to role performance."[7] Such attempts, however, necessarily maintain the structural framework that ties individual action to the structural conditions of role incumbency. Other attempts at redefining role in a manner more compatible with the idea of agency abound. We may think of Ralph Turner and the symbolic-interactive school, whose roots lie in the work of George Herbert Mead and Charles Cooley.[8] In this tradition, social role is defined in much less structuralist terms and more in processual terms, as emerging out of interaction and reciprocity between role incumbents. This perspective has been defined most aptly by Turner as the move from "role taking to role making." Role taking, accordingly, is seen in terms of a "greater degree of selective emphasis" and is oriented less towards established, systemically defined norms and more toward the simple requirement of consistency in role performance.[9] Role expectation, in this view, is a process of interactive, inherently tentative behavior that is not prescribed by systemic constraints but rather is part of a continually unfolding configuration of cultural construction.[10]

To be sure, the two versions of social role assumed in the structural functionalist and interaction perspectives reflect not only two different sociologies but also two different and contradictory readings of human existence. In the one "man is indivisible and free," whereas in the other "man is an aggregate of roles and conditioned."[11] At their extremes the two positions are incompatible: if roles are labile, there cannot be social systems or even social institutions that exist over time; if roles are normatively prescribed only by system needs, one cannot explain the differences between roles and actual behavior or role incumbents.[12] Clearly then, norms exist in various degrees of institutionalization (either in different settings or at different times) and are concomitantly embedded to different degrees in different sets of mutual (role) expectations. Similarly, we have come to learn that the negotiability of roles is not an open-ended process (one does not show up to teach wearing a bathing suit) and that it is carried out within system limits, even though the system itself may come to be redefined (for example, as the women's movement has redefined gender roles in the United States). We have learned too just how important was Turner's original caveat that role behavior be consistent over time, which opens a back door to the establishment of system constraints or institutionalized patterns of behavior.[13]

Other examples could be brought from Anthony Giddens to Margaret Archer, all of whom seek a way out of the same paradox but have not really found it.[14] What has in fact occurred is that the disciplines of the social sciences have themselves divided into those approaches that adopt a more agent-oriented explanation and those that adopt a more structural one. We may take, for example, studies of such macro phenomena as social revolution. Given the reigning definitions of agency as action having "non-trivial consequences" on the workings of social structure, studies of revolution present what is perhaps the best "limit case" of such approaches. Thus we can rather clearly delineate the two approaches. Those of Mancur Olson or Charles Tilly are ultimately reliant on theories of individual action, interest, and agency.[15] And by contrast those of Samuel Huntington, Reinhold Bendix, S. N. Eisenstadt, or even, in a very different vein, Barrington Moore, Jr., Theda Skocpol and Jack Goldstone are structural in nature.[16]

Put most broadly, agent-oriented approaches (also termed individualistic, atomistic, or micro-oriented theories) embody the idea that structure, system, order, or society is ultimately nothing more than a complex function of the actions of individuals and their interactions. Its assumptions presuppose the reduction of system consequences to individual action. Hence it concerns itself with how individual actions combine to form collective action, how individual preferences aggregate to form common values, and how individual interactions become social institutions. Structuralists would argue by contrast that the whole is more than the sum of the parts, that the principles by which the parts (individual actions) are arranged should constitute the primary question of theoretical inquiry. (Are, for example, exchange relations governed by the logic of an international market or of local barter?) Structures, whether materialist or "culturalist," are consequently seen as objective and ordered wholes that exist independent of individual players and whose properties organize individual action.

In sum: Pure action theories emphasize the reduction of structures to actions.[17] At its extreme, a rigid methodological individualist position would always reduce structures to properties of individual people. The hidden assumption would be that the concrete sources of individual actions, values, beliefs, and identities are irrelevant for social analysis because people do always share a similar (if not uniform) psychological makeup, share similar desires, needs, and preference orderings. In contrast, pure structural theories emphasize that structures, not individual actions, determine outcomes. At its extreme, this position is one of methodological holism; structure is taken to be deterministic (given structure, outcome will follow). Hence, as in the quote above, individuals have no choices. Individual actions, beliefs, goals, and identities are determined by structure. People are merely bearers or carriers, "tragers" in that terrible term of Luis Althusser, of social functions. History without a subject.

In their most extreme forms, both pure action-oriented theories and pure structural theories are faulty. One cannot reason directly from individual actions to macrosocial outcomes, nor can one take structures alone and ignore individuals, actions, or agency. The ongoing problem in social science research has been the failure to construct a theoretically coherent project that can accomplish both. Thus far the grandest attempt was that of Talcott Parsons and his theory of the "unit act," from whose corpse the different sociologies of the 1960s and 1970s sprang like the soldiers of Cadmus.

In some sense we should perhaps view the current penetration of economic reasoning into the other social scientific disciplines in the form of rational choice and social choice theories as essentially a retreat from or renunciation of structuralist models (mostly but not exclusively Marxist) of a generation ago. Increasing attention to the calculus of utility maximization and preference ordering assumes a world of discrete individuals making informed choices in the progress of their lives.[18] The most critical of this work assesses how these individual choices combine in untold and unexpected ways to yield those unintended consequences that largely define our shared social life.

If sociological reasoning can be said to have begun with Durkheim's study of suicide and his finding that rates of suicide varied among different populations (urban and rural dwellers, Catholics, Protestant, Jews, and so on), the current popularity of rational choice models explicitly challenges Durkheim's core assumptions about a systemic explanation for the different rates of suicide. For if Durkheim's explanation rests on the structural armature of a conscience collective, current theorizing privileges individual preference orientations as functions of utility frequencies. In this sense contemporary postmodern theory in sociology and its cognate disciplines is analytically of one mind with rational choice and social choice models of rationality in abjuring any metanarrative or any totalizing hegemonic structures of thought or identity. Both posit a host of local or particular identities, interests, and value orientations—a methodological individualism, to use the language of rational choice. One may perhaps characterize postmodern social theory as social choice theory for the statistically challenged.

Whichever discipline they come from, however, most attempts to unite structure and action or structure and agency beg the question, as they dodge the central questions of causality, human nature, and the meaning of human action. Hence the reformation of rational choice theory into social choice or social game theory models endogenizes norms but does not, in the final instance, solve the problem of structure and agency. The revised theory may advance a more plausible reading of the sources of action than the purer, more socially obtuse rational choice theories whose theoretical assumptions are too far from any empirical reality to be useful as a modeling of human action. These limits have been well explored in the work of Martin Hollis.[19] However, once norms are endogenized, preferences pegged for social context, and utility functions properly reformulated to account for the value orientations of different social milieus, one is still left with the question of the human actor—of the meaning of human action and the nature of the acting self. The more psychological and purely rationalist accounts of agency may be tweaked to accommodate structure, but we are still left with the problems of transcendental freedom that are inherent to any structuralist account.

While these problems cannot perhaps be avoided, Dahrendorf's critique of a generation ago has not been heeded, and the philosophical (or epistemological) aspects of these issues remain largely ignored. This is unfortunate, for, if nothing else, it skewers our understanding of the critical concept of human agency. Without presuming to offer greater clarity than that provided by Dahrendorf, it is worth noting one characteristic of the debate over agency and structure that threads through all the contributions: that agency is identified with power, with the ability to effect nontrivial differences in the workings of the world. The implications are wide ranging. Most often we think of agency in term of its power to effect change; hence, the theoretical centrality of revolutions to the structure/agency debate. But it could also be argued with equal logic that agency is as necessary for maintaining a given structure of social relations as it is for changing it. The key issue, however, remains power and the near universal and uncritical identification of agency with power that inheres in all social scientific uses of the term.

At least some aspects of the structure/action conundrum are related to the post-Hobbesian reading of agency as power. In employing such concepts as agency and structure we believe we are using scientific categories whose applicability is universal whether the phenomenon being described is twentieth-century Latin America or second-century Athens. For if they are not generalizable, not theoretically given to a pure or neutral form, and only descriptive of one particular reality, then the whole endeavor would be worthless. (If the term *revolution* could be used to describe only the French Revolution of 1789, say, and not the Russian Revolution of 1917, the Chinese Revolution of 1948, or the Turkish Revolution of 1922, we would not have even the sine qua non of a scientific pursuit, namely, a language in which to pursue it.)

This fundamental point bears repeating only because our use of agency as power itself presupposes a certain model of human nature and action that it purports to explain. This model assumes the individual as autonomous actor in a rather Hobbesian view of the social world, that is, it assumes a social choice man even if the manifest theoretical frame is one of structure. Indeed, such a perspective on agency presupposes this individual as constituted apart from and in contradistinction to his or her social world, and agency itself is posited as the ability to change or even to maintain a given set or sets of such social relations.

And yet, this is not the only possible reading of what a human agent is, nor is it a very sophisticated one. Consider as an alternative the idea of agent as developed by Henri Frankfort and Charles Taylor. As Frankfort has noted, the simple ability to make choices (realize agency) is after all not unique to the human species.[20] Rather, as developed at length by Charles Taylor, human action and agency are defined by the ability to evaluate our desires qualitatively. Our individuality, then, inheres in more than what Frankfort called *second order desires* (our ability to evaluate our desires and privilege one over the other). Rather, following Taylor, the essential component of human agency is the fact that this evaluation can itself be divided into strong and weak evaluations. He draws this distinction as follows:

In weak evaluation, for something to be judged good it is sufficient that it be desired, whereas in strong evaluation there is also a use of "good" or some other evaluative term for which being desired is not sufficient; indeed some desires or desired consummations can be judged as bad, base, ignoble, trivial, superficial, unworthy, and so on. It follows from this that when in weak evaluation one desired alternative is set aside, it is only on grounds of its contingent incompatibility with a more desired alternative. I go to lunch later, although hungry now, because then I shall be able to lunch and swim. But I should be happy to have the best of both worlds: if the pool were open now, I could assuage my immediate hunger as well as enjoying a swim at lunch time. But with strong evaluation this is not necessarily the case. Some desired consummation may be eschewed not because it is incompatible with another, or if because of incompatibility this will not be contingent. Thus I refrain from committing some cowardly act, although very tempted to do so, but this is not because this act at this moment would make any other desired act impossible, as lunching now would make swimming impossible, but rather because it is base.[21]

Strong evaluation thus takes us beyond utilitarian calculations and into a realm of "qualitative constraints." For the strong evaluator "the desirable is not only defined for him by what he desires, . . . it is also defined by a qualitative characterization of desires as higher and lower, noble and base and so on. Reflection is not just a matter . . . of registering the conclusion that alternative A is more attractive to me, or draws me more than B. Rather the higher desirability of A over B is something I can articulate if I am reflecting as a strong evaluator. I have a vocabulary of worth."[22]

Here then is a very different model of agency and of the self who effects such agency or action. Thus, depending on whether our model is drawn from the vocabulary of the game theorists or from Charles Taylor, it comes with its own distinct model of self and of personhood. The particular model of self implies a particular model of agency and vice versa. And thus it is that the social scientific debate over structure and agency is really a debate over the nature of the human self. To accept this conclusion, however, would necessitate opening the door to psychiatrists (which Parsons did in fact do) and perhaps, woe to us, even to theologians. For surely they have a history longer and a vocabulary quite possibly richer than ours for dealing with this issue; and they certainly have one that includes the concept of *will*.

While they wait at the door having their credentials checked, however, it may be helpful to backtrack to the sociological field of *order* to see what implications may be found there for an understanding of agency. For a reading of agency predicated on the morally (and hence socially) constituted agent will yield a very different reading of the social order from one predicated on the power-consummating and utility-maximizing self. Whereas the first posits values, the second posits strategic action as the core of social interrelations and hence of the order that ensues.

In a structural-functional or Parsonian paradigm, the first would lead to role taking, to the patterning of role expectations within reference groups and so ultimately toward the internalization of such expectations in the form of value orientations. By contrast, in the second reading, which is closer to Turner's ideas, all values are in the final analysis labile, negotiated, and simply the rules of the game (whatever the particular game may be). Note an important derivative of this reading: there is no need for values per se. Values are, in the last instance, reduced to negotiation and calculations of strategic action as informed by the power differentials between the relevant actors. Consequently, any attempt to posit structure or ordered relations in this second reading must necessarily be limited to one of two options. Either structure is an emergent property of action and hence is no more than the sum of unintended consequences of individual decision making by actors in pursuit of their individual preferences (a position taken by Hayek, for example).[23] Or structure, that is, patterned action, is held together by power, coercion, and constraint (a point made by Dennis Wrong in his seminal article "The Oversocialized Concept of Man").[24] The task of the social scientist is thus to plot out the steps of the calculus, working out the sum of these individual decisions—which with hindsight and a powerful enough computer would give us understandings not afforded the actors themselves.

These two ways of viewing society may be schematized as follows:

| *Leaning to Structure* | *Agency* |
|---|---|
| role taking | role making |
| patterned expectations | negotiation |
| reference groups | labile roles |
| (consequent of) | (result of external constraints, i.e., of) |
| internalized values | power |

As can be seen, in one reading structure is inherent in action. In the other it is a consequence of action. (Acceptance of the first position does not render the existence of coercion, power, or unintended consequences in the workings of social order impossible. What is at stake is the analytic level at which these processes are posited.) Yet again, we reproduce on the macro level the image of the individual that we began with on the micro level.

The rational actor or social choice model of order doubtless seems to be a much neater and clearer—a more scientific—view of interactive processes than one predicated on internalized moral norms. It also purports (rather hypocritically) to obviate the need for a philosophical anthropology, as the actor is seen stripped of all normative baggage beyond the ability to reason from utility. (This is itself a very particular anthropology, and that is the heart of the problem.) It presumes no conscience collective, no group mind, and no other airy phantoms, and it rests solidly on the foundations of a methodological individualism. With some proper tuning in the direction of the "irrational," such as to incorporate the need for meaning, nonmaterial interests, and so on, such a theoretical perspective should be able to deliver the goods.[25] Of course, once such nonmaterial interests are factored into the calculus of rationality, the very meaning of rational calculation inevitably tends to become fuzzy around the edges, as does the nature of the rationalizing agent, who begins to look more like the agent posited by Taylor and less like that posited by Amos Tversky.

To reiterate our main point: We have two readings of society and of self. In one the agent is a moral decider, in the other a utility maximizer. Again, it is not that moral deciders do not act to maximize the utilities of their decisions, moral or not, but that action assumes a very different type of intentionality than does the moral decision making itself. In one, structure is inherent, more primary, and perhaps even constitutive of action; in the other it is a consequence of action.

The philosophical quandary of the structure/action problem exists only if we adopt the first, structuralist reading. This is, moreover, only a nontechnical problem if we assume with Taylor a strong evaluator as the core of human agency. If not, and we assume the second, agent-oriented position, the "norms" of feudalism, capitalism, or bureaucratic rationality present themselves as no more than preference orientations to be endogenized into the calculative process. The methodological challenges may be immense, but there is no principled problem of taking them into account in the modeling procedure. This changes if we adopt the first perspective, in which norms or value orientations are seen not as standing apart from the self but in a most essential sense as constitutive of the self. To understand what is implicit in this position we must recognize just what is lost when agency is framed in terms of power: put most succinctly, it is the very idea of authority.

The very idea of authority, so inimicable to modern sensibilities, not only challenges the identification of agency as power but also rescues the concept of agency from its simple reduction to preference calculations—however counterintuitive that may seem.[26] Authority is used here in the sense of legitimate power; that is, it is viewed as *just* or fair, whatever the bases of that justice or fairness may be. There are myriad different ways of justifying or legitimizing power, ranging from the givenness of tradition and kinship obligations to the dictates of a transcendent deity (however construed) to those of positive law or modern natural law theory. Again, children will see fairness in the equal distribution of a chocolate cake among all the birthday party attendees or perhaps will accept the fact that the birthday girl gets a bigger piece, or they may contest the latter in the name of the former set of principles. In the end, when parents intervene to point out that they will "all have their turn" at being birthday girls and boys (and so a turn at having a bigger piece), they are invoking the principle of equality as trumping any other (the favored status of the birthday girl, for example) and just demanding a degree of trust to await the reciprocity of a future date. Such is one vision of fairness. When citizens accept the judgments of a court of law or, for that matter, the local tax assessments, they may resent the payment but still accept the authority of the state as fair or just.

But if a certain percentage of the populace rejects such authority and consequently sees its judgments as illegitimate coercion, then social order becomes untenable. This simple fact becomes central in understanding such phenomena as the French Revolution. All regimes at the end of the eighteenth century faced a critical problem of monetary reserves. The English Crown could receive credit, however, whereas the French could not, because the king in Parliament was considered more creditworthy than an absolutist monarch. And it was the latter's continual inability to meet his debts that played such a critical role in the eruption of a revolutionary situation.[27] We may recall Talleyrand's statement that "you can do everything with bayonets except sit on them."

Now, of course, certain social scientists—Mancur Olson, Charles Tilly, and others—would reject the above characterization of social order and see it as solely imposed through coercion and maintained through the difficulty of organizing collective action against ruling elites (the collective action problem, it is called, or, as Mark Lichbach termed it, the "Rebel's Dilemma").[28] Order is no more than a relatively stable coalition of ruling elites capable of coercing the populace (or buying off contenders) through one strategy or another. This reading of social order has no problem with structure slighting agency, but agency itself is equated with nothing more than power, and the idea of fairness, justice, or legitimacy is considered irrelevant to the calculus of social ordering. (Marx came down on this problem in his famous strictures on "ruling class, ruling ideas" and "determination in the last instance.")[29]

Now let us approach this issue of internalized values and coercion or subjugation of the will from the perspective of the social actor, rather than from that of the external authority. Internalized values or indeed any values (for to be values, some element of internalization must adhere to them), if they are to mean anything at all, must mean the acceptance of some propositions—those rules of justice or rules of the game—as

legitimizing certain actions rather than others. And this means, in principle, accepting the idea of some authority as the source of these sets of
principles. In accepting these rules and hence curbing my desires and
subjugating my will, I bow to authority. I may want two candy bars but
have money for only one. I may refrain from slipping another into my
pocket because I am afraid of being caught, or I may refrain from doing
so out of a belief that stealing is wrong or sinful and that doing so will in
fact make me a thief, which is a type of person that I cannot be yet remain
myself. That is because being a thief fundamentally differs from being a
dentist or a plumber or a butterfly collector. It is not some external status
that is interchangeable in nature. (In my youth I was a philologist; now
I am a numismatist. I used to be a salesman of MTV videos; now I am a
patent lawyer.) Rather, being a thief, precisely because of the moral
claims at stake, touches on aspects of one's social self that are essential,
constitutive of self, and not subject to purely instrumental calculations.
Compliance with external reality (here the going market rate for candy
bars) involves some coercion. When that is seen as legitimate (fair or
just, even if I am not particularly happy with the results), I am involved
not only in market relations of a particular nature, but in those of authority as well.

This recalls Peter Blau's important article of a generation ago, "Justice
in Social Exchange," in which he defined principles of justice as the acceptance of the going market rate as the fair rate of exchange.[30] Unfortunately, this formulation begs the question of why and how the rates of
exchange are set. And some very critical aspects of exchange rates are
set beyond the market. This includes all principles of public good, goods
and services that, when provided to one member of the collective must
be provided to all, and principles of the public distribution of private
goods.[31] Also part of this class of goods are entitlements—health care (in
some countries), minimum wage agreements, and child labor laws—all
mechanisms that affect market exchange and are based on principles
that are, themselves, independent of pure market or power exchange
relations. Hence, in the formulation of fair rates of exchange (whether
on the micro or the macro level), factors that go beyond simple supply-
and-demand curves are brought into play. These factors are political in
nature and as such touch on the element of values and of legitimation.
To invoke principles of legitimation is in all cases to invoke the idea
of justice. It is the idea of justice that makes certain types (and rates) of
exchange legitimate and other not. When deemed legitimate, my acceptance of their calculus of value as an aspect of the relevant external reality
(even if against my immediate interest) represents not so much coercion
but the subjugation of my will. Examples of such abound and, as shown
by P. S. Atiyah, the very development of contract law in England reflects

precisely this idea of value external to market structuring the forces of market. Thus, for example, principles of public order came in the late nineteenth century to mediate the workings of pure laissez-faire contract law.[32]

The acceptance of certain actions, structures of decision making and rates of exchange as legitimate (just) is thus an essential aspect of what is implied by the idea of internalized values and patterned expectations. It is precisely this whole edifice that is lacking in a reading of society based only on power, coercion, and a pure calculus of strategic action. That is the issue of the self that inhered in our story of the thief. In a reading of society based on internalized values the act of theft challenges a particular, internalized view of self, while in a model of society based solely on calculations of marginal utility and strategic action, such a problem would not exist. (Of course, it may if one follows John Stuart Mill's later definition of value and utility, but that then subverts the whole explanatory strength of the rational choice model.)

Let us consider here the issues of the rules of the game and how they may be the same as or different from principles of justice. For can one not make the claim that one accepts certain rules of decisions or rates of exchange as no more (but no less either) than rules of the game (something along the lines of traffic lights, say)? Just as one plays chess according to certain rules, indeed can only play chess according to certain rules, one need not invoke any principles of justice or legitimation (or values). Chess is chess and to play it one must play it according to its rules; the same may be said for the game (and consequently the rules) of social interaction. This is the reading of reality affirmed by our column B above, of agency and power, where social norms are no more than instrumental mechanisms that facilitate (with greater or less success) the maximization of preferences by the individual members of society. But the differences in norms reflect no ethical or moral validity, do not represent different ideas of justice, but rather are based solely on utility, what works best where. Thus in some states one can make a right turn on a red light when there is no traffic, while in others one cannot because the nature of traffic or of drivers is different. Compliance here is "external," instrumental, and negotiable; different laws or practices in different places.

In many cases, it will be claimed, this is how we behave: when purchasing used cars (or candy bars, for that matter), choosing a degree program, renting a house, paying taxes—in fact, in the majority of our myriad life ventures. To deny the reality of these calculations would be foolish (after all, we try to take advantage of every loophole in the tax law, and some of us even find ourselves being less than strictly honest in reporting our expenses if we feel we can get away with it). Yet, I would claim, it would be equally foolish to present these types of calculations as the only reality. For while one does participate in different markets (of power, prestige, and wealth) as a purely instrumental player, there is an inherently *finite* regress from one "game"—or set of market relations—to another. There does exist an ultimate referent that most players accept as beyond the different games (those rules that in fact mediate the workings of "pure" market exchange, such as laws against slavery and child labor, mandating a minimum wage, and so on). It is the acceptance of this referent that legitimizes the system as a whole. And the rules of the game ultimately refer to principles of justice, even if these principles are no more than the maintenance of the game itself (as in chess) or, by extension, of society, which, as Durkheim taught, is the essence of the sacred and so, we are forced to admit, of authority itself.

Given this truism, the sociological challenge is to identify the source of this authority—whether rooted, at least in the West, in the transcendent dicta of a monotheistic, Creator God, in a tradition of republican virtue or in the more primordial and ascriptive-based norms of kinship reciprocity. (These are the three sources of authority that we are most familiar with in the West. There are, needless to say ideas of transcendence that do not encompass the idea of a Creator God, such as Hinduism). When the rules of the game are indeed principles of justice and so have an ontological status beyond traffic regulations, they invoke a consideration of society framed in terms of the internalization of values. It is only in such a worldview that the idea of the sacred may exist and with it, its cognate terms of justice, legitimation, and ultimately of authority. Together these terms constitute a set, different faces of a prism, refracting the selfsame reading of social reality and human existence from slightly different angles. Invoking one, we are necessarily invoking all the rest. All are very different from a reading of social order predicated on rational projection of utility functions and the unintended consequences of individual preference maximization.

Again, and not to overstate the case, what characterizes this reading of society is the existence of principles of justice, of the idea of legitimate (and by implication of illegitimate) action and so, *of necessity*, of rules governing market, or better, exchange behavior that are themselves not based on the relations of exchange themselves (such as supply-and-demand curves, existing prestige orientations, and so on). Hence the existence of rules (already beyond the game, metarules, which is precisely what makes the principles of legitimation rules of justice) that are in a sense outside of society, which is, in turn, what gives them their authority (as opposed to the purely coercive property of rules that are only immanent in society and its exchange relations).

Let us consider an example: The meta aspect of this ordering is well expressed in the first chapter of the book of Genesis, in which the very creation of the world is projected as one of division, distinction, and ultimately of classification—with the concrete social rules of classification found in the books of Leviticus and Deuteronomy. Certain forms of division and of classification are thus legitimized while others are delegitimized. In this sense the sacred is society itself, in Durkheim's famous formulation, not the particular individuals who make up a particular society at any particular time but the rules of order that themselves form society. It is, to complete the circle, the subjugation of the individual wills to these sacred rules of order that defines authority.

On the historical level, the work of Karl Jaspers, Eric Voeglin, Benjamin Swartz, S. N. Eisenstadt, and others has contributed to an understanding of that "breakthrough" to transcendence in the period of what Jaspers termed the Axial Age, which saw the development in different world-historical or civilizational religions of the reflexive appreciation of such rules or bases of authority.[33] These, as we know, became the foundations for civilization construction in Judaism, Zoroastrianism, Christianity, Hinduism, Buddhism, Greek philosophy, and later in Islam, for millennia.

What then are we to make of Peter Gay's claim that the Enlightenment (hence modernity) represents the return of "modern paganism," that is, the disappearance of just these types of authority as the ultimate referent for the workings of our daily life?[34] For modernity as a civilizational project is predicated on the wager that transcendence can be represented as no more than transcendental reason yet still maintain its authoritative nature and sacred aura: Immanuel Kant's "starry heavens above and moral law within" or the "self-evident" truths of the Declaration of Independence being this benchmark of modernity.

Is not this reworking of transcendence, however, itself responsible for the increasing difficulty of discussing the "will" or indeed of framing agency in the more moral terms taken from Taylor rather than those of power and strategic action taken from the lexicon of con-game experiments? Does not the modern revolt against the idea of authority, represented most spectacularly in Nietzsche, make it increasingly difficult to speak of a community of norms and values and, for that matter, of the individual as moral evaluator? Can we, moreover, really afford to bury this question in the classificatory categories of *Gemeinschaft* and *Gesellschaft*? Or rather, is the very nature of any community beyond the most purely temporary and instrumental not tied in its essence to the idea of authority? Yes, no doubt, instrumental associations need not invoke authority; they may rely solely on interest, as was Hume's view of the modern world, but does not that already presuppose a very particular vision of the individual self—and so of the relations between selves—whose existence must itself be the point of inquiry?

Is it in fact possible to speak of community in any meaningful sense without the cognate term of authority? Is it possible to speak of individual agency (not power) without such a referent? Is it not rather the case that via Taylor's definition of agency—which roots agentic action in moral evaluation, what he terms "strong evaluations"—we arrive at the notion of individual as moral evaluator that in turn firmly roots the individual in the moral dictates of a shared community, of a shared sacred? Somewhat counterintuitively, we thus find ourselves in the seemingly paradoxical position of affirming an idea of agency connected to a holistic and structured view of society (one that explains social order on the basis of internalized values, shared normative standards of justice) and not, as we first looked for it, in the idea of society defined by power relations and the idea of the autonomous individual pursuing his or her own preference orientations.

This paradox, however, is not simply analytical but also historical. For surely it is only in modernity that we can speak of individuals as value. It is only in modernity, which emerged in rejection of the idea of transcendent authority, that there developed a recognition of the idea of individual autonomy and agency (as, for example, eighteenth-century ideas of freedom replaced seventeenth-century ideas of Christian liberty). How then can agency as moral evaluation be linked to the authority of (what are often traditional) communal forms rather than (of modern) individual choices? To a great extent the following chapters are devoted to these issues, to delineating what has been lost in our sense of self as in our sense of community when our definitions of human agency are restricted to the calculus of power calculations, but also to explaining how a new idea of the individual as morally autonomous adjudicator of value emerges, and the contradictions this entails. What becomes the self in a world shorn of sacred referents, of an authoritative and legitimizing matrix of action and decision making (i.e., of other than immanent rules of exchange relations) is no more nor less than the fruits of modernity's wager.

The disciplines of the social sciences have contributed to this wager by returning the sources of authority to society (this was, after all, the revolution effected by Durkheim in *The Elementary Forms of Religious Life*), making of our laws no more than immanent artifices of the socially constituted.[35] (The dangers of this were darkly understood by Max Weber in his writings on natural and positive law and the problems of modernity in legitimizing legal systems in any other than purely procedural terms.) We witness the consequences of this in such developments as critical legal theory, or critical race theory, all of which, in deconstructing the legal edifice, do no more than affirm not only immanence but a vision of the human actor as no more than a calculating, power-seeking agent.[36] Furthermore, even that structural perspective within the social sciences that accepts the existence of internalized values (and so also the existence of justice, legitimacy, sacred authority, and so on) is based on the epistemological assumptions of a model of self that falls under the rubric of the instrumental rather than the constitutive.

Thus, even though post-Parsonian structural-functionalism accepts the idea of collective norms and values as motivating action, its actual definition of structure assumes something very different. Recall Dahrendorf's discussion of social role in his essay "Homo Sociologicus": structural analyses of society within the structural-functional tradition must assume "role" as the fundamental unit of the social division of labor. Roles are the building blocks of functionalism, whose own grid of organization is the 'stuff of structure' in the structural-functional perspective. There are, of course, other types of structure, from the 'deep-structure' of Levi-Strauss to the linguistic structure of Chomsky, but these slight agency in ways so blatant as to make their discussion irrelevant for present purposes. The very construction of structure from roles, rather than from individuals, is what makes social structure possible. It is also what keeps it from recognizing individual agency as something other than deviance of one form or another—which is the only way a systemic perspective can accommodate individual digressions in role performance.

While there may be no alternative to this methodological construct if we wish to make of the study of society a science, we must not lose sight of the following: By predicating our analysis of social reality on roles, we are, wittingly or no, assuming a generalizable psychology of role incumbents (those who perform role expectations). It is a psychology that is at once simplistic, uniform (in its essentials), and ultimately predicated on the type of behavior patterning and rational calculations assumed by social choice and rational action theories of human behavior. This means that the conflict between rational choice and more culturalist theories of society is, in the end, perhaps more assumed than real.[37] Their differences come down to no more than different emphases rather than different epistemologies. Both assume a similar (simplistic) self and privilege the outcomes of the self's action in different manners. They assume as well a model of selfhood that stands in principled contradiction to a version of self based on moral decision making, constitutive values, and sacralized existence, and to any idea of authority as essential to either individual or social existence. If this holds, so does its corollary, that such a model cannot account for a consistent view of community either. For the question remains: are values the property of roles or of individual selves? On this question there can be little equivocation if the social sci-

ences are to maintain their place as *social sciences*. The costs of this position—hence of the very ability of these sciences to explain reality—are,
however, as we have seen, far from negligible.

The problem with the idea of agency is the Achilles' heel of all social
science perspectives, of those predicated on structure just as much as
those predicated on agency. This is true despite our attempt above to
rescue agency within the structural-functional perspective by following
Taylor and linking agency with moral decision making—to that world of
internalized values upon which such perspective rests. Rather, the social
sciences would seem to mirror society at large and to be implicated in
the assumptions of modernity to such an extent as to make them suspect.
Recall Goffman's work on front and backstage—does this not presuppose
certain ideas of public and private space and behavior that may not in fact
hold for all cultures at all times?[38] Or Garfinkel's ethnomethodological
assumptions on the concern of interlocutors to maintain interaction:
does this hold for individuals bound by kin and territorial obligations
(guest-friendship among the Zande) or only for modern, autonomous
individuals whose interaction with other individuals is essentially voluntary and ruled by external codes?[39] When different autonomous selves
thus meet, their interaction may indeed have to rely on precisely these
mechanisms, as they lack a collective sense which unites them.

I am suggesting here that the epistemological premises of the social
sciences follow those of modernity in general. Perhaps there is no choice.
They do, however, present a post-Hobbesian or at least a post-Humean
epistemology of self that sees individuals solely in terms of their own
individual interests and desires rather than as, as . . . what? That is the
problem, is it not? One can poke fun at "methodological individualism,"
but absent a transcendent locus (being created, let us say, in the image
of God) there is precious little else with which to explain individual existence. Moreover, the road from the transcendent image to a statistical
formula is a well-documented one, passing through the Pauline emphasis on faith (and slighting of law) to sectarian-Protestant ideas of illumi-
nism and of grace, property no longer of a sacramental community but
of individual believers, and ending with the secularized modernity of
transcendental rather than transcendent edicts—in whose very articulation the individual as moral decider both enters the realm of history and,
in the very moment of entry, can glimpse his or her passing as well.

Modernity, as we have said, is based on a wager, the wager of maintaining this individual—emergent from collective definitions yet still defined in constitutive ways by the ethical demands of what is held to be
sacred. Events at the close of this century do, however, raise questions as
to whether the bet has been won. We have witnessed and experienced

both the return to ethnic and religious identities under the rubric of multiculturalism and the dismantling of the individual qua value found in the discourse of postmodernism, in the very idea of "discourse," for that matter.

In all, social theory seems to follow social fact, providing post hoc legitimacy and explanations of events it cannot critically comprehend, sharing as it does the epistemological premises of the society it purports to study. Although this cannot be helped, it does blind us to aspects of life that are not always privileged in liberal visions of modernity. The following chapters attempt to think somewhat differently about the issues of community and individualism and their relation to authority. They draw upon models from the past in an attempt to offer some fresh insights about the present.

## Chapter Two

## AUTHORITY AND THE SELF

As I hope has been made clear in chapter one, attempts at solving the problem of social order all turn ultimately on one's view of what constitutes (or does not) the individual social actor. Rational and social choice theories—like their economistic prototype—all hark back to a more or less Hobbesian view of the individual as a self-contained actor who is director of his or her own passions and interests, chief among which is, for Hobbes, the fear of death and the corresponding right to flee its approach.

This view of the autonomous individual as a self-regulating agent makes for a certain politics, as well as for a certain sociology or even a certain philosophical anthropology. The politics it calls forth is the politics of liberalism—of a principled articulation of rights over good, of the Rawlsian original position, and of the public sphere as a more or less neutral arena where individual interests can be maximized without impinging on the rights (i.e., interests) of others. It is a vision of human nature as one of "methodological individualism," of agent-oriented action, and of social life as a calculus of power and its regulation. Since all there "is" is individual agents maximizing utility functions, power becomes the defining term of interaction between people (hence the current concern with "empowerment"). A fair or justly organized regime is therefore one where power, or at least access to power, is evenly distributed; an unjust, unfair, and often defined as illiberal regime is one where power is concentrated in the hands of a few, who then organize social life through *coercion*, rather than through the *exchange* that is necessitated by the more equal distribution of power throughout the body politic.

In this reading of society, neither the sacred nor authority have any meaning, as both assume a limit to negotiation. Both assume a realm of ultimate reference beyond the intricacies of exchange that organize the division of labor, a point at which such exchange ends and appeal to first principles itself imposes obedience. For while it is true that one cannot play chess without the rules of chess, there is nothing sacrosanct about these rules of chess (or existing rules of exchange), and, unlike Stefan Zweig's hero, we are not "compelled" to play chess, and can easily decide to play freezetag instead.

Now it well may be the case that you, having a much more analytic mind than I, may wish that we continue playing chess, while I, fleet of foot, wish to change the game to tag. How I get you to agree to that, through selective incentives, coercion, trickery, and so on, is another matter. The point is, however, that in an individualist or liberal-individualist reading of social order, the metarules are themselves open to negotiation, not closed in the sense that a sacred text is beyond emendation.[1] The order-defining rules are themselves given to slippage, open to a possible conflation with the process of ordering over which they are purported to rule. The most salient example of this slippage is the phenomenon of postmodernism itself.

Note here, by the way, the subtle difference from the claims made in the previous chapter. There we pointed out how all the rules of the game in their very structural position as metaorganizing categories rested upon some authority, some element of sacrality. Here, however, we are refining the argument to state that, in a truly individualist or radically liberal, perhaps libertarian order, there is no sacred and no authority, and the metarules themselves are open to negotiation. Insofar as this is so in contemporary societies—to an unparalleled degree—we seem to be moving toward a social order in which the problem of authority is replaced with that of the collective action dilemma and the problem of mobilizing contestants to ruling elites.

*Ein begriffiner Got ist keine Got*—a God that can be grasped, a God that can be conceptualized is not a God. A sacred that can be negotiated is not sacred. Or, with Emile Durkheim, we might say a precontractual that is open to the contractual logic of give and take, of exchange and of market relations, is no precontractual. And, more to the point, the idea of the self in a world where sacrality holds and where moral authority is a meaningful concept is a very different self from that predicated on a social order whose ultimate referent and organizational focus is that of methodological individualism. The alternative to the latter, *instrumental* self, which realizes utility functions in the process of social interaction, is a *constitutive* self. Only with this alternative vision of self do the terms *sacred, moral authority,* and even *community* have any meaning. Given such phenomena as the prevalence of a New Age "spiritualism," the worldwide emergence of Evangelical Protestantism, and the balkanization of identities along racial, ethical, and even gender lines in so many contemporary Western societies, one would do well to explore just what is inherent in such concepts. A return to, or search for, such sources of moral authority (however well or ill conceived) does seem to be characteristic of much of contemporary culture.

This would not have surprised Durkheim, who posits an idea of the self whose constituting conditions originate beyond the self and in society, as expressed in the very idea of the conscience collective and the cognate concept of moral authority. If power works through coercing our will, moral authority works through the voluntary subjugation of our will. Consider again the case of stealing a candy bar: either we refrain from stealing it because we are afraid of being caught (and the consequent punishment) or we refrain from stealing it because to do so would make us ashamed of ourselves. All authority is essentially moral authority once we assume that legitimacy which accrues to it and not to simple power.

To steal the candy bar would make me a thief, a particular type of person that I do not wish to be. Were I, in fact, a thief, I could no longer remain who I am. Thus, the very essence of self, that me which touches on that which we conceive as the most personal, turns out to be the most social. What, after all, is more collective than the prohibition of theft, which in our tradition goes back to the decalogue if not before? This was Durkheim's insight. It stands at the foundation of his work on suicide, upon which the disciple of sociology is more or less founded.[2]

From the candy bar theft example we learn that there seems a strong relation between what makes a self and what makes moral authority. That aspect of my very personhood that is violated when I become a thief (but not a plumber, a mountain-climber, a philatelist, or speaker of Hungarian) is defined by overwhelmingly social or collective criteria that we treat as authoritative. Yet this reality is often forgotten or ignored or implicitly denied in models of social order predicated on the perspective of methodological individualism, in the Hobbesian or economistic model of the social universe, which posits the desiderata of social actors as being self-generated. Similarly, all rational actor and social choice models of social order would ultimately have to deny the validity of this model.

There is, however, much more at stake here than simply competing visions of social order. Recall Peter Berger's insight that in traditional societies the individual self was seen to be realized through the fulfillment of given institutional roles, while in modern societies the self is seen to be the most fully expressed beyond institutional roles—the lone ranger model of self.[3] Now, leaving aside the culturally specific nature of this argument (i.e., it seems to be true for one specific form of modernity, that tied up with Anglo-American liberal Protestantism, and may not necessarily be true for those species of modernity identified with Jacobean or more totalitarian, fascist, or communist forms of social ordering), it raises serious questions as to our aforesaid identification of the self with the conscience collective or the overriding ideas of moral authority.[4] For institutionalized roles are nothing more than the specific units that make up the division of labor, that division of labor without which there is no human species. To say that the idea of the self is realized beyond these roles implies as well the realization of self beyond the rules and regulations that structure, order, and organize the division of labor itself. It is in fact a vision of radical autonomy that would seem to divorce the self from all communal referents, from all claims to moral authority—and so, in the reading we have been following, from those, in Charles Taylor's felicitous phrase, very "sources of the self."

What Berger presents as the ideal of traditional societies would seem to be positing an Aristotelian ideal of the fulfillment of specific goods (or virtues) mediated by one's communal referents. It is Aristotelian, but also very halakhic (referring to the Jewish legal code)—resonating with the image of a relational self one would find in rabbinic Judaism, and indeed in much religious thought. This self finds its realization only in the matrix of social relations and so also in the proper fulfillment of the laws and rules or regulations that define such relations—whether the caste relations of Hindu society or the ritual requirements of purity rites followed by Orthodox Jewish women before engaging in conjugal relations. The self is realized through the acceptance of heteronomously imposed laws rather than through the workings of a self-actualizing will. Once posed in these terms I believe we begin to see how very Protestant if not simply Christian is Peter Berger's insight into the modern terms of self. This is not to say that it is wrong, only to say that modern, especially secular, liberal, Western ideas of the self are profoundly Christian. There is, as the astute reader will perceive, something antinomian lurking here, though we are not quite ready to pick up its thread.

In traditional societies the connection between the idea of the self and the existence of moral authority would have been so clear as to be trite. Our own cultural images, as well as our deepest liberal impulses, however, make it not only counterintuitive but also downright difficult to swallow. Yet, the traditional reading also carries with it certain ideas or principles of community and of group participation that most of us would like to make our own even as we would also no doubt shy away from their correlates in other spheres. To what am I referring?

Perhaps the most central correlation that has to be grasped is that between authority and community. Do we not generally tend to think of community as a "good" thing, whereas authority is for us, if anything, seen as the opposite of the "nourishing" image of community. It is, rather, perceived as stultifying and overbearing. While I am dealing here in cultural stereotypes, the basic truth of this dichotomous perception of authority and community is, I think, obvious enough.

The most interesting challenge to our own liberal preconceptions on this matter comes from the Durkheimian perspective, which in essence holds not that community and authority are opposing principles of social organization but rather that they are one and the same principle, as two sides of the same coin. In this reading, to return to the case of the candy bar, to give free rein to desire is to lose the self—that same self who is realized in the (internal) subjugation (as opposed to external coercion) of will. The very violation that sullies the self, for which it feels *shame*, is, of course, a violation of the moral authority of the community. And, without the communal referent, authority as a concept makes little sense. It becomes but the coercion of individual power. What makes the rule legitimate, authoritative, accepted, is that it is a collective dictate, not simply the personal power of the ruler. This collective aspect of authority was represented in the Middle Ages in the idea of the king's two bodies.[5]

Even more significant is the other side of this coin, that of community. What ties individuals together in a community is precisely and only the extent of its own moral authority. A dozen people waiting in line to see a movie are not a community. To some extent they share a minimal set of rules governing their interaction (about queue jumping, pushing, cutting ahead in line, and so on) and subjugate to them their own will (to get the best place in the theater). But, in the case of these people waiting in line, the appropriate analysis (in order to understand the phenomenon) is not that of the "constituted" self but simply of the social choice perspective and the individual costs to each if the line was continually broken and not maintained. The simple fact is that waiting in line involves no expressive component, no symbolization of community (writ either large or small), both of which are intimately tied up with the argument over the constitutive self.

But what is the relation between waiting on line and not stealing candy bars—can we extrapolate from one to the other? Are all or most examples of non–candy bar theft reducible to the same logic of waiting on line? Or are they to be understood in terms of the violation of self, the sense of shame that attends upon such abrogation of communal norms? This, in a nutshell, is the problem of social order, whose most compelling summary can be found in the recent account of Dennis Wrong, who contrasts the Hobbesian and Aristotelian versions of society.[6] The point of the present exercise is solely to emphasize again that different readings of order imply very different models of what a self is.

It is in this context that the present work is arguing not only for the concomitance of authority and community but also for the position that these concepts only really make sense in an explanatory context that assumes what we have been calling a "constitutive" self. For if we eschew this concept of self and remain with a more Hobbesian, social choice, or perhaps Spenserian definition of self, we cannot assume any idea of authority, only an idea of power—as, similarly, we can assume no community, but only contingent groupings held together solely by interests. We can thus posit the contractual relationship existent between people, but not what Durkheim termed the precontractual one. The terms of a "constitutive" self and an "instrumental" self thus correspond with two different views of community—a constitutive group and a participatory one. From here the path is pretty clear to the last term in the set—the idea of the sacred.

Can the term "sacred" have any meaning for instrumental selves, whose modes of group membership are solely participatory, contingent on the play of interests and the calculus of exchange? A world of methodological individualism cannot support the armature of the sacred, for it is a world that in principle does not support the idea of any meaning beyond the play of human negotiation, barter, and exchange (and, of course, violent struggle as well). If the sacred means anything, it is that place where negotiation ends. Like authority (but unlike power), the sacred is a realm defined by what cannot be bartered or bargained. Especially when posited in transcendent and absolute terms, the sacred becomes a point at which all contestation over meaning ceases.

As the foundation of meaning-giving order, the sacred is beyond the play of forces whose negotiation and exchange parse out prestige, status, and wealth to particular roles within the division of labor. A sacred that is seen to be constructed by the division of labor is no more sacred than is a community constituted by allegiances tied to discernible interests alone. Within the Jewish tradition this connection of the sacred and the realm beyond interests is found in the obligations to marry off the orphan and to bury the dead who have no one to bury them. These *mitzvot* are, according to the twelfth-century Jewish philosopher Maimonides, the greatest of all good deeds. Here, then, are obligations performed without an eye to any remuneration, what anthropologists term generalized reciprocity, or what economists term generalized exchange (i.e., a mode of relation beyond those of simple one-shot market exchanges). The correlation of community and authority to the sacerdotal is plainly felt with little need of additional commentary.

It is a correspondence that is self-evident to all anthropologists; students of religious thought; and church, synagogue, and mosque goers, as well as to an unfortunately dwindling number of sociologists and political scientists—decreasing to precisely the extent that social choice perspectives triumph in these disciplines. And that is, of course, the rub, for while social scientists are sometimes willing to acknowledge the existence of these modes of social and individual ordering in ancient (or, for that matter, in more contemporary tribal societies), they are forced into a bind when judging their own modern Western social formations. Few are willing to envision the self as subjugated to an external, heteronomous matrix of rules and obligations through which that self is constituted. Rather, we all seek the core of the self in the image of the self-actualizing agent who realizes his or her autonomous will. The more this will is realized, the more the self does, as it were, exist.

For its part, the feminist movement has contributed greatly to this conception of the person as it has struggled to free a woman from the "constituting" gaze of the man and allow her to join in the construction of a common humanity as an agent in her own right. How ironic, if we think back to the legal roots of the word *agency*, where the agent was, precisely, the doer of another's will (as in "the king's agent"), that is, an individual whose purposes were determined outside of himself, by an external authority.[7] It is precisely this reading of self, as constituted by an external authority—by heteronomous order—that we moderns reject in favor of a more liberal-individualist reading of self, whose relations with others are, in great part, instrumental and as members of communities that are, on the whole, participatory (rather than constituting) in nature. The member of the Brookline Electricians' Association can easily withdraw membership from that organization upon completing her medical certifying examinations without in any way damaging or diminishing her sense of self. The same, however, cannot be said of the Jewish convert to Catholicism. That most famous convert of all, Paul, did indeed become a different self on the way to Damascus, as he left Saul of Tarsus behind and responded, not to any autonomous impulse of his own will, but to a heteronomous call that he could not ignore.[8]

The idea of the self as one constituted by allegiances and obligations that, as it were, precede it and are in some sense constitutive of it is not one that modern liberalism can easily accommodate (or modern sociology, for that matter, which was the point of our earlier chapter). It is, moreover, not my purpose to make the argument that Michael Sandel presented so persuasively in his *Liberalism and the Limits of Justice*.[9] What I wish only to remind us of is that without something approaching such an idea of the self that we have termed "constitutive" it is very difficult to conceive of the meaning of authority or of community or of the sacred. We lose much with an idea of the purely instrumental self, though perhaps we have no choice but to maintain such a vision (as well as of the pragmatic ethics that accompany it). We should, however, remain aware of the baggage that it carries. Normative matters aside, we are left wondering just how adequate such an understanding of personhood is to our understanding of self.

Community and authority are two sides of the same coin, two aspects of the same phenomenon. In the final analysis, one cannot be thought without the other. Both are inherent in any idea of sacrality, which is not far from what Emile Durkheim was evoking with the idea of the conscience collective.[10] No longer the general will, but very much a shared orientation to the phenomena of social life, moral and epistemological both: it connotes an idea very close to that of a self constituted by communal orientations that we have been struggling towards in our own formulations. For Durkheim, this model of personhood was, of course, ahistorical, that is, essential, characterizing human beings at all periods and in all societies. What was different in each setting was not their being constituted by a conscience collective, but the nature of the particular conscience collective playing this role—the tribal solidarities of totemism as opposed to the revolutionary terms of modern citizenship, for example. In the terms of Maine, both *status* and *contract* are forms of conscience collective, though they are, to be sure, different forms.[11]

The contradictory nature of modern citizenship, however, the fact that the very constitutive terms of selfhood in modernity, those of individual autonomy and self-realizing agency, do themselves challenge, if not undermine, the bonds of community, even as they deny the principled existence of authority and remain deaf to the call of the sacred, must not be forgotten. For the very parsing out of the Durkheimian insight on the conscience collective into the twentieth-century sociology of roles registers, in social thought, the same process of institutionalization that, in social practice, has increasingly distanced our understanding of the individual from his and her collective referents. As role theory collapses the individual into the role, so the whole issue of the constituted self is turned on its head as said self is indeed lost in role compliance. There has been a subtle shift of emphasis from the heteronomous dictates of an external moral authority to simply locating the individual in terms of his or her response to the internalization of value commitments that subtly become mere preference orientations. The idea that was so central to Durkheim of individual, voluntary compliance to moral dictates that were not arbitrary is lost. The notion that moral authority was both "obligatory and desirable" becomes, with role theory, transformed into the problem of oversocialization and deviance.[12]

That transcendental freedom that marks the making of moral authority—whether of Antigone before Creon or Abraham binding Isaac—is lost in the reducing of the conscience collective to role expectations and the internalization of value commitments that accompanies such a project. Ironically, the roots of such reduction of self and of society can be found in the very immanence that adheres to the social science project.[13] This immanence is already there in Durkheim's own writing, in his identification of society, or even only of its ideal image of itself, with the sacred. Durkheim's writings provide in fact a secular and "scientific" example of that very *gnostic* nature of modernity that Eric Voeglin and Charles Taylor characterize as the "immanentization" of transcendence that has accompanied the whole project of modernity and without which there could be no social science.[14]

That a fully agentic self (not empowered but rather endowed with agency in the sense of a moral evaluator) is hence dependent on transcendence is, of course, a strikingly unmodern, even illiberal argument. It is, however, in one form or another what this book is about. For if that moral authority upon which the self rests is not conceived of in transcendent terms, its definition can only be immanent, can only rest on society. The consequences of this move in social thought are perhaps one set of fallacies, in social life, however, quite a bit more.

An appreciation of just how significant this immanent move of the moral sense can be may be gained by considering what morality may indeed mean—a necessary step if we are to have a clear conceptualization of what moral authority may mean (let alone its alternative posting in immanent or transcendent terms). Critical to our argument is thus (a) a definition of morality as well as (b) analysis of its institutional or economic role in organizing the division of labor. Once we understand these aspects of morality we can more fully appreciate the different articulations of the sacred not only in transcendent and immanent terms, but more concretely in civil, primordial, and transcendent meanings and identities.

While there are many competing and corresponding definitions of morality, I will rely on that of Bernard Williams, one of the most esteemed moral philosophers in the second half of the twentieth century. The following, then, is found in his highly influential book on morality and ethics, *Ethics and the Limits of Philosophy*. There he notes:

> The purity of morality itself represents a value. It expresses an ideal, presented by Kant, once again, in a form that is the most unqualified and also one of the most moving: the ideal that human existence can be ultimately just. Most advantages and admired characteristics are distributed in ways that, if not unjust, are at any rate not just, and some people are simply luckier than others. The idea of morality is a value, a moral value that transcends luck. It must therefore lie beyond empirical determination. It must lie not only in trying rather than succeeding, since success depends partly on luck, but in a kind of trying that lies beyond the level at which the capacity to try can itself be a matter of luck. The value must, further, be supreme. It will be no good if moral value is merely a consolation prize you get if you are not in worldly terms happy or talented or good-humored or loved. It has to be what ultimately matters.[15]

Morality, in this reading, is a hedge against *fortuna*, against *tyche*, and against the very differentially distributed access to technique (skill), to *techne* that can help overcome the blind and chaotic nature of life. In the philosophy of Immanuel Kant the privileging of the intentional (of that internal state that directs the action) over the course of the action itself, and hence over the opacity of its necessary outcomes, is wedded to the moral virtues in a manner that has come to define most modernist understandings of the term. Morality is thus located within the individual, in individual intentionality. However, if morality is located within the self, the source of moral authority cannot be far afield. For if the morally authoritative is that which is beyond negotiation, beyond the play of barter, contract, and commerce, beyond the realm of meager interest (to use the language of the eighteenth-century moral philosophers), if it is, as noted above, essentially an aspect of the sacred, it is also, in this modernist reading, located within the self. The sources of moral authority are, hence, internalized within the person. Here we turn to Durkheim's famous statements on the individual as being the "touchstone of morality," where the sources of moral action rest on the cognizance of the individual sanctity of each member of society and where "each of us incarnates something of humanity, each individual consciousness contains something divine and thus finds itself marked with a character which renders it sacred and inviolable to others."[16]

Once this "Kantian" project is framed sociologically (with Durkheim), the moral sense achieves an immanent dimension, for it is society itself that is seen as constitutive of the sources of moral action and assessment. Beyond *fortuna* there is only society and hence both the majesty and the degradation of the whole project of modernity, indeed a return to "modern paganism," as Peter Gay characterized the Enlightenment more than a generation ago.

Morality, like the sacred (in that form defined by Durkheim), is what is set apart from processes of negotiation and contestation that define the calculus of power, as well as of prestige and wealth, if not of authority. This very apartness is manifest within the logic of social organization—not only in its symbolic incarnation (in the rituals and rites of collective identity) but more structurally in the very organization of the division of labor in society. It exists even in the economic realm of action as that province of human activity that, while part of the workings of market, is nevertheless not reducible to interest maximization, preference specification, or to the whole set of utility-maximizing actions that we in contemporary societies identify with the market and the contractual aspects of social life. Those actions and principles governing social action that are set apart in this manner are the principles of *generalized exchange.*

Generalized exchange, as distinct from specific or market exchange, provides the conditions of solidarity representing the 'precontractual' elements of social interaction, which include the "obligation to engage in social interaction and to uphold one's obligations; or in other words generalized exchange, if successful, helps to establish the conditions of basic trust and solidarity in society, to uphold what Durkheim has called the precontractual elements of social life."[17] Its existence was perhaps first noted by Marcel Mauss in his famous study *The Gift*, and has been developed in different ways within different anthropological traditions as distinctions between "general" and "specific" exchange (in the works of Claude Levi-Strauss) or "generalized" and "balanced" reciprocity (in the works of Marshall Sahlins).[18] Both authors contrast the direct, immediate, and indeed balanced reciprocity of items transacted (symbolic or material) with a reciprocity that does not demand an immediate return or exchange of such items. In the latter case a form of symbolic credit is granted to the receiver, who benefits from the "trust" of the partner to the interaction that he or she will offer a return in goods received at a later date. In this sense every exchange partakes symbolically of the character of a gift in that reciprocity is not immediately expected.[19]

Moreover, as pointed out by Robert Putnam, Francis Fukuyama, Kenneth Arrow, and others, it is precisely this granting of symbolic credit that makes social and economic life possible at all.[20] And it is this symbolic credit that provides the basis of cooperation in iterated prisoner's dilemma games as well. Its implications for the development of market economies, based as they are on the activities of middlemen, have been studied by scholars such as Janet Landa and Avner Grief.[21] Both have emphasized the necessary role of "reputation" (even intergenerationally) in establishing confidence in trading activities (a point made by Coleman as well).[22] This reputation, based on the iteration of trade activities, becomes the basis for new role expectations and hence for confidence in the system of interacting activities.

Not only do the different terms of symbolic credit make economic life possible, but they also structure social life and exchange in very specific ways. As Eisenstadt has noted, they do so by providing limitations to the free exchange of resources in social interaction, and the concomitant structuring of the flow of resources and social relations in ways that differ from "free" (market or power) exchange. "Such structuring stands in contrast to the purely conditional, instrumental or mostly adaptive, activities that characterize simple or specific exchange. But it does not deny adaptive or instrumental relations. Rather it creates a connection between instrumental and power relations on the one hand and solidarity and expressive relations on the other."[23] These limitations take the form most generally of (1) the establishment of public goods, such that no one member or group in the collectivity has exclusive access to such goods, and (2) the public distribution of private goods, in which the redistributive mechanisms of the collectivity reward groups and allocate resources according to criteria other than those of pure market exchange (priestly tithes, welfare entitlement, or German tax allotment to the church would all be examples of the latter).

Of course, the terms of these generalized exchanges are different in different societies, tied to the way "unconditionality" (that is, solidarity) is articulated in each society (the bases, if you will, of "reputation"). Most of the more penetrating work on this has been carried out by anthropologists working in smaller, relatively undifferentiated or traditional societies where these unconditionalities were formulated in terms of an ascriptive or kinship-based solidarity. However, as the work of Parsons, Mayhew, and Eisenstadt himself has shown, a similar dynamic operates in more developed societies as well, where the different legally defined entitlements of citizen rights play a similar role.[24]

It is thus within the realm of generalized exchange that the play of *fortuna* (not only a becalmed fleet in the eastern Mediterranean but also a sudden fall in stock prices or a rise in mortgage rates) is reined in, or, at the very least, a realm is delineated that is seen as existent beyond its force. It is a realm set apart and separate from the everyday, yet it is very much an organizational and economic realm, not simply a symbolic one. Such a realm defines not only individual conscience (if not consciousness) but social action as well, through the provision of those types of public good noted above.

Significantly, the definition of these generalized exchanges differs in accordance with the different visions of morality, of what is held sacred in society. In one important version of the modernist reading, the Anglo-American tradition of liberalism, the principle of generalized exchange is expressed through the provision of public goods defined in terms of individual rights and liberties (child labor laws, affirmative action injunctions, minimum wage agreements, and so on). All of the above temper the workings of a "pure" market toward the maintenance of some modicum of individual integrity, if not equality (T. H. Marshall's famous conception of "social citizenship").[25] These principles are very different from, say, medieval injunctions against taking interest (among Christians) or usury, which also mediated the workings of pure market forces, but in the name of a more transcendently oriented collective—that of the Christian *ecclesia*.[26] Sumptuary laws based on principles of primordial membership are yet another example of the mediation of pure market exchange in the name of a different set of collectively defined desiderata.

Having reviewed the symbolic as well as organizational aspects of morality, we are now in a better position to appreciate the different implications of what is held to be sacred, as conceived of in civil, transcendent, and primordial terms. For not every morality is defined in terms of individual intention; just as not every set of principles of generalized exchange is organized around the individual citizen, as said individual was not always seen as the sacred locus of society. There have been, historically, other sources or definitions of what is set apart and forbidden, as beyond the play of negotiation and contract. One can be found in the following story told in the Babylonian Talmud in tractate Avodah Zarah (literally "foreign worship," the tractate of laws regulating the relations between Jews and idolaters). It is an eschatological scenario where the nations of the world stand before the Creator of the World in judgment:

> The Holy One, blessed be He, will then say to them: 'Wherewith have you occupied yourselves?' They will reply: 'O Lord of the Universe, we have established many marketplaces, we have erected many baths, we have accumulated much gold and silver, and all this we did only for the sake of Israel, that they might [have leisure] for occupying themselves with the study of the Torah.' The Holy One, blessed be He, will then say in reply: 'You foolish ones among the peoples, all which you have done, you have done only to satisfy your own desires. You have established market-places to place courtesans therein; baths to revel in them; [as to the distribution of] silver and gold, this is mine, as is written: *Mine is the silver and Mine is the gold, saith the Lord of Hosts.*' [Rome departs and the Kingdom of Persia enters the Divine Presence.] The Holy One, blessed be He, will ask of them: 'Wherewith have you occupied yourselves?' and they will reply: 'Sovereign of the Universe, we have built many bridges, we have captured many cities, we have waged many wars, and all this for the sake of Israel, that they might engage in the study of the Torah.' Then the Holy One, blessed be He, will say to them: 'You foolish ones among the peoples, you have built bridges in order to extract toll, you have subdued cities, so as to impose forced labour; as to waging war, I am the Lord of battles, as it is said: *The Lord is a man of war.*'[27]

Note the differential readings that are played out in a parallel manner in the presentations of both Rome and Persia: of the first and second as opposed to the third arguments in each, especially in terms of God's answer. Marketplaces and bathhouses on the one hand, silver and gold on the other, and, with Persia, bridges and cities on the one hand, waging war on the other. In the Holy One's answer the "silver and gold" and "war" arguments are clearly differentiated from the others. God does not say, you are trying to pull one over on me (as in the case of marketplaces, for example, the real reason to build them was to place courtesans inside, so don't tell me stories about letting Israel study Torah), i.e., accuse them of lying, but rather, says that the sources of these accomplishments are in his own works. In this dialogue between God and the nations of the world a special status is accorded the second set of arguments about "silver and gold" and "war." These exist on a separate plane and suggest a reality of deeper import than simply excuses the nations proffer in regard to markets, cities, bathhouses, and bridges—exchange (silver and gold) and warfare being in fact the two realms of human negotiation par excellence, those realms where the conflict of differential attributes, means, resources, skills, and capabilities are most clearly felt in concrete outcomes (again those matters of luck, or *fortuna*). The rabbis, then, are reminding their readers that there is a force that trumps luck, a realm of ultimate meanings that undercuts the meanings of exchange. That realm is the transcendent.

In our first, Kantian or liberal reading it was individual intentionality that trumped luck and so held chaos at bay, through the provision of ultimate "essential" meanings that challenged the contingency of circumstance (and were expressed institutionally through the provisions of generalized exchange, defined in terms of individual goods—provided publicly, of course). In the above story, as indeed for large swaths of human history, it is expressed in terms of transcendence. A third and final expression of this has been in what can most clearly be termed the obligations of primordiality—those specific sets of "given" identities based on birth, kinship, territorial consanguinity that we tend to privilege in giving an account of ourselves.

From Antigone, who heeded the call of these claims in defiance of the political order, to Michael Sandel's description of individuals as "members of this family or community or nation or people, as bearers of this history, as sons and daughters of that revolution, as citizens of this republic," we cannot fail to recognize, as much as we may well normatively reject, those definitions of personhood rooted in the overwhelmingly primordial or ascriptively defined sense of self.[28] However immanent or backward-looking they may be, howsoever their particularism may offend our modern universalist and individualist understanding of what is moral and hence what is authoritative, we ignore these forms of community (and hence, we recall, of authority, of sacrality, and so also of selfhood) only at our own peril. For most of human history has seen societies organized by precisely these particularistic, immanent, ascriptively defined terms of community. Even today, the most telling and compelling forms of moral authority are those rooted in these definitions of the sacred— of a self willed from the warp and woof of his or her own particular familial circumstances. Time and time again, in fact, the political organization of modern polities founded de jure on the revolutionary principles of individual rights and of citizenship have, tragically, slipped and stumbled to reveal the perduring nature of primordial attachments, loyalties, and, hence, of definitions of self. From the Dreyfus Affair to the mutual butchery of the citizens of Rwanda (where the definitions of universal citizenship were less salient than those of tribal membership) and all the horrors of this century in between, the more primordially defined terms of identity have, continually, made themselves felt, often in tragic, if not horrifying circumstances.

Thus we have arrived at precisely those three sources of authority noted earlier—those defined by our modern, liberal, and civil referents, those defined by more primordial identities, and those defined by transcendent dictates. We look at each in turn. As loci of authority, each defines different senses of the sacred as well, itself but an aspect of the differentially defined boundaries and definitions of the self and the collectivity each posit. They define different forms and meanings of that generalized other, that entity that both G. H. Mead and Adam Smith saw as the very source of our sense of self. What relation exists between these different forms of moral authority and different forms of self or personhood if indeed the latter cannot be fully comprehended without the former?

Of the three sources, the one closest to our concerns is, seemingly, the modern, civil, liberal version of moral authority. To grasp the problematic nature of the relation between authority and self-identity here, we must return to the questions of immanence and transcendence found in Durkheim's writings. As he struggled to posit an alternative locus of moral authority to that of the church and the *vrai France* of the ancien régime, he was, at the same time, however unknowingly, undermining his very own project. Most readers will be familiar with Durkheim's formulations on the individual as the source of moral authority and locus of the sacred in modern society, which, in some sense, goes back to the civic humanism of the Renaissance city-states and is most certainly part of that republican tradition that Durkheim himself so defended—as evinced most clearly in the period of the Dreyfus Affair.[29]

Durkheim's formulations, in fact, resonate with our prior claim that modernity rests on a wager that the terms of collective meaning, those of liberal individualism, can be maintained autonomously at the center of the civic polity, without the need for either the armature of a transcendent Deity or the referents of a primordial collectivity. The history of this century has, however, increasingly demonstrated the failure of this idea of civic humanism and of a purely civic virtue. Furthermore, and as J.G.A. Pocock has shown, even historically it has proved well nigh impossible to institutionalize this vision of republican virtue without the aid of a "prophetic" grace, that is, without the aforementioned structure of transcendence.[30] But Durkheim thought he had pointed a way toward just such a possibility—by identifying the individual with the precontractual principle (the principle of generalized exchange) existent in society. As that locus of moral authority existing by definition beyond the bounds of negotiation, conflict, and constraint, it could, Durkheim had hoped, provide the basis for its institutionalization within the politics and society of Third Republic France (that same France of Berlanger, the Dreyfus Affair, and the construction of the Sacré-Coeur in atonement for the "sins" of the Commune of 1871).

Leaving aside the not inconsequential problem of the confusion of the prescriptive and descriptive in Durkheim's writings, another, more significant problem remains in this attempt: the very sources of the pre-contractual, of the sacred, and hence of moral authority. For in identifying these with the existing rules and categories of order, even in their ideal state, Durkheim hobbles the sacred with an immanent dimension. What is lost is the dialectic, the fact that when a truly transcendent understanding of order applies, every concrete social order, as it reached the state of the ideal, would at the same time overcome its finite, labile, and contingent character, that is, overcome itself. However, if the ideal order does not transcend the given one, it is fated to collapse back into it. With Durkheim this collapse was predetermined in his very identification of the sacred with society's ideal image of itself. This heritage has unfortunately defined sociological reasoning for the past hundred years. The problems of role theory discussed above and Dahrendorf's insights on the loss of transcendental freedom that such theory imposes give theoretical expression to precisely this problem.

When liberal individualism thinks of itself scientifically, it does so in terms of role theory, with the attendant loss of any moral authority. Salient aspects of this were noted by de Tocqueville 150 years ago when he pointed out that

> when it comes to the influence of one man's mind over another's, that is necessarily very restricted in a country where the citizens have all become more or less similar, see each other at very close quarters, and since they do not recognize any sights of incontestable greatness or superiority, in any of their fellows, are continually brought back to their own judgment as the most apparent and accessible test of truth. So it is not only confidence in any particular man which is destroyed. There is a general distaste for accepting any man's word as proof of anything.
>
> So each man is narrowly shut in himself, and from that basis makes the pretension to judge the world.[31]

That conformity of mind of which de Tocqueville speaks is rooted in the very terms of liberal individualism as a civic ideal. With nothing beyond the citizenry but the citizenry itself, with no other qua generalized other on which that constituting gaze of the individual can be focused, relations between selves tend to collapse into the instrumental and the pragmatic. And this in turn is the corollary of that tyranny of public opinion, that is, of the mass as opposed to the individual, that so concerned de Tocqueville in the progress of democracy in America, as it did Hannah Arendt one hundred years later. Indeed, a good half century before de Tocqueville a similar concern and distrust had defined Adam Smith's attitude toward public opinion. In his revised 1790 edition of *The Theory of Moral Sentiments* a notion of internal conscience, "the man within the breast," came to replace the man outside, or public opinion, as a guide to moral action and hence to social order.[32] This reflects, I believe, Smith's fear of that retreat or slippage of the sacred into the merely social category of public opinion that is the corollary of modernity's wager.

If modernity is about the predominance of liberal, civic visions of political life, America is surely the most fully institutionalized of such polities, the one where an almost metaphysical equality between members is most fully realized and the one where any presumption of the very existence of authority is most vehemently negated (as opposed to the "authority" of public opinion, which is but the *power* of the self magnified a thousandfold). It is, as well, that place where the self is conceived in the most instrumental of terms and where those very participatory groups that abound in America (in the forms of myriad voluntary associations, charitable societies, and so on) are an ever changing amalgamation of individuals who enter and exit them at will. It is that place where, in Hegel's terms, "A man is counted as a man in virtue of his manhood alone, not because he is a Jew, Catholic, Protestant, German, Italian etc."[33] Leaving aside for the moment the intense Pauline weight of this quote, its referent is, precisely, that no-longer-constituted self that presents itself to modernity as the very model for the individual. If, as Robert Putnam has noted, bowling is out, soccer may well be in, as we await the latest statistical reports on the voting behavior of the "soccer moms." What is significant in all this is not the decline of community in the United States (which was Putnam's point) but rather the *nature* of that community and the accompanying forms of self so well represented in twentieth-century social scientific reasoning. But one should beware of attaching normative value to such a self and of projecting such a self back to other times and other social formations.

The significance of the above for our discussion is how that very civic model of authority tends to realign itself simply into power, to lose its very authoritative nature and become identified in more instrumental and less constitutive ways. This inherent slighting of the constituted self is endemic to modern forms of civic association. It is a central component of what David Riesman described half a century ago as the "other-directed" self.[34] Of this self Riesman noted

> that the feeling of helplessness of modern man results from both the vastly enhanced power of the social group and the incorporation of its authority into his very character . . . the individual is psychologically dependent on others for clues to the meaning of life.[35]

What Riesman terms "authority" is what we are describing as power *simpliciter*, that power of public opinion rooted in conformity to the statistical mean, role incumbency rather than transcendental freedom.[36]

People, however, continually seek to fulfill needs that are slighted by these modern terms of identity and are continually reintroducing other forms of communal affiliation and self-identification. It is, however, possible that the continued reemergence of more primordial and purely transcendent loci of authority (and self and community) have in fact always been part and parcel of modernity for precisely this reason. Whether we think of this as a positive phenomenon or not, we cannot help but recognize the continuing saliency of primordial categories, even in the most modern of societies. These cannot be conceived of simply as "remnants" of less progressive ways of thinking that will pass with time. Indeed, quite the opposite is the case. The very progress of modernity brings with it a reintroduction of primordial (as well as, in different circumstances, transcendent) categories of order. This reality must, I feel, be part of any serious attempt to understand the persistence of racism, of anti-Semitism in Europe (even without flesh-and-blood Jews), and the oft noted balkanization of collective interests and identities at the end of the twentieth century.

The seemingly endemic nature of racism both in this country and abroad points to something a good deal more salient than simply traces of a form of political identity that has not yet been fully overcome. Precisely this new and value-laden reaffirmation of multiple collective, ethnic, linguistic, national, and even gender identities is a sobering side effect of the practice of postmodern politics. If the end of the nineteenth century was the era of the individual par excellence, the end of the twentieth century is witnessing nothing other than the redefinition of the individual in terms of new collective and often primordially defined criteria of membership and identity. Yet, and in a somewhat paradoxical reversal of historical trends, the positive valuation of these new forms of collective selfhood has been taken up as the cause of the left, as they abjure the universalism of past socialist agendas to become advocates of a new particularism. For better or for worse, nobody today is claiming for lesbian Chicanas the role George Lukács arrogated for the world proletariat in his 1922 *History and Class Consciousness*, and, however we evaluate this development normatively, it must still be explained.[37]

And the explanation, I believe, is not a particularly happy one. The story is told of Akiva Ernst Simon, the great religious, Zionist educator of a whole generation of Israeli pedagogues, who, upon hearing the details of the Holocaust, was reported to have said: "We must now begin the really essential work. We must return to a rereading of Immanuel Kant." I have always understood Simon to have been saying that the Kantian wager had failed, that the attempt to base selfhood and moral responsibility on a foundation of individual moral autonomy had self-destructed in the most bestial and evil act ever perpetrated upon hu-

man beings by their own. Henceforth, the moral autonomy of the will
could no longer be seen as sufficient foundation for either personality or civil life. How often in the course of this century have de jure
definitions of citizenship whose referent was some abstract and universal
individual (bearer of universal rights) been stripped away to reveal a
primordial, racial, territorial, or kinship and tribal-based definition of
identity with its attendant unspeakable consequences? It was to this that
Philip Rieff referred when he noted that "Our great Enlightenment, the
slow work of centuries since the Renaissance, has ended catastrophically,
not in the failure of authority . . . [but] in the success of its lowering.
Gulag and Dachau, torture and terror are the dry-eyed children of our
Enlightenment."[38]

Paradoxically, these reversions to a primordial sense of self seem to be
accompanying the growth and further global institutionalization of that
civic ideal of individual rights and ownership that is its very antithesis.
The more successful modernity as a civilizational vision of individual
rights and of the autonomous individual seems to be on the global scale,
the more it appears to call forth its very negation. Today's struggles do
indeed seem to challenge the very domain assumptions of the great
struggles of the nineteenth and early twentieth centuries over the institutionalization of this vision of citizenship (as represented in struggles over
the slave trade in the mid-nineteenth century; over workers' rights; over
extending the franchise, first to the European working class and then to
women; and, finally, the struggles later in this century over colonialism).

Thus, while a primordially defined self has always existed as a real
alternative to modernity (indeed, was to some extent bound up with the
very premises of the idea of the nation-state, especially in the English
and German versions thereof), its appeal has, if anything, widened over
the course of this century rather than diminished.[39] Indeed, the always
existing tensions between primordial (and perforce particularistic)
terms of identity and those rooted in more universalist assumptions have
been, if anything, intensified in modern societies. The absolutism inherent in enlightened reason absolutizes as well the contradictory nature
of pluralistic human goods, including those of particular and universal
identities that are fundamental components of our individual selves.[40]

Primordiality is, in Levi-Strauss's terms, especially "good to think" particular identities with. It is "good to think" identity in terms of the constituted self. What, after all, are more constituting than ascribed criteria
of age, gender, race, or ethnic identities (that is, blood lines), however
construed? These are all aspects of personal identity that we did not,
indeed cannot, choose. They are all *given* aspects of identity and hence
are very handy for symbolizing essentialism. In the search for a *Gemeinschaft,* you can do no better than to parse out kinship identities. With the

horrific examples of fascism and Nazism in this century, we cannot ignore just how important the collectivist and particularist pole has been to modern identities. Just as the individualist pole of self-identity is absolutized in liberal ideology, so the collectivist pole has been absolutized in fascist (and, in other forms, communist) modes of social organization.

The reader must beware of making the mistake of confusing prescriptive and descriptive aspects of an analysis. I am, of course, far from advocating such positions. I am, however, claiming that if we wish to understand the seemingly paradoxical progress of modernity that—most especially in this postmodern age of the global market—seems to combine the impossibly appositional, we must take the above dynamic into account: the heightened institutionalization of the economic and political premises of liberal modernity (as defined by the principles of 1789) together with increasingly more salient espousals of particular racial or ethnic identities (as evinced, for example, in India's nuclear tests of May 1998). Both result from that propensity of enlightened reason to make of pluralistic goods, irreconcilable and absolute oppositions.

Following Simon, we may ask, where do we go when we rethink Kant? One place where we end up, wittingly or no, is with the failure of autonomously defined selves to provide a sufficient foundation for self-identities and the felt need to give expression to a less autonomous, more constituted, more heteronomously defined self. Primordially defined identities and ascriptively maintained aspects of self turn out to be very useful at filling this need. Is this a good, or moral, or desirable aspect of the human condition? Most often not, but that is a different matter entirely. Just as secular modernity called religious fundamentalism into being, so civic identities called up primordiality as an alternative form of selfhood. Indeed, these alternative forms of selfhood are woven into the skeins of the project of modernity and of civic selfhood, called into being by the very needs of people to express the constitutive aspect of their selfhood in a manner that the project of liberal individualism does not really allow, which is precisely the dynamic that gives to these different identities their absolutely irreconcilable and oppositional character.

However tragic the case, the very salience of primordially defined selves, indeed its almost necessary connection to modernity's own project (as evinced, to take only one example, by the critical nature of "the Jewish question" from the late eighteenth through the twentieth century in Europe) would seem to support the contention that the liberal (and as we have been stressing, social scientific—not to mention the classically conceived psychoanalytic) self as autonomous bearer of will is something of a fiction. Such account ultimately fails to recognize other dimensions of individual existence, of a selfhood that, rather than grasp itself in its autonomy, does so rather as constituted by something external.

In a very important sense we are back where we started: with authority and with the necessity of the self to define itself in relation to something authoritative if it is to exist as something beyond a bundle of desires. (Again, this was precisely Durkheim's point about anomie and the infinite nature of human desires, as well as their need to be bounded, reined in by something external—for him, by society itself.) Authority rather than power, and a self rather than a statistical datum. A world where the sacred exists as something nonnegotiable. Here, then, we reengage with externality and with the fact that authority must be beyond the self if it is to play such a role and not collapse into the calculative outcome of differentially distributed resources, as in the Hobbesian solution.

We lack a vocabulary other than a religious one to describe that constitutive function of the primordial, the ascribed, and the tribal. In these cases authority is neither transcendent nor transcendental but rather is immanent. Positing the immanent as authoritative, however, is precisely the definition of idolatry. A self so constituted is precisely what idolatrous activity was taken to mean (offering incense or animal sacrifice to a graven image is but the visible form of the idolatrous act, not its essence). As noted by Rabbi Meir (second century C.E.), people were not really foolish enough to believe that idols were gods, but it excused debauchery. In our terms it excused the loss of the boundaries of social order, of authority, and of a self-imposed morality—of precisely those morally authoritative values discussed in our first chapter. However, if a primordially constituted self is an idolatrous one (which, I hasten to add, is not bad by definition, only in its consequences) and that constituted by an autonomous reason cannot maintain itself, what remains?

What remains is the third form through which authority and community have been defined: the idea of a transcendent and fully heteronomous source of authority, that same conception of authority that came to human consciousness in the so-called Axial Age and that modernity, in the person of the Enlightenment, rejected. The Axial Age, as defined by S. N. Eisenstadt, was that period in which there emerged and became constitutionalized in the period between 500 B.C.E. and A.D. 600.

> a conception of a basic tension between the transcendental and the mundane orders, a conception which differed greatly from that of a close parallelism between these two orders or their mutual embedment which was prevalent in so-called pagan religions, in those very societies from which these post–Axial Age civilizations emerged.[41]

The emergence of these Axial civilizations followed a period of institutional breakdown characterized by a similar breakdown of cosmological symbolism. This period, in Eric Voeglin's terms, of "cosmological disintegration" resulted in a new appreciation of the relations between the individual and society and the cosmic order.[42] The change was accomplished through the fundamental restructuring of the relations between mundane and transcendent orders. As Eisenstadt and others have noted, the emergence of this conception in Christianity, Hinduism, Buddhism, Islam, and the civilizations of ancient Israel, ancient Greece, and China constituted a major force in the restructuring of the terms of collective life and of the principles of political legitimation.[43] For with the conception of a higher, transcendent order to which the political realm had to orient and legitimize itself, the "King-God" disappeared and was replaced by the notion of the accountability of rulers and collectivities to a higher order.

In the context of the present study, the differentiation between Axial and non-Axial civilizations is of utmost importance. For the Axial break (and the emergence of what has in other contexts been termed the great civilizations or historical religions) presumed a fundamental reordering of the nature of relations between society and "the powers governing the cosmos."[44] Breaking down their mutual interpenetration, the Axial Age posited a new conception of the social order, autonomous of, but in tension with, the cosmic (henceforth conceived of as transcendent) sphere. With the institutionalization of such a conception of chasm between mundane and transcendent orders (between society and the cosmos) and the concomitant search to overcome this chasm, the idea of salvation entered human consciousness.

With the invention (or discovery) of transcendence in this period, the magical, rather unitary and undifferentiated vision of cosmic existence became bifurcated by the ethical, by the call of a transcendent Being. Otherness was no longer represented as the otherness of demons, diverse deities, or wandering souls. That *Hinterwelt*, the "world behind the world" formerly given to magical coercion, was thenceforth projected outward beyond the world of daily affairs and events.[45] In this move, the otherness of enchanted nature took on transcendent properties. Within Western religious tradition, otherness was apotheosized in the logos of a personal creator God. This was achieved primarily in the radical transcendence of the Jewish Yahweh.[46] Against this transcendent being and its authority, totally beyond and outside the cosmos as it was, the very historicity of human existence was defined.

It is the authority of this transcendence that Kierkegaard plumbed in the image of the binding of Isaac and that Nietzsche rejected in his *Genealogy of Morals*. It is an authority that may provide an opening for an individual self as moral evaluator, with the absolute, transcendent otherness of God serving as the primary referent for the sense of self. To quote Karl Jaspers:

For the first time *philosophers* appeared. Human beings dared to rely on themselves as individuals. Hermits and wandering thinkers in China, ascetics in India, philosophers in Greece and prophets in Israel all belong together, however much they may differ from each other in their beliefs, the contents of their thought and their inner dispositions. Man proved capable of contrasting himself inwardly with the entire universe. He discovered within himself the origin from which to raise himself above his own self and the world.[47]

Within the Western tradition the individual came to exist primarily as an individual-in-relation-to God, which, as Jaspers noted, is precisely what provided the "resoluteness" of "personal selfhood . . . experiencing the highest freedom in the limits of freedom in nothingness."[48] Each individual became a unique entity "immediately responsible to God for the welfare of his soul and the well being of his brother."[49] The valorization of the individual is through his "consecration to God." It is, in Troeltsch's words, "only fellowship with God which gives value to the individual."[50] As pointed out by Marcel Mauss, the notion of the person—as a rational substance, individual and indivisible—owed its metaphysical foundation to Christianity.[51] And while I would not agree with Mauss about Christianity *tout court*, the connection to the Axial Age and the emergence of transcendence is not to be doubted.

Thus, the transcendent, the first fully generalizable other, becomes the basis for an unnegotiable sacred, one seen to exist beyond all possible social constructions, beyond all negotiation. It provides the definitive description to reality, especially to normative reality or rather the normative aspects of our material reality. Transcendence, or rather the authority inherent in it, reorganizes the relations within the mundane realm. In this it is quite distinct from magic, which relates to the supernatural precisely as another form of the natural that requires its own set of tools to mediate the impact of the supernatural on the world of man. Material tools mediate the effect of the natural world on the world of man (chopping down trees to make a house). Magic does something similar in the realm of the supernatural. Thus one may, in particular circumstances, need to sacrifice one's daughter in order to get the wind up to continue the course of the fleet to Ilium. Indeed, a comparison of the sacrifice of Iphigenia and that of Isaac highlights precisely this difference between a magical manipulation of the cosmos and the bending of the will to the dictates of a transcendent Deity. For transcendence is not about building houses or keeping the wind in one's sails, but rather about reorganizing the mundane world in accordance with principles now deemed transcendent in nature.

In this reorganization the individual emerges as a moral evaluator (as, for example, in the prophet Nathan's admonishment of King David).

True, this individual is conceived differently in different traditions, even within the seemingly similar conceptions of Judaism and Christianity, whose respective understandings of transcendent authority which will be discussed in chapter four. The essential point is that the idea of transcendence provides a locus of moral authority and selfhood, albeit one foreign to modern sensibilities. It provides for much of what would seem to be missing in a purely autonomously conceived model of the self. It does so, moreover, without falling back on ascriptively defined and primordial categories of selfhood. However paradoxical it may seem to us, its very authority calls the self into being as moral evaluator, as agentic in a sense other than of power. Problematizing existence, transcendence drives the self to encounter Being. In this encounter agency can become an existential and moral endeavor rather than simple power.

To summarize: We have considered three possible loci of authority, three different definitions of community—the civic (modern), primordial, and transcendent—about which we may hazard the following conclusions. When the terms of authority, community, and sacrality are defined in more purely primordial terms, the self tends to be undistinguished from the status activities it performs. When ego fails to perform its status commitments, self emerges not even as a deviant, but as something that is perceived as lacking. As an ideal type, this corresponds to some degree with the "tradition-directed" self of Riesman.[52] Missing here is any distance of self from community that would allow for reflection. The near total collapse of self into status—in essence into community and into the very immanence of authority so conceived— blocks the emergence of self that we have argued is constitutive in nature.

In quite a different manner, the civilly constituted self, that self constituted by the authority of a moral individualism, seems to lose the other end of its relational couplet. The very autonomy of self, rather than its collective locus, makes it impossible for it to maintain its separateness, its otherness from the play of contract, negotiation, and power that is, of course, nothing in the end but the work of self in society. Radical autonomy thus defeats itself, but in ways very different from that of a primordially defined authority.[53]

A heteronomously constituted self is, by contrast, constituted in tension with transcendent dictates. This tension was expressed rather movingly by Voeglin as follows:

These experiences [of transcendence] become the source of a new authority. Through the opening of the soul the philosopher finds himself in a new relation with God; he not only discovers his own psyche as the instrument for experiencing transcendence but at the same time discovers the divinity in its radically non-human transcendence. Hence, the differentiation of the psyche is inseparable from a new truth about God. The true order of the soul can become the standard for measuring both human types and types of social order because it represents the truth about human existence on the border of transcendence. The meaning of the anthropological principle must, therefore, be qualified by the understanding that not an arbitrary idea of man as a world-immanent being becomes the instrument of social critique but the idea of a man who has found his true nature through finding his true relation to God. The new measure that is found for the critique of society, is indeed, not man himself but man in so far as through the differentiation of this psyche he has become the representative of divine truth. . . . The truth of man and the truth of God are inseparably one.[54]

Transcendence provides a locus of heteronomy that neither individual autonomy nor group solidarity can provide—one that constitutes authority as such. It is this authority that provides what Charles Taylor termed that "constitutive good" upon which individual selves as moral evaluators can rest.[55]

Hence, I would claim that it is only in light of such heteronomous authority—that transcendent generalized other—that the particularity of individual selves can be said to exist. Not the autonomous will but fully heteronomous obligation forms the basis of the self—as moral evaluator and not simply as one empowered to work the system and so maximize preferences. The particular in its very particularity is here constituted by the general in its generality. This is a point Jurgen Habermas once made in connection with the universality of natural law and the emergence of the bourgeois self.

> The criteria of generality and abstractness that characterize legal norms had to have a peculiar obviousness for privatized individuals who, by communicating with each other in the public sphere of the world of letters, confirm each other's subjectivity as it emerges from their sphere. . . . These rules, because they are universally valid, secure a space for the individuated person; because they are objective, they secure a space for what is most subjective; because they are abstract, for what is most concrete.[56]

In slightly different terms W. H. Auden once referred to the same general civilizational project, remarking that "every high C, accurately struck demolishes the theory that we are the irresponsible puppets of fate or chance."[57] Again, the particular musical accomplishment, like Habermas's law and like transcendence in the realm of the ethical (and hence of individual moral agency), keeps chaos at bay. This is a point we have touched on before and now turn to again, to consider in more general and analytic terms the models of selfhood and their connection to authority. Our stress in this chapter has been precisely on the extent of that generality and on the extent to which it is necessary to maintain an idea of the self as moral evaluator. In the next chapter we will explore some of its modes.

*Chapter Three*

---

# HETERONOMY AND RESPONSIBILITY

IN THE last chapter we studied different forms of externality, of that which is other than self, and we considered the necessity of authority for an idea of the self as something beyond a mere bundle of desires. Moreover, we argued that it was only with the transcendent (what Rudolf Otto termed the *ganz Anderen*, or wholly other) that the self as locus of moral decision making can exist.[1] Only with the emergence of this dimension of existence is it possible to keep the sacred from collapsing into mere idolatry and thereby to sustain those assumptions about a realm free of negotiation, about a fully generalized other, and about values that support a self defined by criteria beyond those of utility maximization.

The otherness of the primordially defined collective or of the Hobbesian alternative (of the other as the mirror of one's own calculus of desire) both fail to support individuality because each continually threatens to collapse authority into simple power. With that collapse the whole edifice of sacrality, and so of a realm beyond the play of power and negotiation, is similarly threatened.

In this chapter we approach the same issue from a somewhat different perspective. Rather than trace the path from authority to externality, we turn the argument around and trace it backwards from externality to authority. First, what is this concept of externality—external to what? Quite simply, external to self. Here perhaps the clearest arguments were made by Bernard Williams and Thomas Nagel in their debate begun nearly twenty years ago on the idea—indeed, the paradox—of "moral luck."[2] How, after all, can matters moral be determined by pure chance or contingency?

Nagel began his argument by quoting the famous dictum of Immanuel Kant in his *Foundations of the Metaphysics of Morals*:

> The good will is not good because of what it effects or accomplishes or because of its adequacy to achieve some proposed end; it is good only because of its willing, i.e. it is good of itself. And, regarded for itself, it is to be esteemed incomparably higher than anything which could be brought about by it in favor of any inclination or even of the sum total of all inclinations. Even if it should happen that, by a particularly unfortunate fate or by the niggardly provision of a stepmotherly nature, this will should be wholly lacking in power to accomplish its purpose, and if even the greatest effort should

not avail it to achieve anything of its end, and if there remained only the good will (not as a mere wish but as the summoning of all the means in our power), it would sparkle like a jewel in its own right, as something that had its full worth in itself. Usefulness or fruitlessness can neither diminish nor augment this worth.[3]

From Kant then, we receive the view that the moral dimension of action exists independent of outcome. For Kant, the realm of intentionality, of the good will alone, is privileged over the circumstances that inevitably hinder or further the will's realization. Nagel responds that, however intuitively plausible this may seem, Kant nonetheless got it quite wrong. Nagel builds his argument case by case to show how one's own moral position is determined, in fact, not by the will alone but also by circumstances quite beyond the control of the will. Thus he notes:

> However jewel-like the good will may be in its own right, there is a morally significant difference between rescuing someone from a burning building and dropping him from a twelfth storey window while trying to rescue him. Similarly, there is a morally significant difference between reckless driving and manslaughter. But whether a reckless driver hits a pedestrian depends on the presence of the pedestrian at the point where he recklessly passes a red light. What we do is also limited by the opportunities and choices with which we are faced and these are largely determined by factors beyond our control. Someone who was an officer in a concentration camp might have led a quiet and harmless life if the Nazis had never come to power in Germany. And someone who led a quiet and harmless life in Argentina might have become an officer in a concentration camp if he had not left Germany for business reasons in 1930.[4]

What both Nagel and Williams tease out of these and other moral dilemmas is that the "morality" of one's actions may well be determined by circumstances over which the actor has no control.

Our own privileging of the internal, of the realm controlled by the individual's own intentionality as circumscribing and defining the moral has a long civilizational history. Ultimately, as I will argue in the following chapter, its sources are to be found in the Christian break with Judaism and the Pauline emphasis on faith over law (and so of the primacy of internal categories over external ones). The words of Jesus to the Apostles in Mark, chapter 7, that it is not what goes into a man's mouth that makes one impure but rather what comes out of the mouth (in reference to the eating of bread without washing hands and saying the benediction), offer what is perhaps the paradigmatic statement of this view of the individual. Clearly the Protestant Reformation of the sixteenth century and the consequent privileging of faith over works and the internalization of grace as practiced by the different Protestant sects—and indeed as found within that very Pietistic tradition from which Kant himself emerged—were all critical carriers of this orientation. We will, in fact, need to explore this particular civilizational trajectory—especially in contrast to those views of the self that can be found in the Jewish tradition over against which Christianity defined itself. This will be the task of our following chapter. Here we note these historical dimensions only to emphasize the important comparative dimension of this view of the self, as internally constituted by a moral dimension defined by a "good will." This is not the only possible view of what a self is and how it is constituted. It is, however, a historically specific one, Western Christian in origin. It is one whose secular, liberal form we are all too familiar with regardless of our own religious affiliation or lack thereof. It is a vision that privileges intentionality over action in awarding its moral accolades and that circumscribes the moral to the internal realm of what transpires within the self's own soul. Interesting in this context is some of Williams' later work as he attempted to dissociate the moral from the ethical such that the realm of ethical action is not dependent on those interior processes of willing that define the moral. Much of his book *Shame and Necessity* is devoted to this issue.[5]

The relevance of this thinking for our own concerns turns precisely on the issue of internal versus external sources of morality and/or ethical action. For as the ethical has collapsed into the moral (intentional) and so the external (*law* or later, *works*) into the internal (faith), it has become difficult to view the individual as anything other than a self-willing agent, constituted of no relational matrix beyond itself. The view that roots the self in internal constructs (of what by the eighteenth century became *conscience*) and gives them primacy in defining that realm of the ethical (now redefined as moral) is dependent on the wholly Other, the transcendent, to support its vision of self as something other than a bundle of desires, passions, and interests. If the locus of ultimate significance is internal to self, then the only way to take the self beyond itself is through the authority of the transcendent.

However, as we cut ourselves loose from the transcendent anchor (what is termed secularization), the whole discussion of values, constituted self, and sacred realm is abandoned. Once the transcendent locus is lost, so also are the ideas of authority and of the sacred that are but its necessary concomitants. One is left with nothing but a set of instrumental relations with the surrounding world, the calculus of wills that defines markets or contracts. It is, in its final guise, the rational actor that emerges. Even if, in this reading, the essence of a self is an agency of internal moral evaluation (rather than, say, pure power or domination), the self that emerges is still one lacking those constitutive components that we have been discussing. It is therefore not surprising that the modern secular version of this view, which maintains the internal definition of ethics as morality but without a transcendent locus, also defines itself in opposition to the very idea of authority. This is precisely the vision of self that we identify with liberal modernity.

Both Nagel and Williams have argued that this reading of self as solely dependent on will and internal intentionality is, in fact, not our own or not our only one (perhaps despite ourselves). Indeed their work has been so influential precisely because it has pointed out the contradictory nature of our own ethical or moral desiderata. These do, on the one hand, accept Kantian injunctions on the good will as defining the realm of the moral. And yet, notwithstanding this position, we all seem to feel a fierce resistance to the total disregard of all external worlds of actions, deeds, and results that this view would in its pure form imply. However much we accept the Kantian injunction as the most "reasonable," we also seem to revolt against such conclusions and demand that the external world of events, deeds, and circumstances be given its due. How can we explain these contradictory impulses and how relate them to our views of the self?

We must begin by reconfiguring Williams and Nagel's concept of moral luck into the more general problem of luck, or fate, or *tyche*—that is, the problem of the contingency of the world. *Moral* and *luck* must be juxtaposed such that morality is considered only one possible way of taming luck, or *tyche*. If the wiles of *fortuna* cannot be tamed in their effects—boats do sink, markets do crash, loved ones die, children are born with Down's syndrome—then they can at the least be tamed in their significance. In this, our predicament is one with that of the ancient Greeks or Hebrews, even if their technology was more primitive and nature therefore seemed more overwhelming. For as history has marched on and nature has come to be more and more managed—as *techne* tames *tyche*—we feel ourselves less and less prey to uncontrolled natural forces. Yet we remain prey to uncontrolled human forces as, for example, with the global economy and disasters such as the explosion of the Challenger that occurred in the technological stratosphere. Indeed this latter showed that at the extremely high degree of differentiation and integration at which systems work today, it is impossible to avoid all technological faults.[6]

Shifting the realm of ultimate significance from what happens "out there" to what happens "in here," over which we (at least as pre-Freudian exponents of free will) do have control, is a way of overcoming the arbitrariness of *fortuna*. Morality, that is, tames luck by redefining the truly important—not those external events that result from the haphazard allocation of resources and contingencies of life, but rather what happens in the realm of intent, inside a person. Challenging this position are Nagel's cases of moral luck and Williams' notion of agent-regret. These are limit cases, where the mechanisms of morality that control luck fail in their efficacy. They fail, for in certain cases the actions and the results are unremittingly present, existing with such brute force and givenness that they cannot be denied or negated by the force of intentionality. Events themselves give the lie to the internalized authority of conscience and the good will. It is, however, very difficult for us to accept that we may be constituted by actions and external events, sometimes even random circumstances, over which we have no control. Precisely because it is so difficult to accept how little control we have over what makes us who we are, we seek respite in belief in personal autonomy, and define the constitutive and the truly significant in terms of our internalized morality, over whose workings we do exert a measure of control. The trouble with this, as we have seen, is that the self cannot constitute itself, cannot provide that other to itself by which it exists.

If our former argument holds, then the constitutive must be based on the truly heteronomous, and not on the randomness of nature nor the chaos of existence clothed in the merely "supernatural," that pretranscendent or pre-Axial idea of otherness, nor again on the posttranscendent, radically secularized idea of the individual who carries a moral compass within. The truly transcendent and heteronomous, by contrast, frames the problem as one of theodicy—justifying the ways of God to man, overcoming the discrepancy between fate and merit. It uses another vocabulary for posing the same problem but now infuses it with a salient ethical moment. The externality that is abandoned with the modern move to an internalized morality, then, is an externality that had already been redefined as heteronomous in the religions of the Axial Age.

Let us recall here the three sacrificial stories that serve as referents in Western culture to the three different modes of externality or otherhood of which we have been speaking: the sacrifice of Iphigenia, the binding of Isaac, and the Passion of Jesus. Each represents a very different response to contingency or, rather, a response to the specific societal and civilizational ways that contingency was framed.

In the case of Iphigenia, following Martha Nussbaum's understanding of Aeschylus's *Agamemnon*, it is to the dictates of necessity that Agamemnon yields up his daughter on the altar of Aulus.[7] External constraint devoid of a moral dimension, though not perhaps of an ethical one. The irreducible force of the world engages the individual with practical problems, the response to which may well lead to tragedy and even ethical condemnation, not only in the choices taken, but in the manner of their fulfillment, which is, as Nussbaum points out so tellingly, at the core of Aeschylus's tragedy.

In the case of Abraham and Isaac, however, contingency has been overcome, not in necessity, but in the dictates of an ethical God. The utter destruction of Abraham's world, defined in terms of a Divine Promise revoked, threatens chaos at an almost unimaginable level. As discussed by Ahron Agus,

> Religious man knows that Abraham had to discover the terrible truth that he had not confronted until that moment when the voice of God called him to Moriah. Finally, theology breaks down in the reality of living. Finally, the world turns out to be not a divinely ordered cosmos, but rather an existence in which the most divine of promises is wrenched away and suddenly dissolved, as if a mere vision. Finally, even our children, as great as their promise may have been, are snatched away from us in the cruelty of chaos that is the real world. God calls upon Abraham to sacrifice his beloved Isaac in order to test Abraham, to see whether he can continue in the world as it really is.[8]

Here then the sacrifice is in heeding the utterly incomprehensible call of an utterly heteronomous God. Heteronomous, external, but no longer mere necessity. The demands are those of the transcendent, the authority is not one of *praxis* but is an authority of the holy, through which action in the world must be judged. And finally, there is the Passion of Jesus, that sacrifice entered into willingly, which therefore subverts death and overturns the natural order of the world. Note, however, the transposed locus of action, from out there in the dictates of a heteronomous God to inside in the willingness of the victim.[9]

In the tragedy of Agamemnon's sacrifice of Iphigenia the will is coerced by practical necessity, as *tyche* is overcome by a particular form of *techne*. In Abraham's sacrifice of Isaac the will is coerced by the dictates of a heteronomous God and in so doing the reality of the world is relativized in terms of a transcendent framework and hence is in a sense overcome. In the sacrifice of Jesus the world is also relativized, *tyche* overcome, and *fortuna* tamed, not, however, by renaming it necessity nor solely by a transcendent relativization (i.e., denuding the world of its significance, though this also happens) but by the power of an autonomous will that transposes the locus of significance from the external to the internal— though, to be sure, one still constituted in transcendent terms, as it would be for another eighteen hundred or so years.

Each offers a way of overcoming the chaos of the world, and each in turn is constitutive of a different idea of selfhood. While the Christian and Jewish perspectives share a transcendent element that the Greek story lacks, the Greek and Jewish sacrifices privilege the external, which in the Christian story is subtly transformed and internalized.

Here let us focus on the external element, even when it is, as in the Christian version, internalized. We must now seek to expand that definition of authority as something external, apart, other than the calculus of interest maximization and instead consider it in terms of the self and its expressive capacities. For while the connection between authority and selfhood (understood as something beyond an infinite bundle of desires) may indeed be clear, the external nature of this authority would still be a matter of some debate. Even if rational choice or economic man can exist without authority in a world where market forces are the sole social tie, one nevertheless recognizes that certain social formations or periods may be characterized by arenas of human interaction that operated to a greater or lesser degree according to terms other than those of exchange and market instrumentality. The institution of marriage in different societies or in the same society over centuries, for example, is an arena in which one can follow the waxing and waning of attitudes rooted in different visions of negotiation and exchange as regards what is holy, set apart, and partaking of an authority beyond individual desire. Thus, one sees the sacramental marriage of the twelfth century and the proliferation of prenuptial agreements at the close of the twentieth.[10] The different stresses are obvious.

Yet, in some sense all this is beside the point. We have already discussed the ideas of constitutive and instrumental self at some length and have shown the necessity of some idea of authority to the first category. The question we pose is whether the relevant authority need remain external to self in order to fulfill the constitutive function. Why, in other words, can it not be internalized to provide the same locus for self as a heteronomous one. After all, the whole of the modern civilizational project turns on the idea of autonomy as constituting self. Why is this insufficient? Thus, I envision the modern liberal reader granting halting agreement, but still not fully convinced, conceding: "Well, okay, fine, I'll buy the argument about authority (candy bars and such), but I still fail to see why the authority must be external. The authority of the moral law, of course, but surely that is the moral law within and not the coercive commandments of a heteronomously imposed authority?"

Modernity, as we have observed, turns on precisely this wager, that an internalized authority in the form of a morality governed by transcendental and hence reasonable rules is sufficient to constitute the self and sacrality. This was Kant's project. In some respects it was the empirical reality that Durkheim set out to demonstrate in his strictures on the transcendent nature of the individual as forming the conscience collective of modern society. It is a view that has been subjected to attack in the epistemological assumptions of social choice theory and rational actor models of social action. For my part, I am questioning it here from the other side: not in support of the paradigmatic individualization of economic theory that questions the idea of a conscience collective, but rather on behalf of an externally constructed conscience collective through whose existence alone the individual can come to exist. Why must the constitutive emerge from an external authority and not from an internalized one?

The force of the external is, first and foremost, in its very givenness, its overbearing quiddity, which makes it phenomenologically incontrovertible. In traditional societies ritual, in its very externality—as something that takes place out there, in the world—is constitutive of the thing itself. Without the ritual, that which it represents does not in fact exist. Romantic love as a bond between individuals exists whether or not it is expressed in a marriage ceremony (religious or secular), but the Jewish notion of *kedushin* does not exist without the proper ritual acts. The same is true, of course, for the myriad of activities that define the life of ritual man. Just to follow the Jewish example, in the life of an observant Jew (today as in the past) the separation of milk from meat, shaking the palm branch on Pentecost, laying phylacteries, and so on all provide the parameters of life. All have a meaning beyond the action itself, but that meaning cannot exist without the ritual action. The meaning depends on the ritual act for its existence. It is the action out there and in the world that constitutes the meaning of the event, not the other way around. Durkheim's work on the history of the contract and of how slowly it has divested itself of its ritual encumbrances and symbols is revealing of just how difficult it is to maintain a relation without symbolizing it.[11] Indeed, there is a massive anthropological literature devoted to the study of ritual and with just this phenomenon in particular—the embeddedness of vast areas of individual and collective experience within external actions, from the pains of childbirth to the trauma of dreams to the festivals of marriage and of exchange to the throes of death. These events are articulated, constituted, and made sensible through praxis.

Today, however, we continue to have rituals, but now our rituals *represent* something else, something that often as not takes place "inside" the self, where we look to the real locus of action. Just as the Lord's Supper became the *seal* of the covenant for seventeenth-century Congregational Puritans, so the marriage ceremony today sets its *seal* on an internally experienced state, the emotional bond that exists prior to and independent of the ceremony itself.[12] Those much trumpeted secular rituals become none other than visible signs of invisible "grace."[13] They are not constitutive of the thing itself.

This is a corollary to the fact that "grace" itself becomes internal, located within the individual as internalized morality from the early eighteenth century on. Indeed, I have used Jewish examples of constitutive ritual functions above precisely because they provide an alternative to the perspective so often adopted by us moderns, while yet maintaining their connection to Western culture, even to the modern world, which Ndemba ritual, for example, would lack. As Jonathan Z. Smith has pointed out, Judaism occupies a peculiar position

> within the larger framework of the imaginings of Western religion: close yet distant, similar yet strange, occidental yet oriental, commonplace yet exotic . . . foreign enough for comparison and interpretation to be necessary yet close enough for it to be possible.[14]

In a sense, however, so much of our thought on these matters is "Protestantized" that it is difficult for us to appreciate the importance of the external, of the other-than-self in ritual acts as constituting and constitutive of self. With us moderns this is manifestly not so at all, and when looking at ritual acts in other cultures we tend to fall into the trap Evans-Pritchard warned us of "in which it is all too easy, when translating the conceptions of simpler people into our own, to transplant our thought into theirs."[15] I think we may even go one step further and theorize the rise of contemporary pagan cults, witchcraft, and the like as very much a reaction to the interiorization of all expressive moments (of ultimate concerns) and the need precisely to find an external, objectified form outside of oneself to express states of feeling that have for too long been deemed an internal affair.

Further, the proliferation of such practices as the household burial of or a woman's eating the placenta after childbirth in the contemporary United States is, I would offer, another reflection of this dynamic—the need to objectify a significant moment in one's life in order to give it meaning.[16] Unrepresented, it is, in some sense, nonexistent. That this representation often takes the form of a modern paganism rather than of transcendent edicts is, of course, one of its major dangers, but that is another matter. This, however, was Durkheim's insight that the symbolic (his concern was with forms of solidarity) takes the place of the thing itself as a locus of meaning and significance. It only exists if it exists "out there."[17]

This is why primordiality is such a good tool to think constitutive identities with. Age, race, and gender lend themselves to constitutive thinking because of their very givenness. This is precisely what ascribed characteristics are. They are given. They are ascribed. They are incontrovertibly *there.* They cannot be changed, won, lost, or achieved. (Achieved characteristics or criteria are, of course, just that, achieved, by the individual's own education, cunning, skill, pluckiness, or determination.) Ascribed characteristics are also, note, invariably collective.

Now it is because of their externality that ascribed criteria of self continue to play a default role—that we continue to fall back on them in defining the constitutive when pressed by lack of sufficient information, feelings of danger, and so on. And it is so because they are external to self—one is born into a race or gender or age cohort, and no degree of intentionality or achievement can change that. Primordial attributes are all visible to others and as such exist out there, in the world, as a form of act, even with nothing really being done. Whether or not we should be color blind, the point is that we are not, and I believe a good argument can be made that race (and gender) are very much equivalent to an act, denoting membership in a constitutive group (providing an easy to way into fooling ourselves with the belief that said group is not, as all groups, of course, are, constructed).

It is the externality of ascribed characteristics that bestows upon them their "givenness," their facticity. But the externally authoritative is not restricted to definition in primordial terms. It can also be defined in terms of transcendence. Our civilizational heritage, however, with its stress on the internal and the intentional aspects of conduct, often blinds us to the constituting nature of the external in much of ritual action. How often is "ritualized" seen to be only a husk or shell devoid of content, devoid of a constitutive core. From the perspective of a ritual culture, of course, it is precisely in that husk that the meaning of the act lies.

Thus we come to a paradox: that same externality which, in the form of worldly existence, presents itself as chaos to be tamed and overcome is, in other forms—of transcendent God, supernatural deities, liberal morality, that which tames, mediates, and orders the contingencies of the world. Ritual systems, I contend, recognize this reality in ways that we moderns, with our purely internal systems of morality, do not. There adheres to the former an understanding that those dynamics through which a self is constructed exist in things done out-there, in the world. Instead, we denigrate such systems as primitive, as somewhat lower down on an imputed moral scale, and as stages on the way to our own developmental apex.

Williams is one who argued against this modernist view and on behalf of a recognition of a worldview that embraces ritual systems as a central aspect of human existence. This then is the point of the expressive—of being-through-expressing and eschewing false distinctions between content and form and a normative privileging of the former over the latter, as we so often do in discussing ritual activity. To recognize the importance of the external is to recognize the constitutive role of the expressive.

Analytically and to an extent historically, I am tracing a movement for framing or taming the contingencies of the world, from the supernatural to the transcendent—hence heteronomous—to the autonomous. It is, moreover, in the heteronomous that an idea of self as other than Hobbesian man can exist, and with it an authority (that is distinct from power) and a morality beyond interest. In the form of transcendence, of Otto's "wholly other," the heteronomous is most fully external to self. The gods of Olympus are not heteronomous, only powerful in their immortality, and neither is the autonomous model of liberal individuality. In the former case the most fully other or external has not yet been achieved, in the latter it has been overtaken as it has been internalized into a form of selfhood (through the autonomous morality of a good will). The dynamics of that move will concern us in the next chapter. Here I only seek a greater appreciation of what externality or otherhood can mean—not in its trendy postmodern guise, but as the essence of a heteronomously constituted self. We are all so thoroughly modern, hence autonomous, that we have become blind to alternative phenomenologies, which are, however, increasingly attractive to more and more people in the West as they experience the expressive muteness of the autonomous self.

Hence, the discussions of moral luck and of ritual are meant to raise questions about what is lost when otherhood is internalized as the deliberations of an autonomous individual will, and the examination of the three sacrifices are offered as an iconic representation of these three moments. I stress the intimate connection between the randomness of the world and the otherhood or externality that must characterize any authority in that realm beyond utility functions. For randomness (lack of control, unknowableness) is what lies beyond the realm of human intervention, as does the Divine with one difference—the idea of divine transcendence posits that order does inhere in the randomness and chaos of the world. It stands the fear of randomness on its head as the unknowability and caprice of the world are projected onto the unknowability of God. As the problem of *tyche* is thus transformed into the problem of a theodicy, some measure of knowability is acquired. Even if it is but a synonym for ignorance, it is at least ignorance of God's will, which is very different from a random fate devoid of any meaning.

Central to this transformation is the time sense inherent in certain transcendent religions and most saliently in the notions of final time, of an *Endzeit*—a cultural orientation that does not exist in pre-Axial social settings. By removing the contingent element (luck) from time, by transforming its existence as brutal fact, eschatology articulates time ethically, as all accounts of a sacred history attest. Thus, we can compare the sacrifice of Iphigenia with that of Isaac and see how the move to appease brute nature has been rearticulated as fulfilling the demands of an ethical God.

And so we can see how the very idea of transcendence (and its concomitant visions of salvation, however varied in different salvational religions,
from Judaism to Hinduism, from Christianity to Buddhism) invests the
temporal with meaning. Time is severed from the meaninglessness of
nature and infused with soteriological significance, as one's actions in
time are linked to salvation. A causal chain roots oneself and one's actions in a set of ultimate meanings. These are, of course, very different
in different religious visions: from the theodicy of the Shema that the
observant Jew repeats every day, to the Hindu belief in reincarnation, to
the place of the Christian *ecclesia* in the progress of salvation, to the calculus of the appearance of the last Imam in Shiite Islam. Common to all,
however, is the radical restructuring of time, as it is severed from the
randomness of being and repositioned in a great salvational drama.

One finds some sense of this change in the writings of Mircea Eliade
and G. van der Leeuw, who pointed out how the primitive (non-Axial or,
in Weberian terms, "magical") man

> knows primordial time, which for him dominates all life, which is renewed
> over and over again in the present day occurrences that are the guarantee
> of this life. As long as he performs the rites correctly, he creates his world
> anew each day, in a manner of creatio continua. The creative world of myth
> renews the world for him.[18]

Compare this characterization with that break in temporal conceptions
that marked the emergence of Axial civilizations:

> On the one side, time takes a cyclical course, on the other it has a beginning
> before which there was nothing and an end with which it stops. On the one
> side every sunrise is a victory over chaos, every festival a cosmic beginning,
> every sowing a new creation, every holy place a foundation of the cosmos,
> every historical event a rise or fall according to the regular course of the
> world and even the law that sustains society is nothing other than the rule
> of the sun's course. . . . On the other side, everything is exactly the same
> except that at a certain point in the cycle someone appears who proclaims
> a definitive event, the day of Yahweh, the last judgement, the ultimate salva-
> tion, or the final conflict as in Iran. The images used are all borrowed from
> the course of nature: day and night, summer and winter. But the ethos has
> changed; a hiatus has been made between a tempus in the strict sense, which
> changes everything.[19]

This conception of final time, of an eschaton, unique to certain Axial
civilizations—a notion of both the beginning and end of historical
time—was also the prerequisite of a full-fledged transcendent orientation of the ethical. However the ethical orientations of these Axial civilizations concerned not the restructuring of a natural order but the anni-

hilation of the temporal and historical nature of both individual and collective existence. Their locus classicus was in overcoming the insecurities and exigencies of any *historical* order through the ethical dictates of a transcendent Deity with its heteronomously imposed injunctions. This dynamic was inherent not only to early Judaism, but continued in the schismatic splits, first of Christianity from Judaism and then of the Protestant Reformation of the sixteenth century. Today, it has been reframed in the internal terms of the autonomous self. The uniqueness of this historical "solution"—secularism—is however such that it ultimately threatens the existence of that very self it wishes to maintain.

Precisely this self, whose identity is nonautonomous yet constituted and whose existence depends on externality, can be approached in a number of additional ways. The issue of moral luck, for example, with its intimations of bearing responsibility for events beyond one's control, approaches the analytically similar issue of collective guilt (or what may be better termed collective responsibility). To what extent, that is, is one implicated in activities simply by virtue of group membership, with no possible connection to intentionality or one's actions? To what extent are essential aspects of self seen as bound up with actions of others, with the progress of things in the world over which we have no control?

In this context, causal chains are set up not only in time, as they are when one is a member of a salvational collective (*ummah, ekklesia,* or *am yisrael*), but also in space.[20] One's membership in certain social groups ties one to others (and in so doing makes us responsible for actions) over which we have no control. One can argue for the very real existence of empirically demonstrable links that connect seemingly disparate acts in ways that were not at first obvious. Take, for example, the assassination of Prime Minister Yitzhak Rabin of Israel by a right-wing religious law student named Yigal Amir in Tel Aviv during a massive peace rally on November 4, 1995. Following the assassination there were a number of reports in the New York media of notices posted in certain kosher New York eating establishments that had called for the death of the prime minister. The argument ran that because Rabin was willing to relinquish parts of the West Bank as a component of a peace agreement with the legitimate representatives of the Palestinian people, he was to be considered a *rodef,* that is, a Jew whose life was forfeit. While the textual basis for this "edict" is highly suspect, a number of influential rabbinic leaders in Israel and the Diaspora had expressed this opinion. It was not quite a Jewish *fatwa,* but it contributed significantly to a climate where Yitzhak Rabin was considered a traitor to the Jewish people who had to be stopped at all costs. Contributing to such a climate of opinion were the types of posters carried at right-wing demonstrations: they depicted the prime minister as Yasir Arafat or even, as at one Likud demonstration attended by Benjamin Netanyahu, in an SS uniform. In this latter case, Rabin was identified—even equated—with the worst enemies of the Jewish people, indeed, with what has come to be the symbol of ultimate evil.

Let us, however, ignore events in Israel prior to the assassination and turn to Washington Heights in upper Manhattan and the hypothetical case of Avraham Stern (fictitious name), who, on his way to his CPA's office, stops in at a local eatery for a knish and a cream soda. On entering the store, he spies a poster comparing the prime minister to Hitler, declaring him to be a *rodef*, in essence, deserving of being put to death for the good of the Jewish people. Now, Mr. Stern was not in a good mood that day. That morning he had been called to an interview with the principal of his daughter's school, where she was threatened with expulsion for being cheeky to a teacher; he had not moved his bowels for two days and was feeling bloated; his wife was demanding that he agree that her mother visit them for a month; and his car insurance had just gone through the roof because of his son's latest accident. On top of everything else it was hot and he was filled with memories of when the neighborhood's lingua franca had been German and not Spanish, which made him sad.

Mr. Stern was thus not an atypical person on the way to the lunch counter. We are all similarly burdened. Mr. Stern's politics, I should add, were a good deal more centrist, even left leaning, than those of most members of his congregation and even his family. He neither liked nor trusted Yasir Arafat but felt that there must be a better solution to the conflict in the Middle East than the continual wars (his brother's son had been killed in the 1982 invasion of Lebanon). And he had an intuition that the Palestinian people were not all so detestable as they were made out by his neighbors and family. Indeed, he could imagine that their concerns were probably similar to his own, and he could occasionally even understand their desire for statehood and independence and even think it just.

So Mr. Stern enters the luncheonette and as he is ordering he notices the poster above the cash register virtually calling for the assassination of Prime Minister Rabin. Mr. Stern is in no mood for a political argument with the proprietor and other customers, and so, even though he vehemently disagrees with the message, he eats his lunch in peace and leaves without comment.

Is there a sense in which Mr. Stern bears any degree of responsibility for the murder of Prime Minister Rabin in Tel Aviv? Not guilt, but responsibility, what Hannah Arendt called "vicarious responsibility."[21] At some point, of course, the question becomes not so much one of ethical responsibility, but of legal guilt, as conspiracy law makes clear. To simply say no begs the question. For we can up the ante to query the position of the proprietor who put up the poster; does he bear any responsibility? Or we may cross the ocean and view a similar scene enacted, not in New York, but in Tel Aviv. Or we may move to the fellow carrying the poster of the prime minister in a Nazi uniform. Or to the rabbi engaging in halakhic (i.e., Jewish legal) discourse on the laws of *rodef* in terms of the prime minister (never outright calling for his murder, which would have been a legal infraction). Do any of these bear responsibility? Most readers would, I assume, admit the existence of responsibility even where the matter of legal guilt does not enter the picture. If so, where do we draw the line? Let us then return to Mr. Stern and to the question of his responsibility—bearing in mind that this is a hypothetical case, the fundamental terms of which concern not an Orthodox Jew in Washington Heights and the murder of the Israeli prime minister but every man and woman in similar circumstances. We could have told a similar story concerning Hamas or the IRA or Indian nationalists; the issue is universal.

Now there are two ways of making the case for some degree of responsibility. Both involve the idea of causal chains, though these are very different in nature. Let me first parse out the one that does not interest us and has no direct bearing on our argument. In this scenario Mr. Stern, in not responding to what he saw as an ethically offensive poster, bears some responsibility for creating the climate of opinion within which the murder took place. In our global culture this climate of opinion crosses borders and even continents. Thus sentiments expressed in Washington Heights do reverberate and influence, to some extent, events in Bnei Brak (the ultra-Orthodox city neighboring Tel Aviv). No doubt Mr. Stern's passive acceptance of the public proclamation puts him in a position of lesser responsibility than the active deed of the proprietor who posted the notice, and both, perhaps, bear a somewhat lesser degree of responsibility than their counterparts in Jerusalem, where similar scenes were played out (to maintain our metaphor, the chain from act to act was longer from New York than from Jerusalem). Moreover, while the assignation of degrees of responsibility would require an expert in casuistry (parsing out the different types of acts, active or passive, proximate or removed, to what degree, etc.), an argument for a real, existing, if as yet hypothetical causal chain, in terms of contributing to a climate of opinion, can be made. It is not irrelevant that most of the public contrition (though by no means all were contrite) among Mr. Stern's coreligionists was expressed along these very lines of the creation of a climate of opinion within which, and, by implication, only within which, the murder could have taken place.

This, then, is one line of argument, which sees the phenomenon of collective responsibility as reducible, in a sense, to collective guilt. That is, there were real acts (including speech acts) that to some, perhaps even infinitesimal, degree aided or hindered a specific event (the assassination). Such acts fall along a continuum, at one end of which is legal culpability, at the other is a moral or ethical responsibility devoid of any ascribable guilt.[22]

Our concern, however, is with the issue of moral luck, with acts or rather with responsibility for acts over which we have *no* control. The case of Mr. Stern's guilt, by contrast, is precisely one where the issue is one of volition and control, however minimal. Recalling our discussion from chapter one, we have in the above argument been dealing with power, with agency as an act of volition that exerts some effect on the world, hence as endowed with some fraction of power. This is very different from the problem of moral luck, of bearing responsibility for acts over which we have no control, and of the type of causal chains that this involves.

Does Mr. Stern bear some responsibility for the assassination simply by virtue of his membership in the group of observant Jews? Are we, in some sense—however symbolic, however unreasonable, responsible for acts of others if these others share with us certain forms of group membership? Is there, in other words, a sense of collective responsibility according to which we are responsible not only for what we do but also for what we are? On the face of it, and, given the majority of groups of which we as moderns are members, the answer would seem to be no. If a fellow member of the Boston Electricians' Union gets up on top of a supermarket with an assault rifle and shoots up the passing populace, we would not be seen as bearing any responsibility for this act. This, of course, would be very different from certain other classes of acts, say, a discriminatory policy against African-Americans that the union had enacted. In such a case my responsibility would be very different. Here I might feel both shame at the collective deed, but also guilt at not taking action when the vote was taken, say, exiting the organization. Indeed in certain cases guilt over such acts may even be legally assignable.

Yet, this possibility of exit brings us to the analytic heart of the matter. For what of those groups from which we cannot exit without losing ourselves, groups from which our withdrawal would in some fundamental sense make us other than we are? What of groups that are constitutive of who we are, rather than simply groups where our membership is voluntary and instrumental toward realizing a certain goal? For if we return to our earlier distinction of instrumental and constitutive groups, we find something very interesting in terms of causal chains and the nature of our own place within them. An instrumental group or voluntary association (the local PTA or MADD or the AAUP) is defined by our own agency, that is, by power. I can enter or exit them at will and use my skills, such as they are, to influence the policy and practice of the group as I see fit. The point of my membership in such groups is to further my own individual interests (again, this is true for groups ranging from the ILGWU to the AMA or the American Numismatic Association), and the assumption is that I may withdraw my membership if my interests are not being served or can be served better elsewhere. (Having read the literature on resource mobilization and the "rebel's dilemma," I may find alternative forms to maximize my utility inputs.) What is critical here is that on exiting these groups I am the same I as I was on entering them and that any changes wrought by my membership are things extrinsic to selfhood (to what psychologists would call ego identity). The conversionary experience of Paul, for example, is a different script.[23] And this is precisely the point, because membership in such groups does not touch core concepts of selfhood. Because such membership is instrumental, it is predicated on assumptions of agency and of power. And hence one's relation to a particularly objectionable practice in such a group would be of assignable guilt. Most of our groups today can be so characterized. Yet there are other types of groups, where membership is not instrumental, not voluntary, and not easily dissociated from the way one views the core values of selfhood.

These groups we have termed constitutive, for the very reason that membership in them does not assume a methodological individualism, where the individual is anterior to the group. A constitutive group of necessity rules out the very idea that an individual can enter and exit as one does a supermarket. Moreover, and as Arendt made clear, the only way any attempt to "escape" this collective responsibility is "by leaving the community and since no man can live without belonging to some community, this would simply mean to exchange one community for another and hence one kind of responsibility for another."[24] It is here that the argument over collective responsibility becomes interesting. For if one cannot exit the group without in some sense transforming the self, one is devoid of precisely that sense of power that can connect one's own individual acts (or one's refusal to act) to the case in question. In these latter cases, as we have seen, what is framed as responsibility is often in fact a form of guilt (predicated on the very power that one does have). In the case of the constitutive group, however, the question becomes more subtle, for, although one cannot exit the group (indeed precisely because one cannot exist the group), one is bound to others by ties that leave us feeling responsible for certain acts of these alters. Certain acts, but not others. A purely individual and self-referential act on the part of another member of such a group would not necessarily leave us with a feeling of responsibility (though it might). It is rather in those acts of the alter that are infused with a collective meaning or character that, when opprobrious, make us cringe. And some degree of responsibility for that which we cannot in any way control is shifted, however minimally, to our own shoulders.

Moreover, as such groups are constitutive in the way they frame our very being in the world (as opposed, say, to simply a particular status position that would be defined by our membership in instrumental groups), we may feel shame even for what on the face of it would be purely selfish or self-referential acts on the part of our comembers. This would not be the case among members of the electricians' union; it would be more the case among Jews or African-Americans (as would the obverse, pride in an individual's accomplishments), though perhaps less so today than fifty years ago. This change is itself a measure of how these very identities are less constitutive today than they were then. We may recall here Robert Wuthnow's respondent in his research on contemporary spirituality—"a 26 year old disabilities counselor, the daughter of a Methodist minister, who describes her religious preference as 'Methodist, Taoist, Native American, Quaker, Russian Orthodox, Buddhist, Jew.' " If one can be all of these, none is constitutive.[25]

Yet the question remains, insofar as these identities do remain and the shame is felt, on what is it predicated? I propose that we envision a different form of causal chain, not a material one but a symbolic one, defined by mutual responsibility. Hence one becomes in some sense responsible for deeds over which, by any common understanding, we have no control. Though no material causal chains can be imputed, a symbolic tie binds us, in however mediated a manner, to deeds that we have no hand in—except that we share with the perpetrators certain fundamental assumptions about who we are and what constitutes our existence in the world. These may be shared religious belief, racial characteristics, or national belonging. There is no essentialism implied in the above. In fact, these modes of identity seem to be decreasing in certain parts of today's postindustrial world. By the same token, however, the very spread of a global culture has reinvigorated such identities elsewhere in the world (as evinced in the rise of nationalist parties from Austria to India and from Indonesia to France). The historical thrust of such modes of collective and individual identity are, however, timeful.[26] For it is these modes of identity that constitute the very essence of transcendent religions and that are the foundation of a Muslim *ummah* or a Jewish *am yisrael* or a Christian *ecclesia*. The connecting ties are ones of responsibility, even indeed across time (though not necessarily in a linear fashion).

In all cases we have a mode of collectivity where membership makes one responsible for others so constituted. Again, in different societies, at different times and places, such identities have run the gamut of primordial, transcendent, and civil, although the latter type tends, with institutionalization, to transform social ties to more plainly instrumental ones.[27] In the case of transcendent religion (and its transcendent edicts), existence is tied to certain ontological premises about the existence of the world and the meaning of human history. And the terms of human existence are redefined in terms of a salvational drama, whose resolution may be expressed in the other-worldly terms of Hinduism or the this-worldly terms of Judaism or Islam. In the process human agency, too, is redefined.[28] The individual begins to emerge with greater distinction (as an aspect of that responsibility imposed by transcendent edicts), but, at the same time, the individual is tied to others in a salvational or soterio-logical program that radically restructures what we may mean by causal chains.

It is, I believe, precisely these types of community that Karl Jaspers had in mind when, following the Second World War and the revelation of the crimes of the Nazi regime, he developed his concept of *metaphysical guilt*, which, similar to our ideas of collective responsibility, involves a "transformation of human self-consciousness before God."[29] Member-ship in a salvational community links one's actions in a project of salva-tion. One's deeds become part of a soteriological calculus that may bring salvation closer or distance it. Saint or sinner. Culpability is assignable. Actions cease to be simple responses to random events in the cosmos but are linked together and to those of others as contributing (or hindering) the progress of salvation. In Jaspers' terms:

> the causal connections of history, cause and responsibility are indivisible wherever human activity is at work. As soon as decisions and actions play a part in events, every cause is at the same time either credit or guilt. . . . [And, with an eye on the issues of moral luck,] even those happenings which are independent of will and decision, still are human tasks.[30]

In transcendence, I would argue, one finds the origin of these forms of causal chains, as symbolic constructs linking us in a unique collectivity. (Not that these ties did not exist in primordially construed collectivities, as we know from Homer, among others, but what constituted such collec-tivities was, or course, very different.) And, as we have observed, these forms of causal chains are articulated very differently in different salva-tional religions. The highly this-worldly and collective nature of Jewish salvational visions, which roots theodicy in collective being (as expressed by the observant Jew each day in his recital of the Shema), is, for exam-ple, very different from the more highly individualist visions of Western Christianity (though, of course, with great differences within these as well). Indeed, and as we shall argue in greater detail in the following chapter, in its liberal Protestant forms this Christian vision undercuts the very idea of such causal chains through the privileging of intentionality over action. This itself is but the final step of the more general privileging of faith over works and the wholesale transposition of the salvational drama from the collective to within the individual (in what eventually became conscience). In this move authority is internalized (as the authority of conscience) and the shame that characterized our response to transgression (our own or another's) is transformed into guilt (over our own).

Let us recall here the main tenets of our argument, of the role of a heteronomous authority in constituting the self as a moral evaluator, with the resultant imputation of responsibility for acts over which we have no control. As we saw, this dynamic, in the form of moral luck, even challenged that most clearly internal of domains, that of morality, which we tend to equate with the internality of intent, rather than with external action. In the case of collective responsibility (and ruling out those forms of causal chains where real linkages between acts can be posited or imputed), the very acceptance of such a formulation led to the idea of constitutive groups whose members can (and do) make claims on us that go beyond those of reason alone and for whose actions we are correspondingly responsible in ways we are not for members of other social groups.[31] To quote Arendt once again:

> This vicarious responsibility for things we have not done, this taking upon ourselves the consequences for things we are entirely innocent of, is the price we pay for the fact that we live our lives not by ourselves but among our fellowmen and that the faculty of action, which, after all, is the political faculty par excellence, can be actualized only in one of the many and manifold forms of human community.[32]

Admittedly, this type of tie is rare today, and beyond family we rarely recognize such forms of communality or of authority, for that matter. Yet family may be a fruitful way to approach the question of how community involves an idea of authority and constituted existence upon which moral individuality must rest. A useful heuristic approach here would be to return to the phenomenon of shame. How many of us feel shame when a coworker, perhaps a fellow lawyer, CPA, or bus driver engages in particularly disgraceful behavior? We may feel offended or angry or we may even worry that our own lives may be affected by the action. But most of us would not feel shame. Compare this to our feelings of shame when our child forgets his lines at the school play or verbally abuses a teacher or is disruptive in church. (We may feel the same, by the way, towards an aged mother taking the liberties of her station with people on the bus, so the matter at hand is clearly not one of its reflection on our child-

rearing practices.) What is this phenomenon of shame, not as a psychological datum but as a cultural artifact? What particular way of being and
of being united to others fosters its emergence? And finally, how does
this issue of shame move us toward a greater appreciation of the issue of
heteronomous authority that we have placed at the heart of our concern
with selfhood?

Shame, then, rather than guilt, leads us to a mode of relation with
others that is far from the economistic or rational actor model of self.
To feel shame for one's own acts (or even for those of others), one must
be tied to others in ways beyond the contractual and in a manner that
presumes more than simply material and causal links between our acts
and those of others. Guilt, as Herbert Morris has pointed out, is a "thresh-
old" morality: one is either guilty of a wrongdoing or one is not. But
shame, as he notes, is connected not to a violation but to a failure or a
shortcoming. He terms it a "scale" morality, the scale in question being
the matrix of our moral identity rather than of any sort of reciprocal
relation with another. His passages in *Guilt and Shame* are among the
most insightful written on the subject:

> Shame, unlike guilt, is not essentially tied to fault. Fault is connected with
> blame and blame is connected with failing to meet demands that others
> might reasonably place on one because they would place it upon themselves
> in like situations. Shame, however, may arise through failure to do the ex-
> traordinary. We may feel either guilt or shame in behaving as a coward. We
> may feel shame and not guilt in failing to behave as a hero. . . . [W]hat is
> valued in shame morality is an identity of a certain kind and not, as is neces-
> sary with guilt, a relationship with others. The whole focus in a shame
> scheme where relationships are valued is the question "Am I worthy of being
> related to others?" With guilt we have a conceptual scheme of obligations
> and entitlements. We have seen how this leads to the idea of owing some-
> thing to others because one has taken something one is not entitled to. With
> shame what is crucial is a failing to correspond with the model of identity. We
> shall feel shame, then, in situations where we do not conceive of ourselves as
> damaging a relationship with others. And where the maintaining of that
> relationship is an element in one's model identity, when one acts in a way
> incompatible with the relationship, the shame response focuses on failing
> to be a worthy person as one conceives it, rather than on failing to meet
> one's obligations to others and needing to restore the relationship. . . . With
> shame there is an inevitable derogation in one's status as a person; with guilt
> one's status is intact but one's relationship to others is affected. The shame-
> ful is not worthy of association; the guilty is still worthy, but a price must be
> paid.[33]

Shame thus admits of no recompense or restitution. Rather, "the steps that are appropriate to relieve shame are becoming a person who is not shameful."[34] It is one's own self, or identity, that must be reconstituted, not a relationship. If it is guilt that we experience when we violate the codes of exchange in a relational matrix, whether material or symbolic, it is shame that we feel when we violate our own constituted sense of self.

At its extreme we can experience this violation of self as threatening our very existence—the popular phrase, we recall, is "to die of shame," not "to die of guilt." (There have always been appropriate venues, from animal sacrifice to tort law to make restitution for acts bearing on the latter set of feelings.) We have traveled far from a worldview where shame (rather than guilt) defines lives and relations. Imagine Homer's Hector about to meet Achilles in battle, motivated primarily by fear of *shame*, as are all the heroes in the Iliad. A modern-day Hector, by contrast, could well exit Troy via the back gate, credit card in hand—a much more reasonable action, in light of what he intuits as awaiting him at the hands of Achilles. But such an option was not open to Hector. The shame of not facing Achilles would have destroyed him in a much more fundamental sense than Achilles could. Indeed, his body was not defiled though Achilles dragged it through the dirt around the Greek encampment.

Shame ties identity to sets of expectations of self that are of necessity role dependent. We may well recall here our earlier discussion of the self in relation to social roles: the modern sensibility defines the true self as existing beyond social roles, whereas more traditional models see self as existent *only* within social roles. Surely, it is this that operates with Hector, whose role as crown prince of Troy mandated certain behavior within which and only within which he could *be*. Greek heroes cannot be petit bourgeois delicatessen proprietors in the way that baseball players can become restaurant owners, or stock managers outerwear purveyors, or yarn salesman social workers. That the self is seen as existing outside the role is indicative of a particular set of relations between individuals— where the *essence* of the self is not in the relation but in itself alone.

When as a shoemaker I produce a poor pair of shoes, I may feel shame. That I later attempt to sell them at an exorbitant price to an unwary customer may lead to guilt.[35] This is the difference between the relational (myself and the customer) and the self-referential—in how I am forced to see myself through the prism of my poor craftsmanship. What shame points to is the fact that I have internalized a set of role expectations or behavior and to violate these expectations becomes a sort of violation of self because I am not living up to my sense of who I am. Williams speaks of the "internalized other," who, he tells us, is indeed abstracted and generalized and idealized, but he is potentially somebody rather than nobody, and somebody other than me. He can provide the focus for real social expectations, of how I shall live if I act in one way rather than another, of how my actions and reactions will alter my relations to the world about me.[36]

Generalized and idealized, yet still potentially specific, particular, and localized. Unamuno's man of flesh and bone perhaps and not quite Adam Smith's third-party observer, "that great inmate of the human breast" who adjudicates a universal morality rather than a set of local expectations.

Leaving Smith aside, the point is that shame registers the violation of an identity or of a sense of self that is posited not autonomously but very much in terms of external referents, heteronomous dictates, and the authority of the sacred—that is, of the other. In Matthew Arnold's dictum, it is "the not ourselves which makes for righteousness."[37] Abjuring recompense or restitution, existing with the sacred beyond the realm of negotiation, the phenomenon of shame calls for reconstituting the self in ways not that dissimilar from Jaspers' idea of metaphysical guilt.

Shame never fails to remind us how mediated our autonomy really is and how dependent it is on acts and experiences that go well beyond the "good will" of Kantian, self-directed action. We see in its manifestation the "eyes of the other" as an authority external to self. Here, shame is to be distinguished from conscience, which, as an indicator of guilt, measures the workings of an internalized authority. Again, as is so often the case, the internal sanctions of guilt are seen as being of a "higher" moral order than the external ones of shame. The ancient "shame culture" of the Greeks is reinterpreted as a way station to our higher morality of internalized guilt and the workings of conscience. We thus reevaluate the past in line with our own normative preconceptions. But as Williams has noted, much of the human experience is lost when shame is relegated to a lower normative status than guilt. Lost is the sense of the individual as positioned within a communal matrix as defined by heteronomous authority. Consider in this context the Japanese saying to the effect that "the traveler leaves his shame behind him" (*tabi no haji o kakisutete*).[38] This is the modern shame culture par excellence, in which shame depends on the communal/relational matrix, the geographic grid of collective existence, through which individual existence is seen to reside.

It is in a very similar sense that shame is often felt when one loses control, when one fails. When we both identify ourselves with our social role and fail at fulfilling the expectations that define that role, we feel shame. The idea prevalent in the USA today that "it's just a job," or, when one is reprimanded, "not to take it personally" is, of course, the obverse of this attitude of shame. The ill-cobbled boot, the badly written book, the ill-fitting dress may all today be interpreted one way or the other. The ill-turned-out son, on the other hand, may well be the cause of shame, indicating the last set of roles that we identity our own selves with. In this case we may feel shame when his faults are pointed out to us, but also when we see them in our mind's eye. Yet, internalization of an external authority is not the equivalent to the constitution of an internal (autonomous) authority. Internalizing the external makes us heed its call at times when we are alone or physically removed from its referents (which are always, we recall, communal). This is very different from those cases where the referents themselves are internal to self and autonomously posited. Loss of control, failure at our role (when indeed the whole of the self and personality resides therein) are all triumphs of *tyche*, of chaos over order, of brute being over the authority that renders it meaningful (and hence controlled). When we lose control, the matrix of meaning within which we exist is rent, the authority of order (and legitimacy) is thrown into doubt by this experience of cosmic disruption, and the sense of shame overwhelms us. What is at stake is not right or wrong in the narrow sense of guilt or culpability, but a violation of meaning and cosmic order—of what is deemed authoritative to one's sense of self.

Shame registers the distance of a self from itself when that self is perceived to exist in relation to an external source of authority and ordering principles. Chaos then looms and with it the loss of that Archimedean point, of sacrality, upon which the process of ordering rests. Not the guilt of wrongdoing but the shame of failure is what attends on such processes. Because we lack such external authority, we moderns no longer feel such shame, only guilt sometimes at wrongdoing. No longer defined by communal obligations that define our roles and status, but carrying authority within our conscience, our worlds are not threatened by collapse if we drop the ball or sneak out of Troy and remake ourselves in the land of endless possibility. (This, by the way, is the true meaning of the first new nation and S. M. Lipset's realization of how important Puritanism— with its notions of conscience—was to the formation of the American character.)[39]

Lacking shame means that we lack pride as well, for one is the concomitant of the other. The cultural images of success—the basketball player spiking a ball, or the successful stock analyst who consummated a deal— reflect not pride but self-satisfaction. There is an important difference. In whom do we feel pride, other than our family members and, more explicitly, our children? We feel pride at their accomplishments as we do shame at their (moral and other) failings. But this is only part of the story. It is a mistake to think of pride only in hierarchic terms, involving, say, relations between parents and children. It is not hierarchy that engenders pride but the sense of an extended self, validated through the acts of others.

To explicate this I would like to share a story that recently drove this point home to me. I had occasion to find myself feeling pride at the success of a colleague and his being courted, at a fantastically high salary, by another university from where he was positioned. At first I felt joy for him and enjoyed the fact that justice was being done and he was finally receiving the recognition he deserved. Sometime later I found myself feeling pride as well and was caught up short by such feelings. After all, who was I to feel pride in his accomplishments (joy for him and envy as well, to be sure, but pride)? What colossal cheek, what unmitigated chutzpah! Indeed, when I told my wife of this feeling she also looked at me as if to say, "And who do you think you are to arrogate to yourself such feeling?" And yet, I did feel pride and so attempted to analyze it. We had, it is true, both grown up in the same neighborhood (though he on the other side of the tracks); went to the same high school (though we didn't know each other then); had worked together for three years; involved one another in knock-down, take-no-prisoner arguments; and even written some papers together. Our discussions enriched me immensely, broadened my understanding of social processes, of theoretical perspectives, and of the nature of the human condition. I would like to hope that something of that nature perhaps had happened to him as well. And here is where I believe pride came to play a role. I had mixed my labor with his, somewhat in the Lockean sense of what makes private property, and in that small sense constructed something, not much, but something, in common with someone, we recall, over which I had and have no control. This allowed me to feel legitimate pride in his accomplishments, just as I would share his shame if circumstances had been different. To the minuscule extent that I had mixed my labor (here intellectual labor) with his and been transformed in the process, I was entitled to feel an albeit small amount of pride quite apart from any joy or happiness I felt for his change of fortune.

I tell this story at some length because I think it is rare to have such feelings outside of the context of the family, yet I also think most of us have had similar experiences and should not ignore the nature of the relationships they indicate. If we moderns, or perhaps postmoderns, rarely feel pride or rarely feel shame, it is because these are not part of our interpersonal calculus. In a state of metaphysical equality where all are equally authoritative centers of agency and moral calculus, there can be neither shame nor pride in the acts of others. Both emotions presuppose a breach in the armor of autonomy. The question that remains then is, whether lacking both, we also lack a self?

We began this chapter by considering the problem of control and the issue of moral luck. We found that issues of responsibility and of one's ethical position cannot be reduced solely to internal states or to intentionality. We are, it seems, tied to others in ways that make us responsible for actions we do not control—a realization that forces us to rethink subjectivity or rather intersubjectivity. This is not a particularly new insight. One finds it not only among the ancients but also informing the thought of the Scottish moralists and thinkers such as Adam Ferguson, Francis Hutcheson, and Adam Smith.

But, it may be claimed, intersubjectivity does not lead of necessity to the idea of authority, let alone of heteronomous authority. Yet precisely the issues of collective responsibility and of shame heighten the truth that if what is intersubjective is not reducible to the partners of the interaction but is itself an autonomous entity (hence something well beyond the shared reality of partners to a contract), then there must also exist an idea of authority to which these subjects do indeed *subjugate* their individual wills. For if such does not exist, then the bonds are indeed no more than instrumental, temporary, and interest oriented, to be abrogated on demand or when the best opportunity presents itself. We are back at the Hobbesian model of self and rational actor theory.

The issue, then, is what type of self exists without either shame or that authority toward which one feels shame? The calculations of the private conscience as "sole arbiter of moral behavior" leaves one, in Agnes Heller's terms, defined by a narcissistic project and deaf to the calls of love, empathy, charity, and sympathy.[40] For it is through the external authority that the communal self, that very sense of shame, enters, to define us in terms of desiderata beyond those of any calculative reason. We note in this context the story Agnes Heller tells of how "inmates of Stalinist prison cells recall that there was only one way to resist, namely, to mobilize the long forgotten *ten commandments*, particularly one of them: 'You should not give false testimony against your neighbors.' This provided them with a *norm* beyond reasoning."[41] Here then we have the invocation of an external, heteronomous authority as the only force capable of providing a strong enough foundation on which a self could stand and withstand the ordeal.

The same self that, to exist, must do so on the plinth of external authority is, paradoxically, also that one which, when violating the norms of community, is banished from its sight, no longer contributing to the skein of mutual existence upon which social life is predicated. This, by the way, raises some interesting questions about the American child-rearing practice of "time out" for unruly or disobedient children, who are left alone to ponder the nature of their transgression. Replacing shame (within the group) with guilt (of the autonomous conscience), this practice is unable ultimately to reintegrate the child on terms other than those of individual ego, conscience, and guilt. In the end it yields a host of conforming consciences rather than an integrated personality.

Recognition. We ourselves are recognized only insofar as we feel shame—as precisely the absence of that recognition and approbation. We may feel this when we lose control in an area where we expect to have competence. We feel this when we do not meet communal (and internalized communal) expectations, when we are viewed in compromising situations. But also when our "hello" is left unacknowledged even by one who is only an acquaintance. This sense of shame has its roots in the lack of mutual recognition.

However, as I have argued throughout, this "recognized self" who can be shamed and who can be held responsible for collective deeds is also, by definition, a self who exists in a world where negotiation does eventually end, where the sacred and its authority of necessity find a place. Moreover, it is posited that this authority must exist heteronomously— beyond conscience, control, and interest. And externality must be an essential aspect of authority if it is not to devolve into idolatry and mere power—again, Matthew Arnold's righteousness of the "not ourselves."

We now turn to a more historical understanding of the process here explored and, perforce, to the religious roots of our current more autonomous and internalized view of authority, as these have evolved from Protestant Christianity and beyond.

## Chapter Four

# THE SELF INTERNALIZED

THE PREVIOUS chapter ended with three themes linked in a somewhat unanticipated manner: *recognition, authority,* and *extended self.* It was very much the need for recognition, as noted by philosophers from Adam Ferguson and Adam Smith to G.W.F. Hegel, that formed the basis of what we are calling here the extended, or nonautonomous, self. Ferguson points to this need for approbation in noting that "what comes from a fellow-creature is received with peculiar emotion; and every language abounds with terms that express somewhat in the transactions of men different from success and disappointment."[1] He continues: "The bosom kindles in company, while the point of interest in view has nothing to inflame. . . . The value of a favor is not measured when sentiments of kindness are perceived; and the least misfortune has but a feeble meaning when compared to that of insult and wrong."[2] This is an idea of the self that would seem to belie the assumptions that later liberal thought developed from the reasoning of the Scottish moralists. The notion of a self validated by others was, after all, at the heart of eighteenth-century Scottish ideas of civil society and found its way, needless to add, into Hegel's *Phenomenology of Spirit.*

We have observed how we today feel a contradiction between such orientations to a community of shared and mutual approbation and orientations toward authority or hierarchy. We have also noted that precisely within community is authority to be found, as subjugation of the will (as distinct from its coercion), which is the essence of mutuality. Community is authoritative, though specific communities define themselves differently, whether in more or less hierarchic terms or in terms of metaphysical equality. Modernity as a civilizational project has, in its Western European and North Atlantic variants, essentially defined community in terms of equality, though we are witness today to variants on the theme of modernity and consequently to different definitions of community.[3]

Western modernity has until now defined itself so thoroughly in secular terms that it difficult for us to appreciate how fully constitutive transcendence has been for most forms of human community. For not only does transcendence transform the problem of *tyche* into a theodicy and thereby organize and frame existence in knowable terms, but it also defines the idea of what is external to self in terms of an absolute authority.

Absolute transcendent authority thus establishes community in terms that transcend not only the particular member but also the community itself. Hermann Cohen noted this in the context of Jewish monotheism, as opening the way to ethics:

> The correlation of man and God is in the first place that of man, as fellow-man to God. And religion proves its own significance first of all in this correlation of the fellowman to God, in which, indeed, man as fellowman becomes a problem and is engendered through this problem. The share of religion in reason is the share of religion in morality, and no problem of morality takes precedence over this problem of the fellowman. The possibility of ethics is tied to this problem.[4]

Compare this with the following by R. H. Tawney, the English historian, to appreciate what is lost when the transcendent dimension is factored out of the ethical calculus:

> What is wrong with the modern world is that having ceased to believe in the greatness of God, and therefore the infinite smallness (or greatness—the same thing!) of *man*, it had to invent or emphasize distinctions between *men*. It does not say, "I have said, 'Ye are gods!'" Nor does it say, "All flesh is grass." It can neither rise to the heights or descend to the depths (these meet in a spiritual exaltation which may be called either optimism or pessimism). What it does say is that *some* men are gods, and that some flesh is grass, and that the former should live on the latter (combined with pâté de foie gras and champagne), and this is false. For what elevates or depresses, what makes man regarded from one point of view as an angel and from another an ape, is not something peculiar to individuals, but characteristic of the species, something which cannot distinguish between men, precisely because it is inherent in man.[5]

And resonances of these perspectives are heard in the work of Rosenzweig and Levinas—that the idea of transcendence allowed an extended self conceived of in fully generalizable (and not solely ascriptive or primordial) terms.[6] We pursue here the particular paths that the idea of transcendence has taken in the West and how its transformations have been accompanied by concomitant transformations in notions of community and authority and so, by necessity, of the self.

We may say that the history of community in the West is its history of transcendence, and the critical link between the two is the idea of representation. With transcendence representation becomes fully generalizable for the first time. This is the moment of the Axial break between the mundane and transmundane orders. Beforehand the "extended" aspect of the "extended self" could not move beyond the particular primordial aspects of tribe or other ascriptively defined identities. Transcendence offered the possibility of a universal orientation (though of course no guarantee of such). We see this in the ancient practice, dating back to the third millennium B.C.E., of translating or interpreting the names of foreign divinities. The Mesopotamian *Listenwissenschaft* listed Akkadian and Sumerian gods in two or three languages. Later, Bronze Age lists were expanded to include Amorite, Hurritic, Elamite, and Kassite names as well. As explained by the Egyptologist Jan Assman: "Treaties had to be signed by solemn oaths and the gods that were invoked in these oaths had to be recognized by both parties. The list of these gods conventionally closes the treaty. They necessarily had to be equivalent as to their function and in particular as to their rank. Intercultural theology became a concern of international law."[7] Here then are the historical rudiments of generalized symbolic exchange as a condition of more particular economic exchange predicated on an idea of the deity as—if not yet fully generalizable—at least translatable.

But there was more to the eventual break with solely primordial criteria of community than just that. There was a transcendent break with immanent modes of representation as well, which meant that heteronomous authority and its associated ethics of individual responsibility became possible. Intimations of this recognition appear in S. N. Eisenstadt's work on the origins of the civilizations of the Axial Age:

> Certainly, the transmundane order has, in all human societies been perceived as somewhat different, usually higher and stronger then the mundane one. But in the pre-axial age 'pagan' civilizations this higher world has been symbolically structured according to principles very similar to those of the mundane or lower one. Relatively similar symbolic terms were used for the definition of God(s) and man; of the mundane and transmundane orders—even if there was a continuous stress on the difference between them. In most such societies the transmundane world was usually equated with a concrete setting, "the other world," which was the abode of the dead, the world of spirits, and not entirely unlike the mundane world in detail. . . . By contrast, in axial-age civilizations the perception of a sharp disjunction between the mundane and transmundane worlds developed. There was a concomitant stress on the existence of a higher transcendental moral or metaphysical order which is beyond any given this- or other-worldly reality.[8]

This was the insight that Cohen and Levinas were approaching, and I would like to argue the same point from a slightly different perspective, also beginning with the Jewish case, though for reasons of historical progression rather than philosophical orientation.

The following story is recounted in the Babylonian Talmud, tractate Avodah Zarah, the section dealing with idolatrous practices and the proper relations between Israelites and idol worshipers.

> Proclos, son of a philosopher, put a question to Rabbi Gamaliel in Acco when the latter was bathing in the bath of Aphrodite. He said to him, ["]it is written in your Torah, 'and there shall cleave nought of the devoted thing to thine hand.' Why are you bathing in the bath of Aphrodite?["] He replied to him, "We may not answer [questions relating to Torah] in a bath." When he came out he said to him, "I did not come into her domain, she has come into mine, nobody says, the bath was made as an adornment for Aphrodite, but he says, Aphrodite was made as an adornment for the bath. Another reason is, if you were given a large sum of money, you would not enter the presence of a statue reverenced by you while you were nude or had experienced seminal emission, nor would you urinate before it. But this [statue of Aphrodite] stands by a sewer and all people urinate before it. [In the Torah] it is only stated, their Gods—i.e., what is treated as Deity is prohibited, what is not treated as Deity is permitted.["][9]

This story bears directly on our theme of representation, for Rabbi Gamaliel's reply offers great insight into the monotheist understanding of pagan worship, of idolatry. He observes that different statues of Aphrodite may well mean different things in different contexts. Some statues are purely decorative, such as, he argues, the case at hand; but other statues in which an aura of sanctity inheres are meant to be worshiped. It would seem that the context in which the statue is situated defines its nature. In one context it is nothing but a decoration (and hence there is no injunction against Jewish presence in their midst) and in another— such as at a pagan cultic site—they clearly take on their characteristics as sacred objects; accordingly, the injunctions of Jewish law take effect and effectively proscribe numerous forms of (Jewish) behavior in their presence. In brief, because the meaning of idols is context-bound, they do not transcend the world in which they are set. A statue of Aphrodite suffers no loss of respect, no act of lèse-majesté if one urinates in its presence. Thus, in some places and at certain times the statue is simply not a sacred object and makes no demands of awe on the part of its surroundings. How different those symbols of transcendent holiness— the Sefer Torah for Jews, the Koran for Muslims, the Eucharist for Catholics. Their essential representative function can never be "turned off" or withdrawn.

This is not to say that the adherents of Jewish rabbinic culture saw all idol worship and acts of idolatry as mere fetishism.[10] There is, for example, the following story recounted in Shemot Rabah:

It may be likened to a choice [piece of wood] which lay in the bathhouse. When the prefect and his attendants came in to bathe they trod on it and similarly all the commoners and everyone else. By and by [the king] sent his bust for the purpose of having an image of himself made. The only suitable [piece of] wood they found was the one in the bathhouse. Accordingly, the artisans said to the governor: "If you want to set up the image, bring hither the wood that is in the bathhouse, for there is none better than it." It was fetched and properly prepared for the purpose. And he [i.e., the governor] brought an artist who designed the image on it and set it up in the palace. The governor came and knelt before it; and the dux, the prefect, the legionaries, the people, and everybody else did likewise. Then did those artisans say unto them: "Yesterday you were trampling this [piece of] wood in the bathhouse, and now you prostrate yourselves before it, but for the sake of the king's bust which is engraved upon it." So the Kings will say: until now we have been treating Israel in an unspeakable manner, as it is written "To him that is despised of soul, detested of nations," and shall we now prostrate ourselves before Israel? But the Holy One blessed be He will answer them: yes, for the sake of my name which is inscribed upon them.[11]

We see here how far the rabbis were from conflating idolatry with simple fetishism and quite recognized the representative symbolic function of idols. Pagans were not accused here (though they were in other texts) of worshiping idols for their own sake but for what was no less deleterious, for worshipping a form of mere earthly power, rather than transcendent authority itself.

The representation of mere earthly power is derided here as an act of stupidity and ignorance to be contrasted with recognition of the superior transcendence of the Lord. The gentile kings are thus led to reject symbols of mere earthly power for an acceptance of the Lord, whose name is inscribed on the people of Israel—which is itself symbolized in the act of circumcision.[12] The absolutism of transcendent authority is here contrasted with the limited, immanent nature of idols, whose representative function is always merely a symbolization of the worldly given and not of the terms of being itself—to which, as Maimonides pointed out some six hundred years later, no positive attributes can be ascribed. It was, we may note, precisely this aspect of monotheistic religions that made them, in Arnaldo Momigliano's terms, disadvantageous to the universal state (i.e., the Roman Empire). The pluralism of peoples and values that was essential to the well-being of the Empire was utterly negated in the univocality of ethical monotheism.[13]

These two rabbinic texts complement one another, highlighting the inherent connection of immanence to the context-bound and hence only partially representative nature of pre-Axial generality. The very absoluteness of transcendent otherness is what permits the representation of a fully generalized other. This is what Cohen means by the correlation of man, fellowman, and God and what Matthew Arnold intends by his assertion that the roots and source of righteousness are in the "not ourselves." Whereas in chapter two we discussed the role of transcendence in more analytic terms, here we follow its historical emergence and development over the past three millennia.

We begin with the insight that transcendence makes moral evaluation possible in new ways, by opening up the possibility of an individual constituted by absolute otherness, rather than solely enmeshed in the skein of worldly power, negotiation, and the calculus of resource mobilization. Not that these cease to exist, not even that a realm of interaction is constituted as totally free from such, but the possibility of such is so constituted and represented (even if the dynamics of its representation are themselves invariably the play of power, negotiation, and so on, as the history of all religious communities to date amply testifies). The world, its power structures, hierarchies, definitions of community, prestige, and participation are, however, all relativized vis-à-vis a new dimension of existence in which the idea of self as moral evaluator can emerge *in the most general and universal of terms.* True, both Philoctetes and Antigone made choices of an ethical nature, but the ethical matrix within which they made them was not fully generalized, not ethically relevant beyond their kin group identities and its honor codes. This was still a mostly particular and immanently ascribed other.

With the idea of transcendence the relevant community or group is broadened and generalized in principle to include what was hitherto the ineluctable other: the fellowman that we find in Cohen, Rosenzweig, and Levinas and whose origins are found in the Noachite commandments of the Jewish religion. These were commandments incumbent on all the children of Noah—all of humanity—and which included the prohibitions of murder, incest, theft, blasphemy, and eating the flesh of living creatures and the injunction to establish courts of law.[14] Only one of these commandments is positive in nature—the establishment of courts of law. And it is to law and the centrality of law that we must look for the very particular form that transcendence took in rabbinic Jewish thought in the period from about 200 B.C.E. to 600 C.E. The ethical self in rabbinic Jewish thought was constituted through the praxis of law and commandments (mitzvot), which bridged the Axial chasm to remake the world in transcendent terms.[15] For the rabbis, ethics was a matter of action *out in the world,* of expressive conduct, ritual as well as interpersonal, regulated by transcendent dictates.

Within the system of halakah (Jewish law/practice) the individual is defined in terms of a relational matrix that grounds individuality within a grid of group behaviors and normative desiderata. The very terms of salvation—or, in the Jewish context, redemption—are collective, affecting the whole of the Jewish people, and this-worldly in promising the restoration of the Davidic kingdom in Jerusalem and of Godly rule.[16] Indeed, the drama of theodicy as represented in the three paragraphs of the Shema prayer, that daily reminder of the covenant with God, is collective in its promise of reward and punishment in the world for the adherence (or lack thereof) to God's commandments. Redemption is not an individual drama, but a collective one. As a collective, as a social group, the terms of the relation between members must moreover be articulated through law, as represented in the 613 commandments.

Indeed, the very terms of purity in rabbinic thought (not the "ritual" impurity of individual status caused by the contact with impure or polluting substances, such as dead bodies, seminal emissions, leprosy, and so on), but the ethical purity or impurity as recounted in Leviticus 18:24–29 is measured as a collective drama.[17] Such impurity pollutes the land itself, which then vomits out its inhabitants. What befell the Canaanites could well befall the Israelites if they succumb to false gods, reject Godly commandments, and so pollute the land. Here, as in so many instances, early rabbinic thought is orientated around a collective representation of the soteriological drama, one which perforce finds its articulation in terms of law, which regulates the actual behavior, the *external* actions, ritual and ethical both, between men and women and between humankind and God. We follow Neusner in avoiding placing undo stress on *ritual* versus *ethical* sources of impurity, as the distinction itself is not a Jewish one and rests on a much later, post-Pauline distinction between the ritual—that is, what is seen as empty and formalized—and the ethical, or moral—that is, what is seen as meaningful and inwardly resonant.[18] This later distinction rests on the type of separation between self and world, internal and external, intent and action, that owes so much to the second-century Christian readings and interpretation of the Pauline break with Jewish modes of being and acting in the world.

Law is a grid for action and not intention. It makes sense of and organizes activities in the world, not states of being or intention that are hidden and internal to consciousness (or, for that matter, conscience). These actions may include those easily understood by modern sensibilities, such as laws regulating justice for the widow, orphan, and the stranger or laws regulating and providing material sustenance to the poor. But these regulations also include actions that may be totally opaque to us, as are many of the "ritual" laws, such as the matter of the red heifer or of the *sotah*. And in all cases the focus is on action prescribed by commandments that define righteousness in the communal setting, among and between selves, rather than what is experienced within the self. The very terms of selfhood are in fact communal, relational, existing within the commandments that define righteousness—for a people. It is in this context that we are to understand Lionel Trilling's observation that "as ethical beings, the Rabbis never *see themselves*—it is as if the commandment which forbade the making of images extended to their way of conceiving the personal moral existence as well. They imagine no struggles, no dilemmas, no hard choices, no ironies, no destinies, nothing *interesting;* they have no thought of morality as drama."[19] As Trilling further notes, there is no "hero" in rabbinic literature or even in the Bible. And as he further observes: "Oedipus confronting the mystery of human suffering is a hero; Job in the same confrontation is not."[20] There can be no hero, for there is in this worldview no individual existing alone and beyond the confines of heteronomous law and its communal embodiment.[21]

These aspects of Jewish religion are, of course, well known—indeed, are often caricatured and sometimes ridiculed. In certain Christian traditions, such as various strains of Lutheranism, an exaggerated version of these principles presented the basis for a virulent anti-Semitism.[22] We are not making claims here for the above description as providing an essentialist reading of Judaism, either in the early centuries of the Common Era or today. There have always been far too many interpretive communities of Biblical texts to allow such a reading. And Jewish mysticism, from the Merkavah literature of the first century C.E. to the medieval corpus, is, of course, very different in its emphases and expressions. Contemporary historical scholarship has also given us a much more refined understanding of Judaism in the period from about 100 B.C.E. to 100 C.E. We have thus broadened our understanding of the allegorizing trends within Judaism, of concepts of "cultic" purity and impurity that extended beyond the precincts of the Temple embraced by groups such as the Yahad (and indeed by the Pharisees as well) and of ideas of sin as actually causing impurity and uncleanliness.[23]

Bearing this in mind, it is nonetheless the case that one of these interpretive communities, one of the twenty-seven or so Jewish sects that existed in the period from about the first century B.C.E. until the first century C.E., did indeed change the world. That was what came to be called Christianity. And while Christian history is, if anything, even less given to an essentialist reading than is Jewish history, one of the striking changes that characterized its emergence and development in the West, first in the Roman Church and then in the many different Protestant sects, was its new mode of representing transcendence in the world. The developing Christian message was one that, especially from the second century on, substituted faith for law, internal states for external action, and the individual for the collective as the locus of the salvational drama. To some extent the impetus for this was the developing tensions polarizing relations between the Jewish and Christian communities.[24] Moreover and clearly, such a transformation of consciousness did not happen in one lifetime or in one century or even in one millennium. Nor are its origins unaccountable: they were well grounded in the practices of such Jewish groups as the Yahad and the Chavura.[25]

However accounted for, however seamless the transition from Jewish to Christian ways of being often seems to be (especially when the later polemics, of both sides, are factored out), a great transformation nevertheless occurred, not least in the imagining of individual selves. For those aspects of purity that later Christian thought deemed "ritual" locate the self in community, since ritual is, after all, primarily concerned with aspects of status—of things, states of being, points in time. One important aspect of the move from Judaism to Christianity therefore was precisely the move from an awareness of both external and internal sources of impurity to a privileging of internal sources alone.[26] Thus the Jesus of Mark's gospel relocates the issue of impurity inward, in his response to the Pharisees' declaration that food eaten with unwashed hands rendered one impure:

> Listen to me, all of you, and understand: there is nothing outside a person that by going in can defile, but the things that come out are what defile. (Mark 7:15)

Defilement and impurity here become the result of internal processes, not external ones. The shift in the locus of self is subtly moved from being constituted by an outside source (the laws of a heteronomous God) to being constituted by an internal one. This move in many ways is a turning point in Western if not in world history, as it lays the basis for a new universalism—no longer that of law, but now of the individual.

Central to this new universalism was Paul's mission to the Gentiles, which opened up transcendent claims and obligations to those not under the law and in so doing provided a turning point in our understanding of individual selves in their relations both to one another and to themselves. The first real Pauline exponent of such individualism was, however, not Paul himself, but his great Western interpreter, Augustine. A fuller perspective would await Luther, in such works as his *A Commentary on Saint Paul's Epistle to the Galatians* in 1575, and the Protestant Reformation, which institutionalized the Pauline vision in a way that the medieval Catholic church had not, indeed could not—given its own overriding solution to individuality and community (in terms of a universal *ecclesia*).

Although it is clearly not possible in the space of this chapter to write a history of the Christian idea of the individual, or even of its Protestant versions, it is imperative for our discussion here to grasp something of this revolution in thinking and its implications. For the idea is too much our own to be ignored, and the claim advanced here is radical in nature and must be substantiated: That is, to understand current rational choice and economic reductionist visions of the self, with the concomitant loss of transcendence and the potential loss of any idea of self as moral evaluator, we must return to Paul and to the substitution of faith for law as the arena in which the theodic drama is played out and wherein *tyche* is to be defeated. The very successful institutionalization of that Pauline vision of self that tied the representation of transcendence to internal processes led, eventually, not only to the loss of transcendence, but with it to the loss of any idea of self as moral evaluator. The great revolution of Christianity was the establishment of a salvational nexus outside the law and universalized in a new sense of individual selves. Preaching salvation (hence transcendent representation) to the Gentiles, Paul preached a conversion to Godly ways through faith in Christ alone. With time, Paul's message was interpreted as creating a breach between law and morality (between external acts and internal states) in a way that had been only vaguely perceived hithertofore (and which he would most probably have rejected).

Such a distinction between law and morality, between the Torah and the moral order, made no sense within Judaism, and to this day would be deemed problematic to observant Jews.[27] As E. P. Sanders reminds us:

> We now make a great distinction between "inner" and "outer," and those of us who are Protestants, or heirs to the Protestant tradition, distrust external forms. It should be remembered that, to ancient Jews, "love thy neighbor" and "love the stranger" were not vague commandments about the feelings in one's heart, but were quite specific. "Love" meant, "Use just weights and measures"; "Do not reap your field to the border, but leave some for the poor"; "Neither steal, deal falsely nor lie"; "Do not withhold wages that you owe"; "Do not take advantage of the blind or deaf"; "Do not be biased in judgement"; "Do not slander"—and so on through the verses of Leviticus 10 and many others.[28]

There is here no privileging of internal over external or its opposite, for the distinction itself hardly exists. Rather, the very act of fulfilling the law, God's commands, affirms the covenantal relationship with God and so existence itself within the covenant. Paul's words, however, would come to structure a civilization out of these very distinctions.

> All who have sinned apart from the law will also perish apart from the law, and all who have sinned under the law, will be judged by the law. For it is not the hearers of the law who are righteous in God's sight, but the doers

of the law who will be justified. When Gentiles, who do not possess the law, do instinctively what the law requires, these, though not having the law, are a law to themselves. They show that what the law requires is written on their hearts, to which their own conscience also bears witness: and their conflicting thoughts will accuse or perhaps excuse them on the day when, according to my gospel, God, through Jesus Christ, will judge the secret thoughts of all. (Romans 2:12–16)

But now, apart from the law, the righteousness of God has been disclosed, and is attested by the law and the prophets, the righteousness of God through faith in Jesus Christ for all who believe. For there is no distinction, since all have sinned and fall short of the glory of God; they are now justified by his grace as a gift, through the redemption that is in Christ Jesus, whom God put forward as a sacrifice of atonement by his blood, effective through faith. He did this to show his righteousness, because in his divine forbearance he had passed over the sins previously committed; it was to prove at the present time that he himself is righteous and that he justifies the one who has faith in Jesus. Then what becomes of boasting? It is excluded. By what law? By that of works? No, but by the law of faith. For we hold that a person is justified by faith apart from works prescribed by the law. Or is God the God of Jews only? Is he not the God of Gentiles also, since God is one; and he will justify the circumcised on the ground of faith and the uncircumcised through that same faith. Do we then overthrow the law by this faith? By no means! On the contrary, we uphold the law. (Romans 3:21–30)

The distinction between *sub lege* and *sub gratia* privileged the realm of grace over the realm of law and, with it, the internal realm of individual conscience. This was the historical result, even if one accepts, as I do, the reading of scholars such as E. P. Sanders and Krister Stendhal, who claim this was not Paul's original intent.[29] Henceforth it would be in the realm of conscience that the workings of grace were to be felt (or not) rather than in the external realm, the world out there, wherein law governed action.

Again, these distinctions did not emerge *ab nuovo* in Christianity. In many ways the type of distinction posited in Pauline texts between inward and outward, between morality and the law, outward purity and inward morality were echoes of extant Jewish positions.[30] As Jacob Neusner points out: "What the Rabbis have to say about the priests is pretty much what the Synoptic's Jesus says about the Pharisees, John's Jesus about 'the Jews,' and Paul about the Law."[31] If indeed the Christians replaced purity laws with their own definition of a new community (as the Temple allegorized), similar positions were maintained by groups such as the Yahad (who had similar views of community but nevertheless maintained the laws of purity) and even by the Pharisees (who also maintained more cultic attitudes towards the Temple, but significantly broadened the purity laws beyond Jerusalem to include all aspects of daily life—Ricoeur's "scrupulous conscience").[32] With Christianity, however, the locus shifts in critical ways as the center moves and the communal context is redefined:

> I know and am persuaded in the Lord Jesus that nothing is unclean in itself; but it is unclean for anyone who thinks it is unclean. If your brother or sister is being injured by what you eat, you are no longer walking in love. Do not let what you eat cause the ruin of one for whom Christ died. So do not let your good be spoken of as evil. For the kingdom of God is not food or drink but righteousness and peace and joy in the Holy Spirit. (Romans 14:14–17)

While the call to justice and peace is certainly prophetic, the move that we must note is the abandonment of the external jurisprudential authority of the rabbinic court for the more inward, individual decision-making process in issues of purity and impurity.

Moreover, just as the definition of impurity moves from the strictures of a communal authority to those of individual conscience, so does repentance move in Christianity from being primarily collective to being primarily individual, from being a continual effort, repeated over the course of one's life, to what is essentially a changed state of Being. Here, then, the soteriological locus is recast, from a this-worldly eschatological vision of collective redemption to a more other-worldly intimation of individual salvation. As the terms of purity and impurity are revised in more purely moral and perforce individual terms, so is the drama of redemption, with both henceforth becoming congruent with a salvation predicated on the other-worldly workings of grace, rather than the this-worldly action of humankind under the law.

From this vision comes as well a new definition of the human community. No longer limited or circumscribed by the tribal bonds of Israelite monotheism, in this new community of nascent individuals, it is precisely their individuality that marks Christianity as a universal religion.

> Is the law then opposed to the promises of God? Certainly not! For if a law had been given that could make alive, then righteousness would indeed come through the law. But the scripture has imprisoned all things under the power of sin, so that what was promised through faith in Jesus Christ might be given to those who believe. Now before faith came, we were imprisoned and guarded under the law until faith would be revealed. Therefore the law was our disciplinarian until Christ came, so that we might be justified by faith. But now that faith has come, we are no longer subject to a disciplinarian, for in Christ Jesus you are all children of God through faith. As many of you were baptized into Christ have clothed yourselves with Christ. There

is no longer Jew or Greek, there is no longer slave or free, there is no longer
male and female; for all of you are one in Christ Jesus. And if you belong to
Christ, then you are Abraham's offspring, heirs according to the promise.
(Galatians 3:21–29)

Paul reconstructs the circumscribed and circumscribing nature of the
law. And the law, as Krister Stendhal reminds us, was but a *paidagogos*, a
harsh, uneducated tutor, a custodian until, through faith, a new dispensa-
tion, and with it a new definition of community would take effect when
all would be "in Christ."

The new community rested on faith, as the old did on law. And just as
the old rested on the relational matrix of individuals fulfilling the law as
a covenantal body, the new rested on individuals whose very faith necessitated the type of distinctions between law and morality that Paul posited.
Paul brings the Gentiles into the Jewish fold—there are as yet no Christians—by redefining the terms of membership in the salvational collective (Israel) by opening it up to those not *sub lege*. This entailed redefining the nature of the collective as well as of its individual members,
recasting both in terms of faith, with the necessary correlate of internalized states of conscience as arbitrators of justification and hence of transcendent connectedness, replacing those "ritual" laws of Pharisaic Judaism. Justification by faith, termed Paul's great insight, has bearing, as
shown by Krister Stendhal, E. P. Sanders, and others, on the relations of
Jews and Gentiles, hence on the definition of community in the time of
the Messiah.

What then are we to say? Gentiles who did not strive for righteousness have
attained it, that is, righteousness through faith; but Israel, who did strive for
the righteousness that is based on the law, did not succeed in fulfilling that
law. Why not? Because they did not strive for it on the basis of faith, but as
if it were based on works. They have stumbled over the stumbling stone. . . .
For, "Everyone who calls on the name of the Lord shall be saved." (Romans
9:30–32, 10:13)

However, as we see, the problem of Gentiles and Jews was also very much
the problem of law and Gospel, of works and faith, and hence also of the
nature of individual selves. For the new community of God's righteousness was predicated on the equality of all in their faith in Jesus. As Paul
famously confessed in Romans 7:18–19:

For I know that in men, that is, in my flesh, dwelleth no good thing: for to
will is present with me, but to do that which is good is not. For the good
which I would I do not: but the evil which I would not, that I practice.

This, then, is the moment when the problem of wrongdoing and shame is transposed to that of sin and guilt. In Judaism what we translate as sin (*het*) means, literally, mistaken action, missing the mark, doing wrong. And a changing idea of self can be grasped in this changing understanding of wrongdoing into sin that accompanied Christianity. Within Judaism, sin is not an ontological state of Being, not constitutive of mankind's essence or existence, but rather exists as a list of violations, of infractions, of 'missing of the mark' as the very word *het*—or *l'hachti*, to diverge from one's mark or goal, indicates. *Het* really does not refer to specific sins but more to characteristic modes of *action*. *Het* itself is something movable from *am yisrael*, to the house of the high priest, ultimately to God. It resonates with motion and action, not with stasis and existence, and to the extent that it exists, it represents in Judaism a violated relationship, a deviation, a straying from the paths of the Lord. Sin is thus removed from ontology, from a category of Being, as ultimate reconciliation is absented from the hands of man. What is left is a worldly arena where we can but struggle to enact holiness in the orders of the world.

Paul's is a radically different vision:

> For I delight in the law of God in my inmost Self, but I see in my members another law at war with the law of my mind, making me captive to the law of sin that dwells in my members. Wretched man that I am! Who will rescue me from this body of death? Thanks be to God through Jesus Christ our Lord! So then, with my mind I am a slave to the law of God, but with my flesh I am a slave to the law of sin. (Romans 7:22–25)

Stendhal convincingly argues that Paul is distinguishing the goodness of the law from the badness of his own sin, the point being that Paul was not making any claims about the human predicament *tout court* as later, especially Protestant, interpreters contended. He was not rejecting the law as responsible for sin.[33] Stendhal's position is significant, especially in view of the anti-Semitic interpretations of this and other passages by Paul. What nevertheless remains in Paul's statement is the differentiation of the corporal or carnal world of man from the law and hence our ultimate inability to fulfill its strictures. Though spiritual, the law is "played out in the flesh, which is unredeemable."[34]

And this is the central point for our own argument, as the distinction between the "innermost self" that delights in the law and the wantonness of his bodily members is the beginning of that view of self which—good or bad, *sub lege* or *sub gratia*, bond or free—can exist independent of actions and external experiences. The emergence of this entity is a tragic unintended consequence of Paul's contradictory aims—to remain within the synagogue but to be apostle for the risen Messiah. As Sanders notes, "He desperately sought a formula which would keep God's promise to

Israel while insisting on faith in Jesus Christ."[35] What emerged was a new *ecumene* whose binding ties of charismatic equality were predicated on grace and internal conscience. And it was the first step on the road to our own predicament wherein the very autonomy of the self calls into question its evaluative capabilities. This trajectory originated with a reading—Augustine's—of Paul's writing not as dealing with the problem of Jews and Gentiles, but as providing an answer to "the quest for assurance about man's salvation out of a common human predicament."[36]

By the time of Augustine, salvation would be formulated in terms of the absolutely unmerited gift of God's grace, whose workings were evinced in the soul of man. It was thus with Augustine in his *Confessions* that the problem of, in Stendhal's terms, "the introspective conscience of the West"—the quest for the basis of salvation—finds its chief exponent. As he put it:

> With Augustine, Western Christianity with its stress on introspective achievements started. It developed in the Middle Ages—with Penitential practice and guidance for self-examination coming increasingly to characterize both monastic and secular life—and man became more and more clever in analyzing his ego. Man turned in on himself, infatuated and absorbed by the question not of when God will send deliverance in the history of salvation, but how God is working in the innermost individual soul.[37]

This shifting focus from the collective problem of salvation in history to the individual problem of the soul's salvation is the move from Paul to Augustine. Still very much the Pharisaic Jew, and practicing his apostolate within the context of Jewish eschatological thought, Paul was concerned with the collective problem of redemption in time. With Augustine, the "first modern man," this was transformed. What had lain dormant in Christian theology for 350 years—justification by faith—was transformed from its Pauline context of intracommunity polemics on the nature of community to the more general and timeless realm of human existence. Using Paul and especially Paul's conversion as a prototype of selfhood and of his new understanding of just what constitutes selfhood (not the sinful doctrine of acts in the world, based on law, but the totally unmerited and *inward* working of grace in the soul), Augustine redefines the doctrine of justification by faith into a new understanding of the relations between self and the workings of salvation. As explained by Paula Fredriksen:

> He thus sees in Paul and especially in Romans the charter for the introspective self as the premier theological category, the setting for the drama of human will expressed in the works of the Law, grace in the unmerited salvation of the sinner (Paul/Augustine) in Christ. Hence, for Augustine, the

inner life of man is the sovereign arena of God's work of redemption, and the chief problem Paul addresses in Romans is the works of the Law and of grace.[38]

Augustine, per Fredriksen, used "his own past experiences as evidence for his new theological propositions" (in his *Confessions*) to effect a radical transformation.[39] Rather than a collective drama, salvation (and so representation of the transcendent) was rearticulated in terms of individual experiences and the inward workings of an undeserved grace. No longer society, which, if it is anything at all, is the laws that regulate the behavior of its members, but the individual member himself becomes the soteriological focus of attention. Emergent with this individual is the problem of the will, which in Augustinian theology is denied any first order role in the progress of salvation, as it would be again among the Augustinian reformers of the Protestant Reformation. Augustine's is a vision of self freed from the constraints of the collective (i.e., the law) and constituted solely in its individuality (albeit by a still transcendent grace), hence an as yet unrealized autonomy (unrealized in the positive sense; the autonomy of the will is as yet but sin). The further refinement of this doctrine would await the Protestant Reformation, but with Augustine the stage was set for the elaboration of the Lutheran doctrine of *sole fide*. And with that formulation, individual will, emerging ever more saliently as the vision of an encumbered or embedded self, gives way ultimately to a vision of unqualified individual autonomy.

We should note as well those historic developments that preceded the Reformation and played a role in the developing sophistication of the idea of an internal or "introspective conscience" as lodestone of individual identity in the West. We will consider, in particular, the renaissance of the twelfth century, not only the recovery of spiritualism in that era, but the establishment of new social groups and the growing individualism that devolved from that.[40] The differentiation of corporate bodies engendered by the papal revolution (the Investiture Conflict), together with the proliferation of myriad new social roles, fostered the development of ideas of an inner life and of intentionality (as opposed to just action) as an aspect of the individual agency and morality. Alongside the growth of new group identities (of which the new corporate identity of the clergy was the most important) and the increase in horizontal mobility as the immediate family differentiated itself from wider kinship groups, there was also the very emic recognition of different orders of knights, clerics, priests, religious orders, married men and women, widows, virgins, soldiers, merchants, peasants, and craftsmen—all with their different talents, institutions, and roles in society.[41] And the era saw the concomitant growth of individual and private modes of self-expression through the revival of the religious tradition of autobiography, confessional literature, and courtly love poetry. Finally, there emerged legal differentiation—a legal corpus no longer bounded by custom or Germanic tribal ideas of honor and fate.[42]

In a manner reminiscent of early Christianity and foreshadowing the Protestant Reformation of the sixteenth century, the twelfth century was characterized by the convergence of a set of structural and symbolic features that coalesced around a greater appreciation of individual identity as incorporating ideas of agency or voluntarism and the workings of conscience. As Benjamin Nelson noted: "The extraordinary stress on the responsibility of each individual for the activity of his will and the state of his soul attained its height in the High and Later Middle Ages."[43] It was not only Abelard in his *Ethica seu Seito Te Ipsum* (*Ethics: or Know Thyself*) and *Sic et Non* (*Yes and No*) who stressed inward intentionality in the conceptualization of spiritual life. Others too evinced such a reorientation—the school of Laon, for example, and even such critics of Abelard as Bernard of Clairvaux.

One institutionalized expression of this change was the decree of the Fourth Lateran Council of 1215 requiring individual confession for communicants at least once a year. Colin Morris observed on this point:

> the attempt to make intention the foundation of an ethical theory is a striking instance of the contemporary movement away from external regulations towards an insight into individual character; a movement which finds its widest expression in the acceptance of private confession as the basis of the Church's normal discipline.[44]

Its other institutional expression was the developing science of casuistry and the proliferation of "specialized treatises tracing the obligations of conscience in the here and now, spelling out how individuals were obligated to act in every case they encountered in the conduct of their lives. . . . In these works conscience extended into every sphere of action, ranging over the whole moral life of man."[45]

This idea of intentionality was not limited to the religious realm alone and resonated both in courtly poetry (for example, in such writings as Chrétien de Troyes's *The King of the Cart*) and in the developing genre of autobiography. It appeared as well in the changing representation of portrait painting.[46] Harold Keller's discussion of portraiture offers an appreciation of precisely that idea of the individual as existing beyond roles and role expectations that we have discussed:

> The portrait, as we understand it today, is one of the new concepts of the late Middle Ages. . . . The characterization of a man, absolutely and unchangeably by his particular physical peculiarities, especially his face, and

not by the insignia of his office or rank or by his weapons—that is a concept
of the portrait which in the second century AD came into question in the
West and which was progressively lost from the time of Constantine onwards.
Only about 1300 did the new conception of man lead to the recovery of the
old idea of the portrait.[47]

Not surprisingly, the new valorization of a self apart from legally defined social roles saw too the valorization of personal relations not so
defined. Hence, there emerged tentative ideas of friendship, albeit still
within the boundaries of the Church, and the conceptualization of love
advanced by the troubadours, both of which, in Morris's terms, "desired
to make personal experience and personal relations the focus of life"
through the process of self-discovery and analysis.[48]

These developments all took place against a backdrop of increasing
structural differentiation characterized by (1) the separation of the no-
bility from the rest of society through its increasing tendency to be defined in hereditary terms, (2) the growth of commerce, of cities with a
vast degree of internal differentiation among the different urban orders,
and (3) the development of the post-Gregorian church, which not only
freed episcopal elections (and elites) from political impingement but
also "created a clergy that was set apart much more radically than before
from ordinary Christians."[49] Caroline Bynum has shown that the Gre-
gorian reform did indeed separate the clergy from the laity, most especially through the campaign for clerical celibacy. But it also led to a proliferation of new institutional religious orders or roles, including the
establishment of the mendicant orders for men and the creation of new
roles for women, such as the Beguine, which was in essence "opposed to
complex institutional structures."[50]

We see in this scenario the Durkheimian correlation between the development of individual identities and the ever-increasing complexity of
social organization and its role expectations. The same period that sees
the "fundamental religious drama" relocated into the self is the period
that sees a proliferation of religious orders, vocations, "callings," and
"lives." The same period that saw a growing literature of private passion
and theories of love—in Southern's terms, "the enlargement of the op-
portunities of privacy, in the renewed study of the theory of friendship,
of conscience and of ethics"—is also a period marked by a greater social
differentiation, complexity, and distinction in the forms of social life.[51]
However, as Southern emphasizes, along with this greater differentiation
came a "changing emphasis from localism to universality," most especially in the rise of the science of logic. The latter, by subsuming all partic-
ularities, made possible recourse to a whole beyond an increasingly par-
ticularized conceptualization of space and time.[52]

The historian Caroline Bynum identifies in this world an "urgency, unlike anything we see in the early Middle Ages, about defining, classifying, and evaluating what they termed 'orders,' or 'lives' or 'callings' (which include what we would term both voluntary religious associations and social roles)."[53] We would disagree with Bynum, however, that the vision of the twelfth century that emphasized inwardness and conscience must be "qualified" by an appreciation of the growth and diversification of the forms of social life.[54] These phenomena, we contend, are not contradictory but complementary, with the latter being the precondition for the former. For only in the developing complexity of social identities can a sense of individual identity flourish. Central to this individual identity as it developed in the medieval West was the idea of conscience expressed in the idea of intentionality in religious life and the gradual construction of a private realm beyond formal social obligations. All the changes of the time—whether in the rites of courtly love, the developing genre of correspondence between friends, or the individual Church confession— foreshadowed, in different ways, the Protestant Reformation of the sixteenth century.

Well studied indeed is the importance of the Protestant Reformation, especially of its sectarian variants, in developing the idea of the autonomous individual whose moral locus is an internalized conscience. Through it, in the words of Benjamin Nelson,

> there developed a new integration of life, both personal and political through the rearrangement of existing boundaries ... older maps were redrawn, fixing new coordinates for all focal points of existence and faith: religion-world, sacred-profane, civil-ecclesiastical, liberty-law, public-private. ... [In this rearrangement] new scope and authority were given to the Inner Light, sparked by the Holy Spirit. This was the Holy Spirit within each individual and within groups. This inspiration came to serve as the basis for vastly expanded involvement of new participants in a variety of different relations of self and world: charismatic activism, quietistic mysticism, covenanted corporate consensualism, natural rights individualism, a religion of Pure Reason.[55]

Here, then, we see a return to Augustinian piety, a break with the sacraments and mediating structures of the Catholic Church, as well as with its symbols—of the Virgin Mary and the different saints. We see instead a reassertion of the believer's unmediated access to the Deity within what became the private space of individual conscience.[56]

The great struggles of Martin Luther were precisely over the foundations of justification, ultimately to be sought solely in the realm of an internal conscience imbued with Divine grace. Again and again in Luther's writings the workings of conscience are contrasted with law and made the bedrock of a good Christian life, in contrast to the cursed doctrine of works and of church sacramentalism. Grace is seen as superseding law (in a manner most probably not intended by Paul), and with this a whole new vision of self and of community is offered. As Luther makes clear:

> Wherefore, when thy conscience is terrified with the law, and wrestleth with the judgement of God, ask counsel neither of reason nor of the law, but rest only upon grace and the word of consolation and so stand herein, as if thou hadst never heard any thing of the law, ascending up to the glass of faith, where neither the law, or reason do shine, but only the light of faith which assureth us that we are saved by Christ alone, without any law.[57]

The Christian man is, for Luther, "free from all laws and is not subject unto any creature either within or without: in that he is a Christian I say, and not in that he is a man or a woman, that is to say, in that he hath his conscience adorned and beautified with this faith . . . which . . . makes us the children and heirs of God."[58] Though far from advocating lawlessness, Luther opened up the possibility of a *principled* antinomianism that has been with us ever since, as the sources of self have contracted inward and their social moorings cut loose from salvational doctrines. Yes, good works and charity must be done, but they bear no relevance to the workings of justification, have no bearing on "the true meaning of becoming a Christian, even to be justified in Jesus Christ and not by the works of the law."[59] For as Luther so clearly parses things out:

> The ceremonial law killeth and bringeth to death. Yea so doth the law of the ten commandments also, without faith in Christ [as] may no law be suffered to rein in the conscience, but only the law of the spirit and life, whereby we are made free in Christ.[60]

With Luther the justified conscience takes center stage in the soteriological drama—and with it an extension of Paul's problem that goes well beyond what the Apostle's words originally indicated.

Beyond Luther, the Reformation as whole, especially in its Calvinist and its ascetic-sectarian varieties (so termed by Weber), evinced an Augustinian renewal that brought new centrality to that problem of self oriented around what Stendhal has termed the "introspective conscience." It brought with it a new image of community. Bonds of a new "communion," in Herman Schmalenbach's sense, would constitute the basis of the new communities forged by religious virtuosi throughout European societies.[61] It was a social restructuring in the relation of the Church and the world, effected by the Reformation in general, but by ascetic Protestantism in particular. To quote from Nelson again:

A fundamental reorientation of the social and cultural patterns of the Western world could not occur until the medieval administration of self and spiritual direction fell before the onslaughts of Luther, Calvin and their followers. So long as a distinction was made between the special calling of monks who lived "outside the world," systematically observing a rule in their pursuit of the status of perfection, and everyone else in the world, who lived irregularly, without benefit of a rule, in the midst of continued temptation; so long was there a brake on the incentive of ordinary men and women to forge integrated characters with a full sense of responsibility. The Protestant notion of disciplined character nourished by a resolute conscience replaced the medieval sense of life as a round of sin and penance.[62]

This new sense of responsibility and of internalized moral authority was expressed in the pursuit of perfection within the orders and institutions of the world.[63] What this implied, however, was the establishment of a new type of moral bond between communal members, and so of a redefinition of the terms of group membership. More than Luther's "priesthood of believers," which posited a break with the church but not with the overriding social definitions of community, followers of Calvinist doctrine in England, Scotland, the Netherlands, France, and Geneva tended to be bound by new ties of fellowship, as well as by notions of a new type of moral authority based on inner conscience.[64]

Calvinism was thus integral in sixteenth- and seventeenth-century Europe to the construction of new symbolic definitions of collective identity and of selfhood. The basis of this new ideal order, the new *ecumene,* was henceforth to be the Holy Community of saints, voluntarily participating in Christ.[65] It was a new definition of community that formed the basis of a new, ideal model of Christian society. Henceforth, the boundaries of Christian community were not those of common participation in the sacrament of the Eucharist, but a common and voluntary subjugation of each individual will to the Will of God. A new community was defined by *willful* participation in the Body of Christ, a community like that of the early Church, existing in the body of the old but distinct from it. Such a code of conduct led to the effective separation within each parish of two bodies of communicants: "On one side there were the true, genuine, faithful and active Christians, and on the other those who were merely nominal and worldly." There thus was effected, in Troeltsch's words, "the separation of the pure body of communicants from the impure."[66]

Fundamental to this separation was the recasting of self and of community on the basis of grace. However, the new type of inner man and justified conscience that resulted demanded a fundamental transformation of the idea of *grace.* "Grace," as the historian R. H. Tawney put it, "no longer completed nature, it was the antithesis of it."[67] The derivatives of this purely theological speculation on the organization of social and political life in Europe were staggering. To quote Tawney again:

> Since salvation is bestowed by the operation of grace in the heart and by that alone, the whole fabric of organized religion, which had mediated between the individual soul and its Maker—divinely commissioned hierarchy, systematized activities, corporate institutions, drops away, as the blasphemous trivialities of a religion of works. The medieval conception of the social order, which had regarded it as a highly articulated organism of members contributing in their different degrees to a spiritual purpose, was shattered, and differences which had been distinction within a larger unity were now set in irreconcilable antagonism to each other. Grace no longer completed nature: it was the antithesis of it. Man's actions as a member of society were no longer the extension of his life as a child of God: they were its negation. Secular interests ceased to possess, even remotely, a religious significance: they might compete with religion, but they could not enrich it. Detailed rules of conduct—a Christian casuistry—are needless or objectionable: the Christian has a sufficient guide in the Bible and in his own conscience. In one sense, the distinction between the secular and the religious life vanished. Monasticism was, so to speak, secularized; all men stood henceforward on the same footing towards God; and that advance which contained the germ of all subsequent revolutions, was so enormous that all else seems insignificant. In another sense, the distinction became more profound than ever. For, though all might be sanctified, it was their inner life alone which could partake in sanctification. The world was divided into good and evil, light and darkness, spirit and matter. The division between them was absolute; no human effort could span the chasm.[68]

Tawney's point is precisely that grace uncoupled from social institutions is therefore ultimately irrelevant for the organization of this-worldly activities; the chasm separating this realm from the processes of grace is absolute and no human effort can span it. The opposition between the Weberian thesis and that of R. H. Tawney is stark indeed. Weber stressed the new interweaving of this-worldly and other-worldly concerns, which imbued this-worldly activity with new meanings and provided new motivations for men and women—motivations critical to the development of capitalist entrepreneurial activities. Tawney, for his part, stressed a somewhat opposite process—not a new interweaving of this- and other-worldly concerns, but rather a more Augustinian separation that relegated social ethics to the realm beyond the pale of soteriological action. This left it free to develop without the constraints of Christian fellowship and universalism that had hampered medieval trade and commerce.

Tawney reminds us that, for the Puritan elect, "it was their inner life alone which could partake of sanctification."[69] Not deeds; not works; not the world of social interaction, exchange, and reciprocity—which would then have to be subject to doctrines of Christian fellowship and the injunctions of the community of love—but the inner self alone, the inner realm of conscience and intention. This is the same realm of individual valuation that since Kant has gained moral priority and sanctity over other aspects of social life, in turn leaving the world of exchange and of the division of labor free from the moral concerns of Christian fellowship. As Tawney reminds us, this is the consequence of the doctrinal rejection of a salvation of works in the external world and the embrace of salvation by faith alone.

With the doctrine of inner faith came, not surprisingly, a new concern with sincerity, the Puritan assurance, Calvin's *cordis sinceritas*, which becomes the only possible limit or test of a faith made totally individualistic and hence subjective.[70] Only by establishing "objective," that is, externally authoritative tests of sincerity could the antinomian and anomic potential of a purely individualistic religiosity be reined in; and even this was not always successful, as the history of the radical Reformation showed only too well.[71] Standards of sincerity provided a way to measure inner states and bring outward behavior and inner intent into at least a rough enough alignment to make social order possible. As Calvin made clear in his *Commentaries on the Epistle of Paul to the Corinthians*:

> Hence Paul does not reckon it enough to declare that his sincerity was perceived by men, but adds that he was such in the sight of God. Eilikrineia (which I have rendered purity) is closely connected with simplicity, for it is an open and upright way of acting, such as makes a man's heart as it were transparent. Both terms tend opposed to craft, deception, and all underhand schemes.[72]

Indeed, a concern with sincerity runs from Calvin's *Institutes* through the English Calvinists, Baxter and Hooker, and into the writings of such New England Congregationalists as Thomas Shepard, John Cotton, Richard Mather, and Cotton Mather. We argue in fact that the more sectarian the group, the greater its concern with sincerity. As the presumption (stated or not) grows that the church visible assumes the shape of the church invisible, so does the need to verify the individual's belief inregenerate grace. Building a social order on justified conscience— precisely that exclusiveness of sectarianism identified by Ernst Troeltsch and Max Weber with sectarian Protestantism—demands some clear signs of justification. The more Puritanism approached its antinomian pole, the more external control over sincerity became the only bulwark against such development.

Precisely these controls were condemned as the "doctrine of works" by the more antinomian element within the Puritan fold, who sought a social order predicated on grace alone. Thus we have, for example, the famous case of Anne Hutchinson in the Massachusetts Bay Colony. She denounced the ministers for preaching a covenant of works and accused them of tricking the people into thinking they were saved "because they see some worke of Sanctification in them." In essence, she turned the covenant of works into a synonym of degeneration and damnation. In place of this "legalistic" doctrine of works and duties, Anne sought the immediate indwelling of the Holy Spirit. In her own words:

> Here is a great stirre about graces and looking into hearts, but give mee Christ, I seeke not for graces, but for Christ, I seeke not for promises, but for Christ, I seeke not for sanctification, but for Christ, tell not mee of meditation and duties, but tell mee of Christ.[73]

The cry was no more than a radical version of a more "respectable" (if still highly suspect) view within Congregational Puritanism of the separation of law and grace, works and faith, bondage and liberty. Thus John Cotton, in his *Treatise of the Covenant of Grace* (1652), offers his own dialectic of salvation:

> In a state of Bondage we were under the Law and the curse of God, but Christ hath redeemed us from the curse of the law (Galatians 3:13) and now sin shall no more have dominion over us, for we are not under the law (Romans 6:14) that is not under the Covenant of the Law, though we lie under the Commandment of it in Christ: we were sometime under the bondage of sin, under the guilt and strength of sin; but by Christ we have redemption, even the forgiveness of our sin: and as the Law was the strength of sin; so sin was the strength and sting of death (1 Corinthians 15:56) but now O death where is thy sting! O grave, where is thy victory! the Lord hath delivered us from him that hath the power of death . . . and from this evil world . . . and from the wrath to come."[74]

In contrast to mainstream Puritan thought, represented by such divines as William Ames, John Preston, and Richard Sibbes in England and Thomas Shepard and Peter Bulkeley in New England, Cotton's conception saw the covenant of grace as effectively replacing the covenant of works and "the continuity of the ontological and moral orders established at creation."[75] This doctrine, holding the covenants of works and grace as mutually exclusive, was understandably viewed with apprehension by the leaders of the Bay colony and by divines in England, who saw in the repudiation of the covenant of works a rejection of "the order of being and morality that compose the substance and rule of earthly life."[76] In their eyes such an interpretation led the way directly to a negation of all morality and respect for Magistracy. And so they insisted that even though the covenant of grace replaced the covenant of works as "the instrument of God's salvific government . . . it does not free the faithful from the law as a rule."[77] In consequence, and as "the doctrine of the covenant [became] the scaffolding and the framework for the whole edifice of theology . . . the essence of their program of salvation," they turned to emphasizing the continuity of nature (as the covenant of works) and the covenant of grace as "mutually implying each other."[78] Mainstream Puritan thought therefore posited a synthesis between the two. In William Stoever's words, the process of regeneration was in Puritanism "approached through a dialectic of nature and grace that preserve[d] the integrity of the one and the efficiency of the other."[79]

An uneasy tension reigned throughout most of the seventeenth century between the antinomian (hence individualistic) pull of Protestant (and especially Puritan) theology and the need to constitute a social order. The participants themselves spoke explicitly of these tensions in terms of the relative place of works and grace, law and faith in the process of salvation. Thomas Weld put the case well for the "order" faction:

> For if a man need not be troubled by the Law, before faith, but may step to Christ so easily; and then, if his faith be no going out of himselfe to take Christ, but onely a discerning that Christ is his owne already, and is onely an act of the Spirit upon him, no act of his owne done by him; and if he, for his part, must see nothing in himselfe, have nothing, doe nothing, onely he is to stand still and waite for Christ to doe all for him. And then if after faith, the Law no rule to walke by, no sorrow or repentance for sinne; he must not be pressed to duties, and need never pray, unlesse moved by the Spirit: And if he fals into sinne, his is never the more disliked of God, nor his condition never the worse. And for his assurance, it being given him by the Spirit, he must never let it goe, but abide in the height of comfort, though he fals into the grossest sinnes that he can. Then their way to life was made easie, is so no marvell so many like of it. . . . Oh, it pleaseth nature well to have Heaven, and their lusts too.[80]

To have "Heaven and their lusts too" is perhaps a somewhat jaundiced view of antinomian intentionality, but it is not unlike the rabbinic view of idolatry—that it served as an excuse for debauchery rather than a principled belief system. It also makes no bones about getting to the heart of the problem: a purely internalized religiosity, predicated on internal processes (of faith alone), makes the constitution of society problematic (if not impossible). And the rabbinic view of idolatry is not unlike Durkheim's view of magic, as an individual social act, without collective import. Within Puritanism, we see, there were those who privileged grace over nature to such an extent that it cut the individual off from all social obligations, responsibilities, and relations.

In theological terms this tension—well illustrated in the contrasting quotes of Cotton and Weld above—was irreconcilable. Ultimately, it was not so much resolved as transformed by the secularization of Puritan thought, which in turn became the foundation of modern social life. As Protestantism and especially Puritan communities underwent a process of institutionalization in the late seventeenth and early eighteenth centuries, conscience and individual agency in the definition of the moral life (i.e., as an attribute of virtue) came to be privileged, such that the individual, the individual conscience, and the realm of the private became *the* arena of religious activity.

Perhaps more than anyone else, Margaret Jacob has developed this argument with respect to English Unitarians, Dutch Collegians, and the increasingly secular French Freemasons.[81] Perhaps the central religious tenet of these groups, as described by Andrew Fix in his study of the Dutch Collegians, was that they "rejected the authority of ecclesiastical institutions and based religious life on the individual believer and his inner ability to know religious truth."[82] By the second half of the seventeenth century this conception, wedded to a belief in the workings of natural reason in the apprehension of truth, led to an emergent belief in the "principle of individual conscience."[83]

Jacob's own work has stressed the role of a particular form of privatized Protestantism in fostering the type of personal autonomy that we identify with bourgeois culture.

> At the heart of this experience lay the encouragement it gave the individual to conceptualize and to experience himself and herself as an ethical being equally engaged in the private and public spheres. . . . This was religion prescribed for the mind where in effect the public disciplined the private, where standards of conduct drawn from social experience and rational argumentation, and not from dogma, ordered and admonished the conscience. In its internalization of ethics and belief drawn from lived social experience, the new religiosity sacralized the public as much as it sanctioned private autonomy.[84]

A further example of this new religiosity, with its deep concern for "creating the conditions for ethical and virtuous conduct," was the case of the New England Congregationalists, who, by the early eighteenth century, had transformed a deeply communal, public, and eschatological religion into one of a privatized morality.[85] The sacred locus of existence had shifted from the public sphere with its collective rites to the private soul of the individual communicant.[86] Similarly, whereas the earlier decades of settlement had symbolically objectified the boundaries of the community as those running between the regenerate saint and unregenerate sinner, by the early eighteenth century, the broadened (more inclusive) definition of communal boundaries was conceptualized as being within each individual. Integrating all communal members in one collective definition, the boundaries between insider and outsider no longer ran through the community, but rather through each individual member. As a result, the move from profane to sacred and from outsider to insider—to membership in the collective—became less a public ceremony and more a private rite. Roger Caillois has termed this type of process the "internalization of the sacred," describing it as the state where "any external criterion seems inadequate, from the moment that the sacred becomes less an objective manifestation than a pure attitude of mind, less a ceremony than a profound sensation."[87]

We may note two developments related to this "internalization of the sacred." The first was an increased privatization of the religious experience evinced in a growing "sacramentalism," that informed the communicant's private meditations prior to approaching the Host. Along similar lines, the period witnessed the growth of what has been termed the "new baptismal piety" and the practice of private baptism. Originally proposed in 1700 by Stoddard in his *Doctrine of the Instituted Churches*, the first private baptism took place in 1718, thus breaking with the New England doctrine that a sacrament must be a "visible gospel addressed to a faithful congregation."[88] This practice (and doctrine) of the private nature of the sacrament of baptism is not unlike the privatization of the Lord's Supper. These previously publicly constituted rituals had, by the early eighteenth century, lost their public and communal function.

The second important transformation was in the affirmation of normative principles, as opposed to the prior criteria of evincing the workings of regenerate grace, as the basis of communal membership. Paul Lucas studied the admittance practices of the churches of Connecticut in the years 1670–1725 and found a marked increase in the use of "moral behavior," as opposed to conversionary experience, as the criterion for judging an applicant's suitability for admittance to the Church.[89] "Moral behavior gradually replaced conversion experience as the most important criterion for membership—and moral behavior was determined by the applicant's ability to abide by the standards of the group."[90] Note here the beginnings of a secular consciousness as locus of communal identity and key to collective membership, slowly replacing purely religious criteria.

Here, too, as in the cases studied by Jacob, we see the concomitant rise of three related phenomena: (1) the increasingly private nature of religious experience, (2) its reorientation along rational-normative lines, and so (3) the growth of a secular rather than a religious morality as the foundation of individual and collective identities. It was indeed at the end of this period that the universal subject qua individual emerges as the new locus of social solidarity and communal identity. As Stephen Darwall viewed this phenomenon in his recent work on seventeenth- and early eighteenth-century moral philosophy: "The most significant development of this period was the fashioning of the concept of autonomy *in tandem with* philosophical speculation about moral obligation."[91] Here, then, we find joined the doctrines of individual agency and autonomous action with ideas of moral obligation and the workings of conscience.

The idea of the moral individual that emerged in the eighteenth century was that of an individual whose autonomy rested on following the dictates of a reason that was both transcendental and constitutive of individual existence. There emerged, especially in the thought of Immanuel Kant, the notion of moral personhood.[92] In his *The Metaphysics of Morals*, Kant sketched out the attributes of this personhood, drawing heavily on the traditions of ascetic Protestantism:

> A person is a subject whose actions can be imputed to him. Moral personality is therefore nothing other than the freedom of a rational being under moral laws (whereas psychological personality is merely the capacity for being conscious of one's identity in different conditions of one's existence). From this it follows that a person is subject to no other laws than those he gives to himself (either alone or at least along with others).[93]

Here we see the eighteenth- and nineteenth-century secular version of the autonomous individual conscience following the dictates of an "inner light" and not the sacramental doctrines of the Church. Here too we see the emergence of precisely those new terms of individual autonomy based on the transcendental qualities of a universal reason and no longer on those of a universal church. It is in a sense the culmination of a process that had begun with Hobbes.

The Catholic church as *Universitas Fidelium* was, through its sacramental doctrine, a potentially universal and inclusive framework, as illustrated in the first fifteen hundred years of Christianity. Protestant sects, by contrast, were rooted in exclusivity and particularism. One was not born into a sect but rather had to undergo an internal transformation— the experience of grace—to attain membership. The universality it espoused was one of particular subjects, each rooted in the experience of grace.

Ultimately, however, the institutionalization of Protestantism resulted in the loss of its transcendent referent. As the community of saints expanded beyond the narrow boundaries of select individuals defined by the experience of grace, secularism was its necessary concomitant.[94] Eschewing the universalism of a sacramental church, what remained was the universalism of reason. And so reason replaced the Deity as the locus of universalist values and moral injunctions in both the ethical and the social (interpersonal) sphere. Less the this-worldliness of Protestant soteriology and more its individual emphasis thus stands at the core of its secularization. The need to posit new universal terms of association between transcendently constituted individual subjects could only be met by a universal reason, which could replace the transcendent Deity (recall the individual-in-relation-to-God) and so constitute individuality. At the same time it united these individuals into a new (universal) community once represented by the Christian *ecumene* and now precluded by the very particularism of grace in Protestantism. What emerged was the idea of the individual whose only transcendence is that of a morality "immanent in [but] transcending" the individual self.[95]

Morality and moral authority came to be founded on the dialectic of reason, inherent in but (as yet) transcending individual conscience. The governing principle of sociability became the autonomous moral subject constituted by transcendental reason and united by compacts or contracts—those critical "promises" upon which early modern natural law theory founded the political community. And if for Grotius the obligation to fulfill promises was an element of natural law, for Kant the "perfect duty" of promise keeping was what unites us in a moral community, itself the woof and weave of those "bonds of mutual respect between members of a moral community."[96] Promise keeping is what allows the constitution of a moral community, indeed of society *tout court.* For Locke "grants, promises, and oaths are bonds that hold the Almighty"; for Hume they were but one of the three "artifices of society" necessary for its constitution.[97] The social ties predicated on such promises thus became the new bonds of society, a community of belief in the act of promise keeping itself and no longer in a shared transcendent deity. Recalling Hutchinson's plea with its heartfelt denunciation of "promises" in the name of *Christ,* we get some sense of just how much was at stake in the process of secularization and the replacement of an internalized faith with an internalized reason as the basis of sociability in the post-Reformation world.

For Protestantism to be institutionalized (universalized, that is), it had to change its terms of inclusion. In its original formulations there was only the individual justified solely by transcendent grace. With secularization, the transcendent referent was replaced by a transcendental one, rooted in the workings of human reason and no longer dependent on divine grace. In this sense, iterated prisoner's dilemma models of social order are simply the final mathematical refinement of the idea of the promise between autonomous individuals as standing at the foundation of the social order. Mancur Olson is David Hume formalized and quantified.

The development we have traced depicts men and women constituted by their individual (as opposed to communal) relation to the transcendent source of meaning and order. This idea, inherent in the Christianity of Paul and later of Augustine, developed through the soteriological doctrines of ascetic Protestantism. It continued in the devotional movements of the late seventeenth century and in the privatization of grace beyond the boundaries of a community of saints. Indeed, a similar movement to that noted above in the North American context can be found in the "ethical inwardness" of the Cambridge Platonists. Their stress on moral activity as partaking of a "universal righteousness" and on individual identity bifurcated into a reasoned virtue (which is "natural") and the vice of excessive appetites marks a similar move toward the interiorization of Puritan beliefs, this time in English Protestantism of the Restoration period. Benjamin Whichcote's dictum was a fundamental tenet among all the Cambridge Platonists: "Hell arises out of a Man's self: And Hell's Fewel is the Guilt of a Man's Conscience." Heaven "lies in a refin'd Temper, in an internal reconciliation to the Nature of God, and to the Rule of Righteousness. So that both Hell and Heaven have their foundation within Men."[98] It resonates with the selfsame interiorization of grace as conscience found in late-seventeenth-century New England and points forward to the ideas of Shaftesbury (who in fact published Whichcote's sermons) and the moral basis of the idea of civil society in the Scottish Enlightenment. Ultimately, these ideas, which stressed the apprehension of God—as the source of our natural goodness—through reason led in the late eighteenth and nineteenth centuries to our more contemporary ideas of the individual as possessing metaphysical and moral value founded on the premise of universal reason.[99]

What emerged together with this modern idea of the individual was, however, a new idea of the ethical or moral no longer rooted in a transcendent and other-worldly sphere but in the immanent this-worldly workings of reason. The result of this process was an individual-as-constructed-by-reason with which there emerged, or rather, reemerged, the problem of society, of how to represent the ties and relations between morally autonomous and agentic individuals. That, of course, is precisely where we began our inquiry into the different forms of social theory in chapter one.

Otto Gierke analyzed this problem in terms of the development of modern natural law theory. He too stressed the change wrought by Protestantism in the defining terms of Christian universalism.[100] The effect of the Protestant Reformation was to replace what Gierke termed the *universitas* (or corporate unity) of the Catholic *ecumene* with a *societas* (or partnership, association) of distinct individuals defined by their particular and individual relationship to the sources of grace and other-worldly transcendence. The hierarchic edifice of the Christian commonwealth had become atomized into one of individuals ("saints"), each containing within his and her own conscience the terms of Christian universalism.

As Christian casuistry lost its role in regulating the activities of Christians in the world, a new set of strictures, institutional and symbolic, replaced them. The maintenance of Christian morality was in essence transferred from the hands of ecclesiastical institutions to those of the state.[101] This shift in regulating mechanisms and agencies was represented by the development of the modern natural law doctrine, in the writings of Grotius (*De Jure Belli ac Pacis*, 1625), Pufendorf (*De Jure Naturae et Gentium*, 1672), Burlamaqui (*Principes du Droit Naturel*, 1747), and Vattel (*Droit de Gens ou Principes de la Loi Naturelle*, 1758). All of them distanced natural law doctrine from its Christian and theological roots and grounded it instead in a doctrine of reason. And with that the importance of honoring one's declaration of will, the *declaratio* or *signum voluntatis*, became the central component of political theory, that is, of the new idea of community.

This grounding of natural law principles in rational constructs aimed at bridging classical natural law doctrines and modern political principles of natural rights.[102] The very appeal of a rationalized theology in the eighteenth century was that it managed to retain the transcendent dimension in the idea of Nature's God among the Deists. Later developments, however, rooted the principles of natural law in pure reason alone, which led to its increasing formalization and the loss of the very transcendent character upon which its claim as an ethical norm had rested for two millennia.

The challenge of modern natural law theory then was to provide a representative vision of the social whole (*universitas*) based on the idea of the individual as an autonomous being whose existence was "logically prior" to the state or society itself. In Gierke's terms:

> The State was no longer derived from the divinely ordained harmony of the universal whole; it was no longer explained as a partial whole which was derived from, and preserved by, the existence of a greater: it was simply explained by itself. The starting-point of speculation ceased to be general humanity; it became the individual and self-sufficing sovereign State; *and this individual State was regarded as based on a union of individuals, in obedience to the dictates of Natural Law, to form a society armed with supreme power.*[103]

To a great extent this was the logic of the United States' founding. Consequently, it is not surprising that the very construction of the political community on the basis of natural law and the autonomous moral individual has had its greatest success in the United States, where, according to Albrecht Wellemer, Hegel's understanding of individual "right" is given concrete existence.[104] Hegel's characterization of modernity, as we saw earlier, is that "a man is counted as a man in virtue of his manhood alone, not because he is a Jew, Catholic, Protestant, German, Italian etc."[105] The fact that Hegel's quote resonates with the words of the Apostle Paul should not surprise us, for this is precisely the new universalism of the individual as moral entity that replaced the earlier Christian idea.

What we have traced, in however schematic a manner, has been the construction, through Christianity, of a historically unique form of the generalized and universalized other. The irony, however, is that this universalization threatens the very idea of boundaries within which, and only within which, an idea of community (and hence authority) and of mutual approbation and responsibility makes sense. If community is to have meaning beyond a set of compacting or contracting individuals, if it is to foster constituting roles replete with values, internalized norms, the mechanics of shame, responsibility, and so on, it must be bounded. Trust demands limits (as does Durkheim's notion of the *precontractual*). But the universalization of otherhood in Christianity and most especially in its institutionalized Protestant versions undercuts this very aspect of the construction of community.

Note that the idea of transcendence by itself, though clearly universal, does not of necessity lead to this outcome. In the Jewish reading of law (or works, if you prefer), the external element is preserved and with it the specificity of group boundaries, individual status, and the unique obligations incumbent upon different solidarities within society. Though generalized and indeed generalizable (as evinced in the Noachite commandments as well as the laws regulating obligations of the stranger and the sojourner, those "fellow travelers" of the late second Temple period and beyond), the external and action-oriented nature of legal injunctions maintained both the heteronomy of authority and the constitutive elements of the group "called" by that authority.

Ultimately, it was the interiorization of the ethical sense in terms of a morality of faith and conscience that destroyed both the idea of community and the idea of authority. (As argued in chapter one, neither can exist without the other. If a community is not authoritative, it is not a community; and if the dictates of authority are not girded within communal or collective standards and obligations, it is but brute power.) This interiorization was, as we have seen, the legacy of the Puritan sects. The triumph of conscience is the necessary concomitant of the Hobbesian vision of the autonomous self—as Hobbes himself realized! The brute power of individual selves, held in check no longer by an external *authority*, could only be contained by a supreme *power*. Hobbes was painfully aware of the antinomian potential that was unleashed by a society of sectaries, each proclaiming a justified conscience. The liberating effects of conscience came at a price—the loss of communal obligations and, in essence, of heteronomous authority. And this is what Tawney was getting at in his *Religion and the Rise of Capitalism.*

The irony of these developments is great. For none can accuse either Luther or Calvin or their adepts in the sixteenth or seventeenth centuries of being deaf to the calls of heteronomous authority. Nor indeed were the calls of communal obligation lacking among the Puritans in the Old and New Worlds (or indeed among the myriad of other sects that formed on the Continent in the sixteenth century and later). What we have, rather, is a case of the unintended consequences of institutionalization. As conscience triumphed and as public order secularized in the eighteenth and nineteenth centuries, the full institutionalization of the original Christian vision essentially broke out of its own meaning-giving framework. Both heteronomous (transcendent) authority and constitutive community were replaced with a transcendental reason mediating (through contract, i.e., promises) the actions of a *societas* of morally autonomous selves. And we have been struggling with the consequences— and reaping the benefits—ever since.

This dynamic has profoundly affected the dual issues of authority and the self. For without an authoritative source of the sacred, any idea of the self as moral (or perhaps ethical) evaluator loses its cogency. Without the concomitant idea of community, any idea of a relational self loses its sense and suasion. Authority may be internalized as conscience, to be sure. It may also, however, be internalized simply as desire ("Heaven and their lusts") and as such becomes a purely private directive. It may then become increasingly difficult to establish a sense of self that is anything other than an idiosyncratic bundle of desires (and even these desires are more and more a mass phenomenon and no longer individual constructs). In some cases these mass phenomena have lent their weight to collectivist movements and ideologies within which any realization of individual identity is lost. Thus was the expressive dimension of existence as propounded by Herder and the German romantics given an often brutal social articulation. Indeed, the results of such movements in this century have, on the whole, been rather ghastly. For all their ghastliness, however, they are resultant of the aforementioned tendency of modernity to absolutize the tensions between individual and collective modes of identity—including its expressivist components.

A further consequence of this absolutizing dynamic of Enlightened reason has been the increasing contemporary concern with the issue of recognition that has emerged at the center of political thought and action on both the national and international scenes. Interestingly, this is also concerned with the expressive aspect of existence, though in a

somewhat different manner. *Multiculturalism and the Politics of Recognition,*
the title of a short and influential book by Charles Taylor, expresses what
is after all at the core of many current agendas: from the courts (in briefs
over affirmative action) to international funding agencies such as the
Ford Foundation, to QUANGOs and NGOs from South Africa to Prague.
The problem of recognition with which we ended the previous chapter
is nothing other than the problem of the self, or rather of selves devoid
of an authoritative locus of value. For the problem of recognition, like
that of community, is that it is always only specific, particular. There is
no generic recognition of otherhood (which is the absurdity of so much
in contemporary politics), only recognition of specific differences, of
specific selves (the feminist issue of difference, we may note, is, like much
else, subsumed in an older polemic and problem, which is really that of
Jewish and Christian consciousness). Yet it is precisely the context within
which such individual selves can exist and be recognized that is lacking.
An internally constituted self cannot be recognized as such because recognition can only occur in a shared and common framework, which is
precisely what has been undercut by those very developments that, as
described by Bernard Mandeville, have left us in a situation where "every
individual is a little World by itself."[106]

Unless such frameworks are authoritative they cannot provide the
shared and common basis for mutual recognition. If they are not, they
are a very different type of framework (like the rules of queuing or Ping-
Pong or the selling of shares in a company, but not those of community).
And it is precisely with this issue of authority that we moderns have a
problem, indeed are confronted with a paradox, which is the paradox
of modernity. For modernity's own autonomous and value-laden individual—that moral personality outlined by Immanuel Kant—is itself constantly threatened with collapse into either a communal self (whether in
totalitarian politics, racist identities, or even the phenomenon of mass
man, what Hannah Arendt termed the "rise of the social") or into itself.
In all cases (though the differences between them are vast) what is lost
is the idea of the self as moral evaluator, which was precisely the modern
contribution to our idea of what is sacred and of ultimate concern.

Another way to grasp this paradox is through recalling Max Weber's
discussion of charisma in terms of authority. He noted that if the sacred
or charismatic is not authoritative it cannot very well be sacred. However,
if we follow the writing of scholars like Edward Shils and S. N. Eisenstadt,
who speak of the dispersal of charisma in modern societies, we find ourselves observing nothing less than the dispersal of authority throughout
society, which, of course, is what democratic equality is all about.[107] However, and this is the rub, when authority is so dispersed it is no longer
authoritative. Its call is no more heeded than are symbols of ancient

heraldry. Recall the definition of authority as legitimate power. If the power of all members of society is legitimate in the same measure (consequent of that very "metaphysical equality" of democratic regimes), then the calculus again becomes one of pure interests and of power *simpliciter.* Durkheim, in a tragic sense, got it profoundly wrong. Yes, indeed, as he claimed, there is most certainly a sacred locus in modern society, that of the individual. Yet once sacrality (or the charismatic) is defined in terms of the individual, the worm is already in the apple.[108] For with the individual as sacred, the "pre" of the precontractual continually threatens to unravel and leave said individuals with nothing between them but the contract itself.

Where this becomes most visible and most illuminating of the problem of recognition is in the arena of social roles. As noted earlier, Berger has observed that one of the big differences between traditional and modern notions of selfhood is in the relation of self to roles. He specifies further that "the concept of honor implies that identity is essentially, or at least importantly, linked to institutional roles. The modern concept of dignity, by contrast implies that identity is essentially independent of institutional roles." Thus "in a world of honor, the individual discovers his true identity in his roles, and to turn away from the roles is to turn away from himself. . . . In a world of dignity, the individual can only discover his true identity by emancipating himself from his socially imposed roles— they are only masks, entangling him in illusion, "alienation," and "bad faith."[109] Contemporary ideas of personal identity, he asserts, exist "apart from and often against the institutional roles through which the individual expresses himself in society." Thus,

> the reciprocity between individual and society, between subjective identity and objective identification through roles, now comes to be experienced as a sort of struggle. Institutions cease to be the 'home' of the self; instead they become oppressive realities that distort and estrange the self. Roles no longer actualize the self, but serve as a 'veil of maya' hiding the self not only from others, but from the individual's own consciousness. Only in the interstitial areas left vacant, as it were, by the institutions (such as the so-called private sphere of social life) can the individual hope to discover or define himself.[110]

The dispersal of charisma is, in the end, so widespread as to vitiate even the social aspect of self (the role) from any authoritative component. Left is only an almost disembodied individual severed from any sense of social constraint. And this brings us back to that most contemporary of complaints, the need for recognition. For if roles are voided of meaning, are distanced in any meaningful sense from selves, what is left to recognize? When authority is internalized, it becomes impossible to seek mutual recognition, and we are trapped in increasingly solipsistic forms of self-recognition, actually often only acclaim. The search for recognition from others becomes nothing more than a continual affirmation of selves by themselves. Whatever else this is, it is not mutual recognition and is much closer to the narcissistic self characterized by Christopher Lasch than to the introspective conscience of the apostle.[111] Short indeed is the route from here to anomic spending patterns and a search for self-validation in material objects that theorists from Thorstein Veblin to A. O. Hirschman have studied.[112]

Once external, ultimately heteronomous authority is gone; so too is any fixed hierarchy of norms and values and a shared, communal sense of the supreme virtues. These or an approximation of these could be found in social roles and their proper fulfillment. We are, of course, on firm Aristotelian ground here. However, when internalized authority becomes the ultimate arbiter of social life and practical decision making, any meaningful sense of mutual recognition and approbation is lost. It is very well to call for a politics of recognition, but for that call to be meaningful it must countenance social conditions and orientations that are, more often than not, inimicable to the logic of modern life.

It is, however, this very logic with its seemingly inexorable tendency to conflate all value positions and pluralisms into the logic of an instrumental rationality (what Max Weber termed *Zeckrationalität*) that is responsible for our dilemma in the first place. After all, an instrumental, ends/means rationality of utility calculation is precisely what is called for in a world defined solely by mutual negotiating acumen and the calculus of resource mobilization and exchange. Hence our contemporary predicament and the continual demand for recognition, which, however, implies as well a recognition of other value positions and rationalities (what Weber termed *Wertrationalität*) as well. What these demands therefore evince are the limits of our liberal and autonomous view of the self (however much those making such claims may not recognize this).

How then to reconstitute a self without reconstituting authoritarianism and without returning to the brutal, oppressive, and servile aspects of authority relations that have marked so much of the historical record? How to return to heteronomy (if at all) without fundamentalism and without the intolerance and the intransigence that characterizes so much of religious thought and practice—certainly in the West among the adherents of the three revealed religions, though not only among these? How to return to community, to a society with boundaries of trust and membership, without returning to the exclusiveness, hatred, and intolerance that we see today from the Balkans to Indonesia and from the Middle East to the Central Asian republics? These are real questions that cannot be shied away from if the foregoing analysis is to be treated with any degree of seriousness.

We began this chapter by noting the univocality of ethical monotheism and end it with the totalizing (and hence univocal) character of Enlightened reason. It may just be, however, that by bringing these two inherently hegemonic and totalizing conceptions into dialogue and tension with one another (rather than their mutual exclusion, which has been the case since the French Revolution), some new synthesis may be broached. In the following and concluding chapter I offer some modest suggestions along these lines.

## Chapter Five

# TOLERANCE AND TRADITION

THE PREVIOUS chapter ended with the problem of recognition, which lies at the core of the "politics of identity." With authority internalized as individual right, mutual recognition becomes an elusive goal as, in de Tocqueville's words, "each man is narrowly shut in himself and from that basis makes the pretense to judge the world."[1] With recognition lost, the self comes increasingly to rest solely on the calculus and negotiation of power. Wills are, to return to the nomenclature of our opening chapter, coerced from without, rather than subjugated from within. The result is a situation fraught with paradox: the very individualist assumptions of moral autonomy upon which modernity is predicated frees the individual from collective restraints even as it ultimately destroys said agency by reducing it to a calculus of pure power and utility calculation. Moral evaluation is lost.

Thus, and though individualism becomes a value in modernity, it is precisely within contemporary modernity—what is often termed postmodernism—that the very ability to denote moral values becomes open to absolute questioning and relativism. Moral evaluation, as we have argued throughout, rests on communal approbation. However, in absolutizing the tensions between collective and individual desiderata (what Rousseau termed the general will and the will of all, the *volonté générale* and the *volonté de tout*), the course of modernity has tended to either collapse the individual into the collective (as in fascism, Nazism, and, in different forms, in various examples of state socialism) or, in its liberal variants, to obscure the very matrix of their connection. Hence the paradox (noted above and) at the end of chapter one, that individual autonomy emerges in modernity, as individuals are freed from those previously existent collective constraints and sanctions, yet these sanctions and constraints are themselves necessary for autonomous reason to function practically in the world. The very totalizing and univocal propensity of Enlightened reason to absolutize the tensions of social existence is here manifest in the dualism of individualist and collectivist positions. Such absolutization, however, makes both the resultant positions untenable.[2]

Above, in chapter four, we traced but one historical strand of this development whereby the very idea of a constituted self that is essential to any idea of authority was undermined by the full institutionalization (and hence universalization) of Christian individualism, first in Protestantism and then in secular liberal thought. With the loss of the idea of a Christian life constituted by its transcendent referent, lost too was the very basis for a self constituted by that which is external to it. What remains is our overriding concern with individual autonomy, which leaves us at the mercy of the vagaries of power differentials, of *fortuna*, and of our negotiating acumen.

This book has argued for the need to take authority seriously in order to maintain a more rigorous and morally thick notion of autonomy. Viewed from the perspective of group sanctions, this is represented in the idea of legitimation (of a social order), which is more than something to be scrutinized by an ethic of suspicion and questioned by the perennial *cui bono*. Rather, inhering in the idea of legitimation are allied concepts of sacrality, authority, and internalized values, without which we would do but poor justice to the human condition.

This is not to say that worldly power, in the very act of invoking authority, does not often corrupt itself as well as the authority invoked.[3] To be sure, we see in the examples of Iran, Israel, and too often the Roman Catholic and Orthodox churches the corruption of religion and religious authority by their alliance with state power. Over the course of history this has been the rule more than the exception in all the monotheistic religions, but, of course, not only in these. Caesaro-papist regimes, on the whole, are not known for their commitments to tolerance and democratic rule.

More importantly, from the era of antiquity and the wars of the kingdoms of Israel and Judah (beginning 900 B.C.E.), the role of transcendent religion in the establishment of peaceable and tolerant regimes has been far from salutary.[4] Israelite Yahwists were no more tolerant of alternative truth claims than were the Muslim conquerors of the Sassanian, Zoroastrian Empire fourteen hundred years later.[5] The Axial revolution and the breakthrough to transcendence and absolute heteronomous authority that it called forth provides as well the source for a new intolerance. In this sense the 'corruption' of authority is almost, as it were, built into its very constitution, in its claims to reorganize worldly existence in the name of a higher truth. When, following that insight of Voeglin quoted earlier, in chapter two, "the truth of man and the truth of God are inseparably one," there is, as well, a strong impetus to impose this truth on others as a uniform and incontrovertible grid of existence, often by force of arms. The well-known tolerance of Roman polytheism, which could adapt itself and merge with different religious traditions, stands in marked contrast to these claims of Axial religion (though we should heed Arnaldo Momigliano's warnings in not attributing too much to this Roman tolerance, especially in practices touching on political rule).[6]

Transcendent authority, which allows the constitution of individual agency in the form of moral evaluation, has also, ironically, provided serious threats towards its realization within the concrete political and social orders of the world. Its own univocal claims are no more given to temperate realization than those of Enlightened reason—at least so the historical record shows.

We must note, however, that certain strains of sectarian Protestantism did devise an ingenious solution to the problem of authority and power. By internalizing the religious experience, they obviated the necessity for state power to promulgate religious dictates. By saving religious authority from the corruption of this-worldly *power*, the citizenry was also rescued from religious coercion. Within the history of world religion this was a somewhat unique and radically innovative step towards solving the often dangerous conflation of worldly power and transcendent authority. Roger Williams, we may note, was one of its most important advocates in this country. It was, however, a solution arrived at with a cost. For the solution was premised on that morally autonomous self (of justified conscience), which, as we have argued, underpins the process of secularization through which heteronomous authority is ultimately lost, and with it the very idea of authority per se.

Clearly, however, the very same trajectory was also the one that generated individual rights, choice, and the freedom of conscience upon which so much of what we consider morally, even ethically, irrevocable in the modern world rests. These secular and liberal political orientations owe a large debt to the structures of Protestant belief.[7] An important example of this was the interweaving of religious and secular dimensions that came to characterize the reconstruction of natural law doctrines in eighteenth-century America and the related idea of the individual as constitutive of the political community. This development was analyzed by Georg Jellinek, whose work served as an inspiration for Weber's own. Already in 1895 Jellinek compared the American Bill(s) of Rights (from different states), the French *declaration des droits de l'homme et du citoyen*, and, more significantly, the English Bill of Rights of 1689, the Habeas Corpus Act of 1679, and the 1628 Petition of Right. His conclusions are worth quoting, as the United States has become in so many ways the "ideal" type of Western modernity:

> The American bills of rights do not attempt merely to set forth certain principles for the state's organization, but they seek above all to draw the boundary line between state and individual. According to them the individual is not

the possessor of rights through the state, but by his own nature he has in-
alienable and indefeasible rights. The English laws know nothing of this.
They do not wish to recognize an eternal, natural right, but one inherited
from their fathers, "the old, undoubted rights of the English people."[8]

As Jellinek sees it, English law offers no autonomous grounding of individual rights in a set of natural principles but grounds them solely in
tradition, in "the laws and statutes of this realm."[9] He looked to the defining traits of Congregational Puritanism to explain how the "inherited
rights and liberties, as well as the privileges of organization, which had
been granted the colonists by the English kings," were transformed in
the New World to "rights which spring not from man but from *God and
Nature.*"[10]

The very success of natural law doctrine—based on self-sufficient individuals endowed with reason—as the foundation of the American political community rested on the synthesis of these ideas with the tradition
of the Holy Commonwealth of visible saints, the transcendent subject of
Protestant belief. Not only (transcendental) reason but also (transcendent) grace, redefined in the inner-worldly terms of individual conscience, continued throughout the eighteenth century to define the
terms of individual and social existence in the civil polity. It was the very
continuity of this religious heritage that made the positing of a political
community of individuals—united by compacts—possible in eighteenth-
century America and beyond. And so Jellinek concluded as well:

> In the closest connection with the great religious political movement out of
> which the American democracy was born, there arose the conviction that
> there exists a right not conferred upon the citizen but inherent in man, that
> acts of conscience and expressions of religious conviction stand inviolable
> over against the state as the exercise of a higher right. This right so long
> suppressed is not 'inheritance,' is nothing handed down from their fathers,
> as the rights and liberties of Magna Charta and of the other English enact-
> ments,—*not the State but the Gospel proclaimed it.*[11]

As Jellinek realized, individual rights in America were not derived
solely from positive law, but had acquired a transcendent justification
unique in the modern world. Indeed, this situation constituted the foundation of modernity itself.

Any attempt to return to a politics of authority and an experience of
constituted self must therefore acknowledge the experience of individual choice and freedom of conscience that few today would forgo. On a
theoretical level such a move would necessitate a return to a faith mediated by reason, to an idea of authority that survived the rigors of Enlight-

enment skepticism, doubt, and rational inquiry. Some reintegration of belief and understanding, of faith and reason, rather than their absolute incompatibility, would be called for. The ineluctable contradiction of reason and revelation that, as Stephen Toulmin argued, defined the seventeenth-century "quest for certitude" and that has continued to define modern civilizations would needs be transformed.[12] Rather, tempered by reason, faith would need to temper reason in turn. Choice would then be interpolated as uncertainty and the arrogance of knowledge replaced by the humility of fideist belief. Something of this point is intimated in Leo Strauss's comments on the context of Spinoza's critique of religion:

> If orthodoxy claims to know the Bible is divinely revealed, that every word of the Bible is divinely inspired, that Moses was the writer of the Pentateuch, that the miracles recorded in the Bible have happened and similar things, Spinoza has refuted orthodoxy. But the case is entirely different if orthodoxy limits itself to asserting that it believes the aforementioned things, i.e. that they cannot claim to possess the binding power peculiar to the known.[13]

Humility then in all directions—of both faith and of reason. The absolute and univocal claims of both must thus be brought together in a dialogue that would, of necessity, question the very "givenness" of each's certitudes.

On the more practical level a post-Enlightenment faith would perhaps be one founded on casuistic processes of moral reasoning, rather than on unassailable principles. Such a faith could be approached through a skepticism that I would like to call a skeptical toleration—an epistemological modesty whose very uncertainty would prevent intolerance of the other. Authority remains, but presumptions of its knowability are held in perpetual abeyance by the very heteronomous character of said authority. Choice and freedom are preserved—not by the privatization of the sacred in individual conscience, but by the very unknowableness of the truly external, of the other-than-self. In the more theological terms of Paul Ricoeur, not the "justified conscience [which comes to] understand its past condemnation as a sort of pedagogy, but, the conscience still kept under the guard of the law, its real meaning unknown."[14]

The reference to casuistry was deliberate, for casuistry is predicated on the recognition of the discrepancy between general and universal moral rules and their concrete, particular implementation. For as ever more realms are brought under the rubric of a particular principle of ordering, and the more diverse these realms, the more the principles themselves become attenuated. This in essence is what is meant by the paradox of institutionalization.[15] In terms of moral reasoning there exists a similar paradox. As parsed out by Albert Jonsen and Stephen Toulmin:

The fact that every moral maxim, rule or other generalization applies to certain actual situations centrally and unambiguously but to others only marginally or ambiguously, makes the latter situations just as problematic in their own way as the situations in which different rules or maxims come into conflict. . . . In a nutshell, once we move far enough away from the simple paradigmatic cases to which the chosen generalizations were tailored, it becomes clear that no rule can be entirely self-interpreting. The considerations that weigh with us in resolving the ambiguities that arise in marginal cases, like those that weigh with us in balancing claims of conflicting principles, are never *written* in the rules themselves.[16]

There is, then, no space free from interpretation. And as with moral reasoning, so with authority. What is needed is a process of *phronesis*, a practical ethics and a wisdom that is continually subjected to rebuttal and counterfactual challenges, that is hesitant in its approach and modest in its claims. As argued most recently by Menachem Fisch, such an almost Popperian approach can be found in the religious discourse of the Babylonian Talmud.[17] It can also be found, as Toulmin has argued, in pre-Reformation Europe, that is, in societies before the wars of religion and the consequent obsession with and quest for certainty.[18] The thought and personhood of Michel de Montaigne is perhaps the paradigm of such a position of contextualized belief embedded within the practical experience of life itself. Having, as Montaigne teaches us in his *Apology for Raimond Sebond*, "no intercourse with being," we must be forever vigilant against both the "vanity" of our reason as well as the self-certitude of faith, which is but the play of chance.[19] As he reminds his readers,

Another country, other testimony, similar promises and menaces might, by the same means, impress on us a very different belief. We are Christians by the same title that we are Perigordins or Germans.[20]

What is demanded, then, is a midpoint between nihilism and postmodern relativism, on the one hand, and absolutist claims of both faith and reason, on the other. As an example of what can be gained through such a reintegration of both modern and traditional understandings of self and society rather then their absolute differentiation, we end this inquiry with a brief explication of one particular issue, that of toleration. A skeptical toleration of modest claims, of faith tempered by reason and tempering reason in turn may in fact permit a return to a principled authority, without resurrecting the authoritarianism of the past.

Many would counter that the matter of toleration or what might even be called a sacred pluralism (that is, a pluralism of authorities) is no longer relevant at the end of the twentieth century. They might perhaps even argue that the problems evoked by issues of toleration, insofar as they exist at all, are no more than "remnants" or "traces" of insufficiently modernized cultures or insufficiently modernized subcultures within a broader society. In any case, they would say, these are problems destined to disappear with the final triumph of Enlightenment principles.

True enough, rarely are the myriad examples of intolerance, bloody-mindedness, and evil in today's world seen as part and parcel of modernity itself, as a concomitant of the universalist vision. Rather, most people do tend to view these situations as ones wherein the actors are operating according to rules other than those of the modernist world view. But they also view the situation as amenable to amelioration by proper education, change of political regime, international pressure, or other means. More to the point, certain principles are seen as the hallmark of a properly functioning modern liberal political and social order. These principles are *the privatization of religion, a politics of rights over a politics of the good,* and, in the broadest of terms, the triumph of a secular *liberal-Protestant vision of selfhood* (the sort of Kantian self-actualized moral agent) together with a *secularized public space.* Furthermore, as the popular wisdom goes, if only those intractable, fundamentalist Jews, Christians, Muslims, or Sikhs could accept these eminently reasonable principles, we would solve the problem of intolerance. And the sooner the better.

My argument here is that this vision is no longer tenable, for at least two reasons: First, the progress of secularization—one of the central sociological hypotheses of the 1960s—is more than called into doubt by contemporary events. More than that of anyone else, David Martin's work has documented the spread of evangelical Protestantism, most markedly in Latin America but also in Southeast Asia, Korea, China, Africa, and increasingly in Eastern Europe.[21]

Peter Berger has tended to see this phenomenon in terms of processes of globalization and as a development sui generis—though there is some debate here; for instance, on the spread of a new Confucianism among certain elites in China and of Islam in Africa, or the return to Orthodoxy among a whole new generation of affluent American Jews.[22] So there may well be many comparative cases after all. The point is that we are witnessing a major reorientation of belief structures that puts the lie to any simple belief in the march of secularization.

It is also clear that the Islamic world has not secularized in ways that were long thought to be necessary to the development of modern economies and societies. And while the Western press tends to focus on instances of Islamic fundamentalism, there are, as we all know, significant phenomena of a very different nature—the movements of a "liberal" Islam in Indonesia, counting some twenty-two million members, being a case in point.[23]

The problem, then, is apparent on the empirical level. If the only source of tolerance is a secular liberal political and social order, we may all be in for some difficult times, for secularism seems to be in retreat, and liberal assumptions of self and society are under attack in many places.

With this we come to the second problematic aspect of the "Enlightenment as end of history" argument: that the very institutionalization of modernity calls forth its own antithesis. This old sociological insight into the paradox of institutionalization calls to mind the history of the Catholic church, as well as of sectarian Protestantism. And it is just as relevant for the development of secular modernity.

The flip side of secularization is fundamentalism: both are inventions of modernity. The very institutionalization that brings more and more realms of social life under the rubric of an abstract and universal reason will sooner or later evoke a reaction, as modernity calls forth its own antithesis. This reaction can take many forms—the growth of primordial, racial politics being perhaps the most malevolent. But we see it as well in the blossoming of gender and sexual preference as modes of identity and as political statements. And, of course, we see it in the return to religious identities and commitments as an increasingly important affective aspect of individuals' lives in different parts of the world.

In this sense these identities may well be a clear concomitant of globalization. There seems to be a widespread dynamic at work, in the production or even the reproduction of what some had come to think of as "pre"-modern forms of identity and commitment. There is, it seems, a need to express constitutive aspects of the self and of personality. Whereas the self predicated on autonomous reason cannot adequately meet this need, both primordiality and the idea of heteronomy do it very well. So regardless of the reason, the return to religion that we are witnessing today is often a return to religion in its most primitive, unsophisticated, blind, and ignorant versions.

In the Jewish tradition there exists the notion that evil is produced by *ru'ach stut*, a spirit of folly or foolishness. Often enough today's return to religion is done in such a spirit, and, if not of foolishness, then of ignorance—with the expected results. By foolish and ignorant, I intend ignorance of precisely those aspects within the different religious traditions that point the way not to a self-satisfied and comfortable validation of oneself and one's belief structure—that certitude that leads to acts like the murder of Yitzhak Rabin—but rather to an openness to the stranger, to the other, and hence to ethical behavior informed by the principle of tolerance. Those aspects of belief open us as well to doubt and uncertainty and to the responsibilities demanded by that very uncertainty. In fact, the obligations that uncertainty imposes are arguably greater than those imposed by certainty itself.

Moreover, it is more than possible that historians in another hundred or hundred and fifty years' time will look back on the period from roughly 1750 to 2050 as a brief three-hundred-year secular parenthesis in a history of humanity that was always religious. However, if it indeed comes to be that rationality gives way to a return to faith, it will be a faith of a different order from that of the faith of prerational times. It will be a faith that has passed through the crucible of the Enlightenment understanding of reason. While we cannot know the nature of such faith, at least two possibilities do present themselves to our understanding. The one would be an intensification, if not absolutization, of the modernist tensions between faith and reason. In such a scenario a fundamentalist religiosity would prevail as a reaction to a fundamentalist reason. Intimations of this are unfortunately not too hard to perceive in many contemporary societies. Mass demonstrations in Israel for and against the Israeli court system (seen as *the* institutional realm of modern liberal-democratic assumptions) following the conviction of the leader of Israel's fastest-growing religious party on charges of bribery and corruption is a good case in point. Almost all the demonstrators in favor of the courts were secular Jews; almost all the demonstrators against the courts were religious. Other examples can, of course, be brought from other societies, whether of the religious right in the USA, the situation in contemporary Turkey, Algeria, Egypt, or, for that matter, Indonesia.

The other possibility is, however, of a faith in perpetual dialogue with the dictates of reason and with its justificatory procedures. To be sure, a simple return to the Deism of the eighteenth century or to the beliefs of the Cambridge Platonists is no longer possible. Yet, the emergence of a self-reflective faith where reason is no longer alien, but integrated into its very domain assumptions is a real possibility. Certainly, the recent papal encyclical letter *Fides et Ratio* bears witness to a perceived need within the hierarchy of the Roman Catholic Church to further this very integration, as do similar moves within the Jewish and Islamic worlds as well.[24]

If we wish to avoid a return to the worst excesses of the past, we need to chart a new course and bring to light possibilities only dimly realized at present. Too often today religion is dismissed as fundamentalist with a sweeping condemnation. This reflects willful ignorance of other aspects of religion. It reflects that totalizing propensity of reason to absolutize the tensions between sacred and profane realms (as well as of pluralist normative injunctions), into irreconcilable contradictions between which no compromise or dialogue is possible. This then makes it very difficult to articulate a position of principled toleration or an acceptance of pluralist value commitments predicated on anything other than some form of indifference or (absolute) relativism. In contrast to this, it is precisely within a religious orientation that one can find the foundation of a very different sort of orientation, one of a real toleration. Indeed, one could claim that the bases of a principled toleration can be found only within a religious perspective (though the concrete venues of such are not always those most stressed in religious education). How so?

Tolerance of something, we must never forget, implies tolerance of practices and beliefs whose validity or normative status we reject as wrong, unreasonable, or undesirable. Otherwise we would not need to be tolerant of it. Tolerance does not, however, involve coming to accept these beliefs as correct or somehow less wrong. Rather, it involves the ability to abide beliefs we continue to think of as wrong or misguided.

Yet if one group of people simply hates another, we would demand of them not tolerance but rather the abandonment of their hatred. Moreover, we do not consider the bigot tolerant if, through a vast expenditure of psychological energy, he refrains from acting on his prejudice. The fact that, though he had the opportunity, he did not go down to a church in Alabama and burn it down does not make him a tolerant individual. This is not to say that toleration does not involve restraint, but it is a restraint of more than action. It is a restraint of thought, a restraint quite possibly of judgment, as John Horton pointed out some time ago.[25]

Thus, toleration involves some tension between commitment to one's own set of values or principles or religious edicts and a willingness to put up with, to abide, those of the other who adheres to beliefs that one thinks are wrong. Moreover, the tolerance we would presumably be looking for would be a principled one, not some sort of unprincipled tolerance. Thus we would not be advocating

1. a tolerance simply of indifference (where one's tolerance of the other's belief is akin to a "tolerance" of his taste in bathroom tiles, say);
2. or a sort of Hobbesian calculus of differential *power* (tolerant because we cannot impose our will);
3. or toleration as a sort of second best solution (though we often must settle for this. Thus, if we cannot get the racist to overcome her racism, at least we can get her to tolerate those others whom she despises).

Finally, there is a rather counterintuitive thread that runs through the above arguments—that people do not become more tolerant by finding certain behavior less objectionable. Quite the opposite, for approved conduct does not need to be tolerated. It is rather in behavior found objectionable, yet unjudged, that tolerance would seem to rest. Just what sort of beliefs or judgments are suspended in this act of *tolerance* toward what we consider wrong is admittedly not always obvious. I wish to make clear that this itself does not imply any sort of relativism. It does, however, involve a certain skepticism or tentativeness, a modesty perhaps toward our own epistemological claims. That such a position can be developed from within a religious perspective is, I believe, a crucial point, precisely because the alternative—modern and liberal—bases for tolerance are themselves somewhat shaky.

As we well know, for the past two hundred years or so, tolerance in the Western world has rested, not on religious bases, but on a decidedly secular foundation. The privatization of religion—which can be seen as one aspect of its secularization—is itself rooted in the institutionalization of Protestant religiosity. It has led to the circumscription of religious truth claims to the realm of the private rather than that of shared, public culture. The epistemological foundations of this orientation were, in part, laid by John Locke, who claimed that since religion was a matter of belief, any coercion of the will would simply not work in enforcing religious conformity—for the structures of belief were not subject to the workings of the will.[26] This is fine, as far as it goes; however, it does also betray its own particular religious assumptions in its stress on belief as standing at the center of religious consciousness, reflecting the type of Protestant religiosity discussed above. For while belief cannot indeed be coerced, practice, and most especially public practice, certainly can. And there are religions where the public practices are a good deal more central than the structure of individual belief systems. If we look to Hinduism, Islam, or Judaism, we immediately see this to be so. No small number of people continue to be engaged in violent, illegal, and often repressive behavior in many parts of the world over precisely issues of religious practice; if coffee houses can be open in Jerusalem on the Sabbath, if women must go veiled in public, if they can attend university, and so on.

Similarly, we should note that the tolerance advocated by Thomas Hobbes, the tolerance of a minimalist morality and of a skeptical consciousness (note, though, that it is a secular skepticism rather than a religious one), was one predicated on a *pragmatic politics* that—in given situations—could also deny tolerance for dissent in the name of the same principles of public order and civil peace in whose name it was promulgated.[27]

With Hobbes, even more than Locke, religion is privatized, and so, while I may have every right to repel my neighbors' attempts on my person or property, I cannot take up arms against him to impose my own conception of his salvation. The *state, however,* may well have the right to suppress the public expression of heretical beliefs for the same reason that it may suppress walking naked in the streets (the Quakers in mid-seventeenth-century England and New England, we may recall, did both and were duly suppressed). Such suppression is but a police matter and has nothing to do with belief. What results, however, is the idea of a potentially intolerant state upon which social peace and order could rest.

If belief was not a basis for coercion, neither was skepticism towards belief a guarantee of dissent and tolerance (at least in the seventeenth century). For the skepticism of the seventeenth century was tied to the stoic notion of *ataraxia*, that is, imperturbability—as a good to be strived for in life.[28] Such a stoic sentiment led one to distance oneself from wild passions and beliefs and assume a form of skeptical consciousness. However, as the ultimate good was not seen as tolerance itself, but of *ataraxia*, in certain circumstances, of religious contestation, for example, tolerance itself could be sacrificed to ensure imperturbability—a tolerance then of a practical nature rather than of a principled position.

It is, nevertheless, from these positions that our contemporary Western and liberal assumptions on tolerance to a large extent are seen to rest. In fact, note that the liberal synthesis and the way toleration has developed in the Western European and North Atlantic communities over the past two hundred years have embedded within them aspects of both intolerance and indifference. In the first instance, the liberal distinction between public and private realms is, among other things, a distinction in realms and types of toleration: certain beliefs and/or practices are deemed private and so almost by definition are to be tolerated. Here, then, is not quite indifference *simpliciter* but more of a principled indifference. For one has no *right* to intervene in private matters or even to judge them. In this reading, all conflicting views are reduced to matters of taste or aesthetics. But is this in fact tolerance? No, principled indifference or neutrality toward different conceptions of the good is not tolerance.

Similarly, the politics of rights over good, of individual autonomy over shared public conceptions of the good, often leads to tolerance not in principle but simply as a temporary expedient, until such non-autonomy-valuing subgroups come to share the assumptions of liberalism. Liberalism's much vaunted toleration may then well be more complicated and problematic than we often take it to be, as it tends in fact to be constantly in danger of slipping into either indifference or intolerance.

There is, however, one critical basis of toleration within the liberal tradition. It is directly related to the theme of this whole book, and this is the basis of individual autonomy. Toleration as a practice flows from autonomy as a virtue or a good. If this is so, however, then the supposedly liberal indifference to the idea of the good is therefore untenable. As Bernard Williams has stated: "Only a substantive view of goods such as autonomy can yield the value expressed by the practice of toleration."[29]

The positing of a social good, however, always involves us in that familiar situation of a "conflict of goods," which liberalism does not address but nonetheless cannot really avoid.

A liberal foundation for tolerance seems then either to be not tolerance at all but indifference or to involve us in a contradiction. And that is the contradiction between the practice of tolerance predicated on a politics of rights, rather than of the good, and the very principle of individual autonomy as a prime good upon which such toleration is to be based. This principle, however, is contradictory, for it involves a refusal to advance a politics of the good while at the same time resting on at least one very clearly defined principle of the good, that of individual autonomy. The very practice of toleration from this perspective thus contradicts the basis of the practice itself. At the very least, it leads to a discussion of conflicting goods that we had hoped to avoid. If such is the case, then in such a debate over conflicting goods, a good other than individual autonomy may become accepted as of greater value, as "trumping" autonomy—say, the view that abortion is murder and the prevention of murder is the greater good and therefore takes precedence over individual choice.

Our own concern at present, however, is not to rescue liberalism from its own contradictions. Further, we must acknowledge that liberalism as a philosophical program holds in only certain societies and not in others. Moreover, the very principle of individual autonomy is under attack in many venues and societies and at different levels of social praxis, from the so-called "Southeast Asian" model of development to evangelical Protestantism in Korea to the postmodern politics of English professors in Berkeley. If tolerance is to continue to exist as a virtue, it would thus seem to need to rest on a foundation independent of individual autonomy.

And here we come to the theme of this concluding chapter. For there has historically been another foundation posited for toleration, one that for a period even shared the stage with what became the liberal argument for autonomy but then retreated to the background. This was the argument based on *skepticism.* Both arguments emerged out of the Protestant Reformation, the wars of religion, and the challenge that the Reformation posed to the faith and practices *and criteria of justification* of Catholic Europe.

The path that eventually led to the liberal argument of individual autonomy has been studied by generations of historians, sociologists, and philosophers, from Troeltsch and Weber and Jellinek down to Dumont, Nelson, Blumenberg, Schluchter, Pocock, and others.[30] This was the path that wound its way through the secularization of the ideas of inner light or Holy Spirit to the internalization of the idea of grace, and by the eighteenth century to the further secularization of these ideas in more contemporary notions of morality and civic virtue and often romantic nationalism as well.[31] It is a body of scholarship rich in insights into the historical, religious, and most especially Protestant sources of modernity as a civilization.

The other path, that of skepticism, has been less studied and less well marked, especially outside of the history or sociology of science. The early work by Richard Popkin, now almost forty years old, still stands as a monument to this mode of inquiry.[32] Very briefly, Popkin shows how the Reformation, in challenging the church's infallibility, challenged as well existing ideas of certitude. (We should recall here that what constituted probability reasoning in the seventeenth century was nothing close to what we consider probability today, but only the veracity of received authorities.) The sixteenth and seventeenth centuries were also characterized by arguments over sufficient evidence. Ultimately, the failure to justify faith on the basis of knowledge led to pure fideism on the one hand (that is, belief by faith alone) and a sort of mitigated skepticism on the other. This was the position of Castellio in his condemnation of the burning of Servetus by Calvin—that since we cannot be sure of truth, we cannot be sure of the nature of heresy, and hence cannot go to such extremes as burning heretics.[33]

This debate and others took place in an atmosphere characterized by the revival of classical Pyrrhonism—the doubting of all propositions, including that of doubt itself. This position was itself called up by the search to justify an infallible truth via a self-evident criterion; thus while the Protestants contested papal authority, the Catholics made short shrift of inner conscience. François Veron was one of the masters of the Counter-Reformation polemic who showed how (1) the Protestant claim that Scripture was self-evidently clear was manifestly false and in need of interpretation and (2) predicating interpretation on individual conscience opened the floodgates to sectarianism and antinomianism. That "search for heaven and their lusts as well" was how one early-seventeenth-century Congregationalist described the pursuit of his more enthusiastic neighbors.[34]

The one side claimed that the Catholic demand for infallible knowledge led to the discovery that no such knowledge exists and hence to complete doubt and Pyrrhonism, while the other claimed that the very proliferation of opinions engendered by Protestantism ended in complete uncertainty in religious belief and hence to total doubt.

From this debate certain positions emerged. As noted above, one of these was fideism—faith justified by no structure of knowledge, which provides a way to toleration via a diffusion of those realms ruled by faith and those ruled by rational knowledge. This could offer a way to reconceptualize the public/private distinction without incorporating the liberal Western idea of self and society. Another position was the faith advocated by Montaigne, who understood tolerance with a most modern of sensibilities arising out of Pyrrhonist principles and as—lived nature and custom—a Christian *Sittlichkeit* perhaps and an interesting position from which to develop tolerance.

Historically, the emergence in the West of the argument for a tolerance based on skepticism was overtaken by three developments: (1) the liberal argument for autonomy and (2) the process of secularization itself, which obviated the very need for a religious tolerance. To these we must add (3) the Cartesian revolution, which reoriented the whole issue of certitude as well as the position of the knowing subject.

The contingency of history aside, a principled tolerance is indeed a difficult position to maintain, as it would seem that people have a marked preference for some sort of certitude. To maintain a position of belief while at the same time maintaining a position of skepticism as to its truth claims—indeed, a skepticism so great that one is tolerant of other such claims—is a truly stoic position. But it is one that first and foremost must rest on some belief; otherwise the whole issue of tolerance becomes moot.

What becomes clear from the above is that the critical "variable" for tolerance is some sort of pluralism of value positions and orientations. Now, Peter Berger has made us all aware of how the very fact of pluralism undermines the taken-for-grantedness of beliefs and values.[35] Most social scientists, however, have all too uncritically identified this pluralism with modern secular reality, and the taken-for-granted beliefs and values with traditional religious worldviews. But the truth of Berger's statement is that it works both ways, and the pluralism of religions or even (and this is my point) of a single religion, with its built-in tension between reason and revelation, between knowledge and faith does also tend to undermine the taken-for-grantedness of the beliefs and values of modernity. These latter are, after all, identified with a rather totalizing Jacobean project, one that has all too often conflated a substantive rationality with an instrumental one and has sought to promulgate an overarching, totalitarian, and all-encompassing ideology (whether of the right or the left). The very homogenizing tendencies of the modern worldview can themselves be brought to question by the pluralism inherent in religious doubt—that necessary concomitant of faith itself.

In this pluralism, in this that cannot be subsumed into the universalism of the modern worldview lies what may well be the necessary sources of tolerance in the twenty-first century. Some light can, I feel, be shed on this, at least in metaphor by recalling the reality of Sarajevo before the 1992–95 war and the nature of commensality there: the move between the particular neighborhoods, or *mahalas*, and the city center, or *Charshiya*. As explained in an evocative work by Dzevad Karahasan:

> Upon leaving the Charshiya, all Sarajevans retreat from human universality into the particularity of their own cultures. Namely, every *mahala* continues the enclosed lifestyle of the culture that statistically prevails in it. Hence, Byelave, for example, is distinctly a Jewish *mahala*, whose everyday life completely realizes all the particularities of Jewish cultures, life in Latinluk goes on in accordance with the particularities of Catholic cultures, in Vratnik in accord with Islamic cultures; and in Tashlihan according to the particularities of Eastern Orthodox Cultures.[36]

In this move between cultures, with its almost enforced pluralism, a new form of tolerance may perhaps be found. It would be one that abjures the false universalism of Jacobean modernity. It would be one that must admit of the particular as well as of the universal and which, in the move between them, would bracket that certitude of knowledge upon which all tolerant attitudes must in the end founder.

It may be the case that the very necessity imposed by a religious consciousness of the move between faith and reason can play a role in bracketing out this certitude in a way equivalent to that bracketing which I believe is imposed by the practical concerns of commensality. What may be involved in this process, how certitude is, as it were, bracketed out and people schooled in a praxis of uncertainty and modesty is a question not only sociological and philosophical in nature, but one rooted in the internal orientations of different religious traditions.

There has yet to appear for other religious traditions the type of history of their skepticism that Popkin brought to Western Christian thought. Yet some preliminary efforts are in evidence. The work of Menachem Fisch, for example, on the role of counterfactual evidence in Talmudic discourse and on the tension between reason and received authority in the redaction of the Babylonian Talmud is a case in point. The paradigmatic case discussed by Fisch, and by others as well, is that of the excommunication of Rabbi Eliezer ben Hyrcanus described in the Babylonian Talmud as follows:

> We learned elsewhere: If he cut it into separate tiles, placing sand between each tile: R. Eliezer declared it clean, and the Sages declared it unclean and this is the oven of Aknai. . . . On that day R. Eliezer brought forward every imaginable argument but they did not accept them. Said he to them: 'If the *halakhah* agrees with me, let this carob tree prove it!' Thereupon the carob tree was torn a hundred cubits out of its place—others affirm four hundred cubits. 'No proof can be brought from a carob tree,' they retorted. Again he said to them: 'If the *halakhah* agrees with me, let the stream of water

prove it!' Whereupon the stream of water flowed backward. 'No proof can
be brought from a stream of water,' they rejoined. Again he urged: 'If the
*halakhah* agrees with me, let the walls of the schoolhouse prove it,' whereupon the walls inclined to fall. But R. Joshua rebuked them, saying: 'When
scholars are engaged in *halakhic* dispute what have you to interfere?' Hence
they did not fall, in honor of R. Joshua, nor did they resume the upright, in
honor of R. Eliezer; and they are still standing thus inclined. Again he said
to them: 'If the *halakhah* agrees with me, let it be proved from Heaven!'
Whereupon a Heavenly Voice cried out: 'Why do you dispute with R. Eliezer,
seeing that in all matters the *halakhah* agrees with him!' But R. Joshua arose
and exclaimed: '*It is not in heaven.*' What did he mean by this? Said R. Jere-
miah: That the Torah had already been given at Mount Sinai; we pay no
attention to a Heavenly Voice, because Thou hast long since written in the
Torah at Mount Sinai, *After the majority must one incline.*

R. Nathan met Elijah [the prophet] and asked him: What did the Holy
One Blessed be He, do in that hour?—He laughed [with joy], he replied,
saying, 'My sons have defeated Me, My sons have defeated Me.'[37]

To understand the full import of this story one must realize (1) that Rabbi
Eliezer was *the* expert on laws of purity and impurity, upon which this
dispute turned; (2) that he was reputed to be an almost superhuman
storehouse of received wisdom and would not utter a pronouncement
on law that was of his own making, but all his wisdom was received wisdom
that could be traced to the revelation of Moses on Sinai; and (3) the
quote from the Pentateuch noted at the end (in Exodus 23:2) is in fact
taken out of context and used to make a point quite at odds with the
obvious meaning of the text. Thus, the story has assumed its rather paradigmatic place in the Jewish corpus as a defense of the use of reason
(through the debates and decisions of the majority) over against a simple
appeal to received authority in the practicalities of moral reasoning.[38]

A resource of reason is also always a resource of skepticism, and so I
would maintain of a true toleration that can indeed be found in all of the
religious traditions. The Islamic *kalam* no less than the Jewish halakah
presents a method of reasoning and legal interpretation based on what
John Clayton has termed "localized reasoning," instances of which he
labels "group-specific reasoning."[39] That is, they rely on processes of
moral reasoning that in addition to recognizing sacred authority also
recognize the limits of human reason and hence the inherent abyss between general principles and their instantiation in the orders of the
world. Again, then, the *phronesis* of casuistry or, for that matter, of Jewish
halakic or (in Islam) neo-mu'tazalite thought may provide a basis for
toleration from *within* a recognized authority rather than from a world

defined solely by power, where tolerance can never be more than a contingent balance of forces.

This, then, is the challenge facing us all. If the secularization thesis has indeed been proved incorrect and the further progress of modernity—and perhaps even postmodernity—is not to be accompanied by the further spread of a secular consciousness but by some sort of return to religious orientations, then how can a principled position of toleration be maintained? For such a return, I maintain, is almost mandated by the human need for self-expression, by the need for at least a certain aspect of self to be seen as constituted by a heteronomous authority and not simply as autonomous. As people return to positions of principled belief, there is the possibility either of returning to some of the most horrendous authoritarian terrors of the past or, as I believe is preferable and possible, of resurrecting a language of toleration based on skepticism towards one's own principled beliefs. To do this we must enlist the help of precisely those beliefs—chief among which are beliefs in revealed, transcendent truth—of the three revealed monotheistic religions. In a discussion of this once with Peter Berger, he elegantly glossed the problem as being not what one believes but how one believes. And that *how* must be sought in the nature of belief itself, though no doubt a skeptical one as well.

# *NOTES*

## INTRODUCTION

1. Max Weber, *Economy and Society*, ed. Guenther Roth and Claus Wittich, 53.
2. Ibid., 33.
3. Max Weber, "Politics as a Vocation," in *From Max Weber: Essays on Sociology*, ed. G. H. Gerth and C. W. Mills, 78.
4. See S. N. Eisenstadt, *Max Weber on Charisma and Institution Building*, 11 n.
5. Ralf Dahrendorf, *Class and Class Conflict in Industrial Society*, 168–69.
6. Brian Barry, *Sociologists, Economists and Democracy*, 9–10.
7. Samuel Huntington, *The Clash of Civilizations and the Remaking of World Order*, Benjamin Barber, *Jihad vs. McWorld*; David Martin, *Tongues of Fire*.
8. Bernard de Mandeville, *Fable of the Bees: or Private Vices, Public Benefits*, 2:178.
9. David Hume, *A Treatise on Human Nature*, 520.
10. Adam Smith, *The Theory of Moral Sentiments*, 110.
11. Ibid., 135.
12. On these distinctions see S. N. Eisenstadt and Bernard Giesen, "The Construction of Collective Identity," *European Journal of Sociology* 36, (1995): 72–102.
13. See Adam B. Seligman, *The Problem of Trust*, 75–100.
14. S. N. Eisenstadt, ed., *The Origins and Diversity of the Axial Age Civilizations*; Karl Jaspers, *The Origin and Goal of History*.
15. Marcel Mauss, "A Category of the Human Mind: The Notion of the Person, the Notion of the Self," in *The Category of the Person*, ed. Michael Carrithers, Steven Collins, and Steven Lukes; Luis Dumont, *Essays on Individualism: Modern Ideology in Anthropological Perspective*; Charles Taylor, *Sources of the Self*.
16. Emile Durkheim, "Individualism and the Intellectuals," in *Emile Durkheim on Morality and Society*, ed. Robert Bellah, 52.
17. Ibid., 46.
18. Max Weber, "The Sociology of Law," in *Economy and Society*, 880–95.

## CHAPTER ONE
## THE SELF IN THE SOCIAL SCIENCES

1. We may note in passing that the last serious attempt to unite both was in the sociology of Talcott Parsons and, more specifically, in his concept of the 'unit act', which, however, elided the conflicting epistemologies rather than actually synthesized them. See Talcott Parsons, *The Structure of Social Action*, 1:20–51.
2. Philip Abrams, *Historical Sociology*, 2–3.
3. Ralf Dahrendorf, "Homo Sociologicus," in his *Essays in the Theory of Society*.
4. Ibid., 77.
5. Ibid., 77–78.

6. Ibid., 80–81.

7. Arthur Stinchcombe, "Merton's Theory of Social Structure," in *The Idea of Social Structure*, ed. Lewis Coser, 11–33; Robert Merton, "Social Structure and Anomie," in his *Social Theory and Social Structure*, 125–49.

8. Ralph Turner, "The Role and the Person," *American Journal of Sociology* 84, no. 1 (1978): 1–23; idem, "Role Taking: Process Versus Conformity," in *Human Behavior and Social Processes*, ed. A. Rose, 20–40.

9. Turner, "Role Taking," 28, 36.

10. Ibid., 22.

11. Dahrendorf, "Homo Sociologicus."

12. See Adam B. Seligman, *The Problem of Trust*, 11–42.

13. This point has, in fact, been recognized by Richard Hilbert, "Towards an Improved Understanding of Role," *Theory and Society* 10, no. 2 (1981): 207–26.

14. The debates on these issues are enormous. Some of the most relevant to our concerns are Margaret S. Archer, "Morphogenesis versus Structuration: On Combining Structure and Action," *The British Journal of Sociology* 33, no. 4 (December 1982): 455–79; William Sewell, Jr., "A Theory of Structure: Duality, Agency and Transformation," *American Journal of Sociology* 98, no. 1 (July 1992): 1–29; Warren Handel, "Normative Expectations and the Emergence of Meaning as Solutions to Problems: Convergence of Structural and Interactionist Perspectives," *American Journal of Sociology* 84, no. 4 (1979): 855–81; Piotr Sztompka, ed., *Agency and Structure: Regrounding Social Theory*; Sharon Hays, "Structure and Agency and the Sticky Problem of Culture," *Sociological Theory* 12, no. 1 (March 1994): 57–72; and, on the Giddens controversy, Jon Clark, Celia Modgil, and Sohan Modgil, eds., *Anthony Giddens: Consensus and Controversy*.

15. Mancur Olson, Jr., *The Logic of Collective Action: Public Goods and the Theory of Groups*; Charles Tilly, *From Mobilization to Revolutions, European Revolutions 1492–1992*.

16. Samuel Huntington, *Political Order in Changing Societies*; Reinhold Bendix, *Kings or People: Power and the Mandate to Rule, Nation Building and Citizenship: Studies of Our Changing Social Order*; S. N. Eisenstadt, *Revolution and the Transformation of Societies*; Barrington Moore, Jr., *Social Origins of Dictatorship and Democracy: Lord and Peasant in the Making of the Modern World*; Theda Skocpol, *States and Social Revolutions: A Comparative Analysis of France, Russia and China*; Jack Goldstone, *Revolution and Rebellion in the Early Modern World*.

17. These paragraphs are taken from work originally developed together with Mark Lichbach on the structure/action problem in historical sociology.

18. The similarity of this reading to tobacco advertisements may be more than coincidental.

19. Martin Hollis, *Reason in Action: Essays in the Philosophy of the Social Sciences*.

20. Harry Frankfurt, "Freedom of the Will and the Concept of the Person," *The Journal of Philosophy* 68, no. 1 (January 1971): 5–20.

21. Charles Taylor, "What Is Human Agency?" in his *Human Agency and Language: Philosophical Papers*, 1:18–19.

22. Ibid., 23–24.

23. Friedrich Hayek, *The Fatal Conceit*.

24. Dennis Wrong, "The Oversocialized Conception of Man in Sociology," *American Sociological Review* 26 no. 2 (April 1961): 183–93.

25. Max Weber, "The Social Psychology of World Religions," in *From Max Weber: Essays in Sociology*, ed. G. H. Gerth and C. W. Mills.

26. For a similar, multidimensional view of agency, see Richard Wolheim, *The Thread of Life*.

27. Simon Schama, *Citizens: A Chronicle of the French Revolution*.

28. Mark Lichbach, *The Rebel's Dilemma*.

29. For different formulations of this see Karl Marx, *The German Ideology* and the 1857 introduction to *Grundrisse: Foundations for the Critique of Political Economy* as well as Engels' letters to Schmidt and Bloch.

30. Peter Blau, "Justice in Social Exchange," *Sociological Inquiry* (spring 1964): 153–206.

31. S. N. Eisenstadt, *Power, Trust and Meaning*.

32. P. S. Atiya, *The Rise and Fall of the Freedom of Contract*.

33. S. N. Eisenstadt, ed., *The Origins and Diversity of the Axial Age Civilizations*; Benjamin Swartz, ed., "Wisdom, Revelation and Doubt: Perspectives on the First Millennium," *Daedalus* (spring 1975); Karl Jaspers, *The Origin and Goal of History*; Eric Voeglin, *Order and History*.

34. Peter Gay, *The Enlightenment: An Interpretation*, vol. 1.

35. A rather detailed form of this critique can be found in John Milbank, *Theology and Social Theory*.

36. A good example of this type of writing can be found in Patricia Williams, *The Alchemy of Race and Rights*.

37. This with the understood provision that we are dealing with those "culturalist" theories that still attempt to explain an institutional reality.

38. Erving Goffman, *Presentations of Self in Everyday Life*.

39. Garfinkel, *Studies in Ethnomethodology*.

CHAPTER TWO
AUTHORITY AND THE SELF

1. In the Jewish tradition, for example, all emendations are viewed as but technicalities. See Moshe Halbertal, *People of the Book: Canon, Meaning and Authority*.

2. Emile Durkheim, *Suicide*.

3. Peter Berger, "On the Obsolescence of the Concept of Honor," in *Revision: Changing Perspectives in Moral Philosophy*, ed. Stanley Hauerwas and Alasdair MacIntyre.

4. S. N. Eisenstadt, *Fundamentalism, Sectarianism and Revolution: The Jacobean Dimension of Modernity*.

5. Ernst Kantarowitz, *The King's Two Bodies*.

6. Dennis Wrong, *The Problem of Order*.

7. Frederick Pollock and Frederic Maitland, *History of English Law before the Time of Edward I*, vol. 2.

8. I do not mean to enter here into the debate raging among scholars of early Christianity as to whether Paul can properly be termed a convert or not, certain

aspects of which can be found in Alan Segal, *Paul the Convert.* Paul's theology will indeed be discussed in chapter four.

9. Michael Sandel, *Liberalism and the Limits of Justice.*

10. Emile Durkheim, *Sociology and Philosophy.*

11. Henry Sumner Maine, *Ancient Law.*

12. Durkheim, *Sociology and Philosophy,* 36; Talcott Parsons, *The Structure of Social Action,* 1:384.

13. See John Milbank, *Theology and Social Theory.*

14. Eric Voeglin, *The New Science of Politics,* 120; Charles Taylor, *Sources of the Self,* 95.

15. Bernard Williams, *Ethics and the Limits of Philosophy,* 195.

16. Emile Durkheim, "Individualism and the Intellectuals," in *Emile Durkheim on Morality and Society,* ed. Robert Bellah, 52.

17. S. N. Eisenstadt, *Power, Trust, and Meaning,* 212.

18. Ibid.; Marshall Sahlins, *Culture and Practical Reason.*

19. On the interesting idea of how the very idea of the gift is self-contradictory, see Jacques Derrida, *Given Time I: Counterfeit Money,* 34–70.

20. Kenneth Arrow, *The Limits of Organization*; Francis Fukuyama, *Trust: Social Virtues and the Creation of Prosperity*; Robert Putnam, *Making Democracy Work: Civic Traditions in Modern Italy.*

21. Janet Tai Landa, *Trust, Ethnicity and Identity: Beyond the New Institutional Economics of Ethnic Trading, Networks, Contract Law and Gift Exchange*; Avner Grief, "On the Political Foundations of the Late Medieval Commercial Revolution: Genoa During the Twelfth and Thirteenth Centuries," *The Journal of Economic History* 54, no. 2 (June 1994): 271–87; idem, "Historical Perspectives on the Economics of Trade: Institutions and International Trade: Lessons from the Commercial Revolution," *American Economic Review* 82, no. 1/2 (May 1992): 128–33; idem, "Reputations and Coalitions in Medieval Trade: Evidence on the Maghribi Traders," *The Journal of Economic History* 49, no. 4 (December 1989): 857–82; idem, "Contract Enforceability and Economic Institutions in Early Trade: The Maghribi Trader's Coalition," *American Economic Review* 83, no. 3 (June 1993): 525–48.

22. James Coleman, *Foundations of Social Theory,* 91–115.

23. Eisenstadt, *Power, Trust, and Meaning,* 212–13.

24. Talcott Parsons, "Christianity and Modern Industrial Society," in *Sociological Theory, Values and Sociocultural Change,* ed. Edward Tiryakian.

25. T. H. Marshall, *Class, Citizenship and Social Development.*

26. Benjamin Nelson, *The Idea of Usury: From Tribal Brotherhood to Universal Otherhood.*

27. Tractate Avodah Zarah 2b. (All quotations from the Babylonian Talmud follow the Sonchino translation.)

28. Sandel, *Liberalism,* 179.

29. See Steven Lukes, *Emile Durkheim: His Life and Works,* 320–60.

30. J.G.A. Pocock, *The Machiavellian Moment.*

31. Alexis de Tocqueville, *Democracy in America, ed.* J. P. Mayer and Max Lerner, 394.

32. See Knud Haakossen, *The Science of the Legislator: The Natural Jurisprudence of David Hume and Adam Smith*; Adam B. Seligman, "Animadversions upon Civil Society and Civic Virtue in the Last Decade of the Twentieth Century," in *Civil Society, Theory, History, Comparison*, ed. J. Hall.

33. G.W.F. Hegel, *The Philosophy of Right*, trans. T. Knox, 134.

34. David Riesman, *The Lonely Crowd*.

35. David Riesman, *Individualism Reconsidered*, 106.

36. This insight can be found as well in the writings of Philip Rieff, *The Feeling Intellect: Selected Writings*.

37. George Lukács, *History and Class Consciousness*.

38. Rieff, *The Feeling Intellect*, 331.

39. On different versions of nationalism see Rogers Brubaker, *Citizenship and Nationhood in France and Germany*.

40. I am most grateful to S. N. Eisenstadt for pointing out to me this critical aspect of the Enlightenment, its tendency to absolutize as irreconcilable tensions and contradictions what were once conceived as of manageable dimensions, perhaps not solved, but not at all irreconcilable (such as, for example, the tension between reason and revelation as it presented itself to twelfth-century philosophic thought in any of the monotheistic traditions).

41. S. N. Eisenstadt, "The Axial Age: The Emergence of Transcendental Visions and the Rise of Clerics," *European Journal of Sociology* 23 (1982): 294, 296.

42. On the symbolization of cosmic order and on times of troubles see Eric Voeglin, *Order and History*, (Baton Rouge: Louisiana State University Press, 1954), 1:1–13, 52–110.

43. Eisenstadt, "Axial Age," 300–301.

44. For this terminology and additional perspectives on religious evolution, see Robert Bellah, "Religious Evolution," *American Sociological Review* 29 (1964): 358–74.

45. Wolfgang Schluchter, "The Paradox of Rationalization: On the Relations of Ethics and the World," in *Max Weber's Vision of History: Ethics and Method*, ed. Guenther Roth and Wolfgang Schluchter, 23.

46. On this see Peter Berger, *The Sacred Canopy*, 113–18.

47. Karl Jaspers, *The Origin and Goal of History*, 3.

48. Ibid., 63, 65.

49. Benjamin Nelson, "Self Images and Spiritual Directions in the History of European Civilization," in *On the Roads to Modernity: Conscience, Science and Civilizations*, ed. Toby Huff, 43.

50. Ernst Troeltsch, *The Social Teachings of the Christian Churches*, 1:55.

51. Marcel Mauss, "A Category of the Human Mind: The Notion of the Person, the Notion of the Self," in *The Category of the Person*, ed. M. Carrithers, Steven Collins, and Steven Lukes, 19–20.

52. David Riesman, *The Lonely Crowd: A Study of the Changing American Character*.

53. In a recent and enlightening book, Hannah Fenichel Pitkin has analyzed the way in which Hannah Arendt struggled with these categories in her own writings. See her *The Attack of the Blob: Hannah Arendt's Concept of the Social*.

54. Voeglin, *New Science of Politics*, 66–69.

55. Taylor, *Sources of the Self*, 93.

56. Jurgen Habermas, *The Structural Transformation of the Public Sphere*, trans. Thomas Burger, 54.

57. W. H. Auden, "Notes on Music and Opera," in his *The Prolific and the Devourer*, 71–72.

CHAPTER THREE
HETERONOMY AND RESPONSIBILITY

1. Rudolf Otto, *The Idea of the Holy*.

2. Bernard Williams, "Moral Luck," *Proceedings of the Aristotelian Society*, supplementary vol. L (1976): 115–35; Thomas Nagel, "Moral Luck," in his *Mortal Questions*, 24–38.

3. Nagel, "Moral Luck," 24.

4. Ibid., 25.

5. Bernard Williams, *Shame and Necessity*.

6. Nichloas Rescher, *Complexity: A Philosophical Overview*.

7. Martha Nussbaum, *The Fragility of Goodness*, 32–41.

8. Ahron Agus, *The Binding of Isaac and Messiah: Law, Martyrdom and Deliverance in Early Rabbinic Religiosity*, 29.

9. Perhaps, rather than refer to volumes of Christian theology, it would be more relevant to recall C. S. Lewis's *The Lion, the Witch and the Wardrobe* to realize just how pervasive this theme (of voluntary martyrdom as overcoming fate) has become in Western culture and consciousness. Lewis both tapped a pervasive theme in Western thought and transmitted it to generations of schoolchildren (of many different religions), who continue to read his books.

10. On sacramental marriage see George Duby, *The Knight, the Lady and the Priest: The Making of Modern Marriage in Medieval France*.

11. Emile Durkheim, *Professional Ethics and Civic Morals*, 176–83.

12. For some perspectives on the Lord's Supper in Puritan theology see Francis Clark, *Eucharist Sacrifice and the Reformation*; Patrick Collinson, *The Elizabethan Puritan Movement*; David Hall, *The Faithful Shepherd*.

13. On secular rituals see Sally Falk Moore and Barbara Myerhoff, eds., *Secular Rituals*.

14. Jonathan Z. Smith, *Imagining Religion*, xii.

15. E. E. Evans-Pritchard, *Theories of Primitive Religion*, 109.

16. My wife's placenta was offered to us by the hospital in Boulder, Colorado, for precisely these purposes after our daughter was born there in the mid-1990s.

17. Talcott Parsons, "Durkheim on Religion Revisited," in his *Action Theory and the Human Condition*.

18. G. Van der Leeuw, "Primordial Time and Final Time," in *Man and Time: Papers from the Eranos Yearbook*, 337.

19. Ibid., 339.

20. On the more general notion of causal chains in the more strictly legal context, see H.L.A. Hart and A. M. Honore, *Causation in the Law*.

21. Hannah Arendt, "Collective Responsibility," in *Amor Mundi: Explorations in the Faith and Thought of Hannah Arendt*, ed. James W. Bernauer, S.J., 43–50.

22. Different aspects of these and the differences between them are explored in Larry May and Stacey Hoffman, eds., *Collective Responsibility: Five Decades of Debate in Theoretical and Applied Ethics*; Larry May, *Sharing Responsibility*.

23. It would only be fair to mention, however, that the case of Justin Martyr does raise some interesting questions regarding the type of distinctions I am attempting to make here.

24. Arendt, "Collective Responsibility," 45.

25. Robert Wuthnow, "A Reasonable Role for Religion? Moral Practices, Civic Participation and Market Behavior," in *Civil Society and Democratic Civility*, ed. R. Hefner, 123.

26. I am indebted to Barry Mesch of Boston Hebrew College for having coined this term, which so aptly carries the historical into the present.

27. On the problems of institutionalization of civil identities, see my *The Problem of Trust*.

28. See S. N. Eisenstadt, ed., *Origins and Diversity of the Axial Age Civilizations*; Eric Voeglin, *Order and History*.

29. Karl Jaspers, *The Question of German Guilt*.

30. Ibid., 85

31. See Michael Sandel's formulation of this in his *Liberalism and the Limits of Justice*.

32. Arendt, "Collective Responsibility," 50.

33. Herbert Morris, *On Guilt and Innocence: Essays in Legal Philosophy and Moral Psychology*, 61–62.

34. Ibid., 62.

35. On this see the following astute observation of R. H. Tawney on occupational norms in his *The Acquisitive Society*, 94:

> The difference between industry as it exists today and a profession is, then, simple and unmistakable. The essence of the former is that its only criterion is the financial return which it offers to its shareholders. The essence of the latter, is that, though men enter it for the sake of livelihood, the measure of their success is the service which they perform, not the gains which they amass. They may, as in the case of a successful doctor, grow rich; but the meaning of their profession, both for themselves and for the public, is not that they make money but that they make health, or safety, or knowledge, or good government or good law. They depend on it for their income, but they do not consider that any conduct which increases their income is on that account good. And while a boot-manufacturer who retires with a half a million is counted on having achieved success, whether the boots which he made were of leather or brown paper, a civil servant who did the same would be impeached.

36. Williams, *Shame and Necessity*, 84.

37. Matthew Arnold, *Collected Prose Works*, vol. 6, ed. R. H. Super, 196.

38. I am grateful to Ronald Dore for giving me the correct version of this folk saying.

39. S. M. Lipset, *The First New Nation: The United States in Historical and Comparative Perspective*.

40. Agnes Heller, *The Power of Shame: A Rationalist Perspective*, 47.

41. Ibid., 46.

CHAPTER FOUR
THE SELF INTERNALIZED

1. Adam Ferguson, *An Essay on the History of Civil Society*, 5th ed., 53.

2. Ibid.

3. Theoretical perspectives on this process of identity formation can be found in S. N. Eisenstadt, "The Construction of Collective Identities: Some Analytical and Comparative Indications," *European Journal of Social Theory* 1/2 (1998): 229–54.

4. Hermann Cohen, *The Religion of Reason out of the Sources of Judaism*, 114.

5. *R. H. Tawney's Commonplace Book*, ed. J. Winter and D. Josline, 54.

6. Franz Rosenzweig, *The Star of Redemption*; Emmanuel Levinas, *Otherwise than Being*; idem, *Totality and Infinity*.

7. Jan Assman, *Moses the Egyptian: The Memory of Egypt in Western Monotheism*, 46.

8. S. N. Eisenstadt, "The Axial Age: The Emergence of Transcendental Visions and the Rise of Clerics," *European Journal of Sociology* 23 (1982): 296.

9. Avodah Zarah, 44b; Sonchino translation.

10. On this theme see Moshe Halbertal and Avishai Margolit, *Idolatry*.

11. Shemot Rabah, XV.17, taken from Shaul Lieberman, *Hellenism in Jewish Palestine*, 125.

12. On this aspect of circumcision see Sharon Koren, "Mystical Rationales for the Laws of Niddah," in *Woman and Water: Menstruation in Jewish Life and Law*, ed. R. Wassefall, 104.

13. Arnaldo Momigliano, "The Disadvantages of Monotheism for a Universal State," in his *On Pagans, Jews and Christians*, 142–58.

14. Babylonian Talmud, Sanhedrein, 56–58.

15. True of rabbinic thought, the following description does not encompass all Jewish communities, such as the Essenes or Qumrom sects.

16. Though there are, to be sure, intimations of individual salvation in the Bible, see, for example, the last chapter of the Book of Daniel.

17. Jonathan Klawans, "Idolatry, Incest and Impurity: Moral Defilement in Ancient Judaism," *Journal for the Study of Judaism* 29, no. 4 (1998): 391–415; idem, "Notions of Gentile Impurity in Ancient Judaism," *American Jewish Studies Review* 20, no. 2 (1995): 285–312; Adolph Buchler, *Studies in Sin and Atonement in Rabbinic Literature of the First Century*.

18. Jacob Neusner, *The Idea of Purity in Ancient Judaism*, 1–2.

19. Lionel Trilling, *Sincerity and Authenticity*, 85.

20. Ibid., 86.

21. A rather different reading of rabbinic culture can be found in Yonah Frankel, *Iyunim b'olamo Haruchani shel Sipor HaAggada* (Hebrew, Tel Aviv, Kibbutz Hameuchad, 1981).

22. Some of these interpretations are discussed in Daniel Boyarin, *A Radical Jew: Paul and the Politics of Identity*.

23. Neusner, *The Idea of Purity*, 53–54.

24. A fascinating arena where both overlaps and tensions between these communities may be found is in the interpretation of the Passover story. On this see the important article by Israel Yuval, "haPoschim al Shtei Hasi-ifim: HaHagada shel Pesach v'haPascha haNotzrit" (Hebrew), *Tarbitz* 55, no. 1 (1996): 1–28.

25. For general perspectives on some of the different groups in Judaism at this time, see Joachim Schaper, "The Pharisees," 402–27; Gunter Stemberger, "The Sadducees," 428–43; Otto Betz, "The Essenes," 444–71; Kurt Rudolph, "The Baptist Sects," 571–600; Morton Smith, "The Troublemakers," 501–68; Stanley Isser, "The Samaritans and Their Sects," 569–95; W. D. Davies, "Paul from the Jewish Point of View," 678–730; J. Carleton-Paget, "Jewish Christianity," 731–75; all included in W. Horbury, J. Sturdy, and W. D. Davies, eds., *The Early Roman Empire*, vol. 3 of *The Cambridge History of Judaism*.

26. Klawans, "Idolatry, Incest and Impurity."

27. To be sure, the only possibility of arguing a nonbinding or legal yet ethical position within the Jewish tradition is through the status dicta of *lifnim mishurat hadin* (beyond the line of the law), upon which nearly all attempts to argue an ethical orientation autonomous of the law have rested. Just how extralegal or extrahalakic (referring to the corpus of Jewish law) the injunctions of *lifnim mishurat hadin* are, however, has been a point of continuing controversy. Though this is not the place to enter into this controversy, we should note that, on the whole, Orthodox commentators have stressed the seamless web that binds the legal injunctions of the halakah with those of *lifnim mishurat hadin*, while liberal commentators have tried to use the concept in order to argue for an extrahalakic standard by which the halakah itself could be critiqued.

However much I would like to support the liberal reading, I am afraid that I am unconvinced. We must note, for example, that none of the (nine) examples given in the Babylonian Talmud for *lifnim mishurat hadin* involve breaking the law to follow the dictates of conscience. All, in fact, turn on acts of supererogation, the forgoing of legal rights and waiver of benefits, usually by rabbis of extraordinary piety and virtue. The concept of *lifnim mishurat hadin* thus sanctions certain acts that the law does not require, but never acts that the law does not permit!

Indeed, for Maimonides *lifnim mishurat hadin* represents nothing more nor less than the standards of saintly behavior that are neither required nor even desired for the majority of the populace. For Maimonides, natural morality was both incorporated and superseded with the Sinitic revelation. Indeed, so much has the unity of halakah and *lifnim mishurat hadin* been the majority view, that even statements that would seem to point in other directions—such as R. Yohanan's lament that the Temple was destroyed because the populace only followed the law and did not "go beyond its limits"—have been interpreted to point to a *halakically mandated* edict to "go beyond the law." Indeed, the writings of both Nachmanides and the Maggid Mishneh (commentator on Maimonides) have explained the presence of areas unspecified by law as existing only to permit casuistic interpretation of general principles, not autonomous or pluralistic directives. The realm of independent ethics is, throughout, seriously circumscribed. As argued by one contemporary commentator: "The very character of halakha as both legal system and divine revelation . . . blurs the distinction between law and ethics. Ethical obligations, like all divine imperatives within the tradition will be understood as part and parcel of the halakha, that divinely revealed law that governs the ongoing life of Israel. Moreover, the close relationship in Judaism between ethics and piety, between doing the right thing and doing the holy or godlike thing, tends to blur the distinction between moral obligation and supererogation." (Louis Newman, *Past Imperatives: Studies in the History and Theory of Jewish Ethics*, 43.) Again, heteronomous dictates as prescribing normatively binding action define Judaism's attitude towards the halakah as well as towards any behavior that may be adduced from *lifnim mishurat hadin*. A more detailed discussion of these issues may be found in Ahron Lichtenstein, "Does Jewish Tradition Recognize an Ethic Independent of Halakha?" in *Modern Jewish Ethics: Theory and Practice*, ed. Marvin Fox, 62–87.

28. E. P. Sanders, *Jewish Law from Jesus to the Mishnah*, 271.

29. Krister Stendhal, *Paul Among Jews and Gentiles*.

30. This argument is made forcefully in Ellis Rivkin, *A Hidden Revolution: The Pharisees' Search for the Kingdom Within*.

31. Neusner, *Purity*, 78.

32. See Paul Ricoeur, *Symbolism of Evil*.

33. Stendhal, *Paul*.

34. Alan Segal, *Paul the Convert*, 248.

35. E. P. Sanders, *Paul, the Law and the Jewish People*, 199.

36. Stendhal, *Paul*, 86.

37. Ibid., 16–17.

38. Paula Fredriksen, "Paul and Augustine: Conversion Narratives, Orthodox Traditions and the Retrospective Self," *Journal of Theological Studies*, n.s., 37, pt. 1 (April 1986): 27.

39. Paula Fredriksen, "The Body/Soul Dichotomy in Augustine on Paul against the Manichees and the Pelagians," *Recherches Augustiennes* 23 (1988): 104.

40. Following précis based on R. W. Southern, *The Making of the Middle Ages*; Caroline Bynum, "Did the Twelfth Century Discover the Individual?" *Journal of Ecclesiastical History* 31 (1980): 1–17; idem, *Jesus as Mother: Studies in the Spirituality of the High Middle Ages*; Walter Ullmann, *The Individual and Society in the Middle Ages*; Harold Berman, *Law and Revolution: The Formation of the Western Legal Tradition*; Marie D. Chenu, *Nature, Man and Society in the Twelfth Century*.

41. Bynum, "Did the Twelfth Century Discover the Individual?"

42. Peter Brown, *Society and the Holy in Late Antiquity*, 302–32.

43. Benjamin Nelson, "Self Images and the System of Spiritual Direction in the History of European Civilization," in *The Quest for Self Control: Classical Philosophies and Scientific Research*, ed. S. Klausner, 43.

44. Colin Morris, *The Discovery of the Individual, 1050–1200*, 75.

45. Nelson, "Self Images and the System of Spiritual Direction," 45. See also Odon D. Lottin, "Synderese et conscience aux XIIe et XIIIe siècles," Première partie, *Psychologie et morale aux XIIe et XIIIe siècles*, 104–350.

46. On these developments see as well: John F. Benton, "Consciousness of Self and Perceptions of Individuality," in *Renaissance and Renewal in the Twelfth Century*, ed. R. Benson and G. Constable, 263–95.

47. Quoted in Morris, *Discovery of the Individual*, 88.

48. Ibid., 118.

49. Bynum, *Jesus as Mother*, 11.

50. Ibid., 15.

51. Southern, *The Making of the Middle Ages*, 221.

52. Ibid.

53. Bynum, *Jesus as Mother*, 89.

54. Ibid., 95.

55. Benjamin Nelson, "Conscience and the Making of Early Modern Culture: The Protestant Ethic Beyond Max Weber," *Social Research* 36 (1969): 16–17.

56. Adam B. Seligman, "Innerworldly Individualism and the Institutionalization of Puritanism in Late 17th Century New England," *British Journal of Sociology* 41, no. 4 (December 1990): 537–58.; idem, *Innerworldly Individualism*.

57. Martin Luther, *A Commentary on Saint Paul's Epistle to the Galatians*, 83.

58. Ibid., 98.

59. Ibid., 100.

60. Ibid., 102.

61. Herman S. Schmalenbach, "The Sociological Category of Communion," in *Theories of Society*, ed. T. Parsons, E. Shils, K. Naegele, and J. Pitts, 331–47.

62. Nelson, "Self Images and the System of Spiritual Direction," 71.

63. The development of a sense of moral responsibility at this time was not restricted to Puritan or even Protestant societies. A similar development characterized the Jansenist religious elites in France. On these see Bernhard Groethuysen, *The Bourgeois: Catholicism vs. Capitalism in Eighteenth Century France*; Nigel Abercrombie, *The Origins of Jansenism in France*; and, for comparison to the Puritans of England, Robin Briggs, "The Catholic Puritans: Jansenists and Rigorists in France," in *Puritans and Revolutionaries: Essays in Seventeenth Century History Presented to Christopher Hill*, ed. D. Pennington and K. Thomas, 333–57.

64. On these aspects of Calvinism see Harvo Hopfl, *The Christian Polity of John Calvin*; Sheldon Wolin, "Calvin and Reformation: The Political Education of Protestantism," *American Political Science Review* 51 (1957): 425–54; Ernst Troeltsch, *The Social Teachings of the Christian Churches*, 2:576–690; David Little, "Max Weber Revisited: The Protestant Ethic and the Puritan Experience of Order," *Harvard Theological Review* 59 (1966): 415–28; idem, *Religion, Order and Law: A Study of Pre-Revolutionary England;* Michael Waltzer, *The Revolution of the Saints*. For an opposing view to those of David Little and Michael Waltzer see John McNeill, "Natural Law and the Teachings of the Reformers," *Journal of Religion* 26 (1946): 168–82; On the place of Calvinism in the history of Western European political thought see Quentin Skinner, *Foundations of Modern Political Thought*, 1:189–348. On some of its social implications see Steven Ozment, *The Reformation in the Cities*; Norman Birinbaum, "The Zwinglian Reformation in Zurich," *Archive Sociologie Religion* 4 (1959): 15–30; J. E. Ellemers, "The Revolt of the Netherlands: The Part Played by Religion in the Process of Nation-Building," *Social Compass* 14 (1967): 93–103.

65. Troeltsch, *The Social Teachings*, 2:590–92.

66. Ibid., 596–97. In Calvin's thought the freedom within which the true body of believers lived must be differentiated from the state of existing political society

and from the unregenerate, among whom the command of God had to be enforced by coercion until the coming of the Kingdom of God. At its coming, according to Calvin, the separation between those 'in Christ' participating in the
world of freedom and those still subject to coercion would be dissolved.

67. R. H. Tawney, *Religion and the Rise of Capitalism*, 98.

68. Ibid.

69. Ibid.

70. I am grateful to Marwood Harris for pointing out to me the importance
of sincerity within the major strains of Reformation and especially Calvinist
thought.

71. On the radical Reformation see George Williams, *The Radical Reformation*;
Michael Mullett, *Radical Religious Movements in Early Modern Europe*.

72. Jean Calvin, *Commentary on the Epistle of Paul to Corinthians*, 2:126

73. In David Hall, ed., *The Antinomian Controversy: A Documentary History*, 17–
18.

74. John Cotton's *A Treatise of the Covenant of Grace* was preached in the 1630s
but not published until 1652 in London. See Phyllis Jones and Nicholas Jones,
eds., *Salvation in New England: Selections from the Sermons of the First Preachers*, 49.

75. William Stoever, *A Faire and Easie Way to Heaven: Covenant Theology and
Antinomianism in Early Massachusetts*, 11. William Ames's *The Marrow of Sacred Di-
vinity* (1642) and Richard Hooker's *Laws of Ecclesiastical Polity* (1594) were to a
large extent the pillars of English Puritan thought. For good insights into the
lived, experienced world of Thomas Shepard's Puritanism see his *God's Plot: The
Paradoxes of Puritan Piety, Being the Autobiography and Journal of Thomas Shepard*, ed.
M. McGiffert. The definitive work on Puritanism in New England is still Perry
Miller, *The New England Mind*, 2 vols.; as well as his *Orthodoxy in Massachusetts*.

76. Stoever, *A Faire and Easie Way*, 180.

77. Ibid., 93.

78. Perry Miller, *Errand into the Wilderness*, 60.

79. Stoever, *A Faire and Easie Way*, 8. The tension between these two interpretations and the never fully resolved contradiction between nature and grace that
ran through the heart of Puritan theology runs, of course, through the heart of
the Christian tradition as a whole, existing, as it does, "in a tension between
legalism and antinomianism, between the belief that religion, taking its impetus
from revelation, through reason achieves forms and laws which are essential to
the aiding of weak human nature and to the continuity of divine law upon earth;
and the belief that since man's relation to God is super-rational, consisting as it
does of the Lord's gift of grace to the individual believer, laws and rituals are dead
except insofar as they are directly informed by the Holy Spirit acting through the
individual believer." (Lazer Ziff, "The Literary Consequences of Puritanism," in
*The American Puritan Imagination*, ed. S. Bercovitz, 34.)

80. Thomas Weld, preface to *A Short History of the Rise, Reign and Ruine of the
Antinomians, Familists and Libertines*, by John Winthrop, 74.

81. Similar developments emerged among different groups of English Puritans of this period, such as the Cambridge Platonists.

82. Andrew Fix, *Prophecy and Reason: The Dutch Collegiants in the Early Enlightenment*, 118.

83. Ibid., 119.

84. Margaret Jacob, "Private Beliefs in Public Temples: The New Religiosity of the Eighteenth Century," *Social Research* 59 (1991): 64.

85. Adam Seligman, *Innerworldly Individualism.*

86. The critical ritual regulating boundaries was the "test of relation." See David Hall, *The Faithful Shepherd: A History of the New England Ministry*; Charles Cohen, *God's Caress: The Psychology of Puritan Religious Experience.*

87. Roger Caillois, *Man and the Sacred*, 132.

88. E. Brooks Holifield, *The Covenant Sealed: The Development of Puritan Sacramental Theology in Old and New England 1570–1720*, 192.

89. Paul Lucas, *Valley of Discord: Church and Society Along the Connecticut River, 1636–1725*, 242.

90. Ibid., 126.

91. Stephen Darwall, *The British Moralists and the Internal 'Ought', 1640–1740*, 17.

92. This aspect of Kant's thought and the interrelated nature of personhood, conscience, and moral action are discussed in Ludwig Siep, "Person and Law in Kant and Hegel," in *The Public Realm*, ed. R. Shurmann, 82–104.

93. Immanuel Kant, *The Metaphysics of Morals*, 50.

94. On this process in New England see Seligman, *Innerworldly Individualism.*

95. Emile Durkheim, *Sociology and Philosophy*, 54.

96. A. I. Meldon, *Rights and Persons*, 43.

97. John Locke, *Two Treatises on Government*, pt. 2, ed. by Peter Laslett, 396; David Hume, *A Treatise on Human Nature*, ed. L. A. Selby-Bigge, 455–534.

98. Benjamin Whichcote, "The Uses of Reason in Matters of Religion," in *The Cambridge Platonists*, ed. C. A. Patrides, 46.

99. Marcel Mauss, "A Category of the Human Mind: The Notion of the Person, the Notion of the Self," in *The Category of the Person*, ed. Michael Carrithers, Steven Collins, and Steven Lukes.

100. Otto Gierke, *Natural Law and the Theory of Society 500–1800.*

101. Ibid., 102.

102. See Richard Tuck, *Natural Right Theories: Their Origin and Development.*

103. Gierke, *Natural Law*, 40.

104. Albrecht Wellemer, "Models of Freedom in the Modern World," in *Hermeneutics and Critical Theory in Ethics and Politics*, ed. M. Kelly, 238.

105. G.F.W. Hegel, *The Philosophy of Right*, 134.

106. Bernard de Mandeville, *Fable of the Bees, or Private Vices, Public Benefits*, 178.

107. Edward Shils, *Center and Periphery: Essays in MacroSociology*; S. N. Eisenstadt, ed., introduction to his *Max Weber on Charisma and Institution Building.*

108. On congruence of sacred and charisma see Talcott Parsons, *The Structure of Social Action*, vol. 1.

109. Peter Berger, "On the Obsolescence of the Concept of Honor," in *Revision: Changing Perspectives in Moral Philosophy*, ed. Stanley Hauerwas and Alasdair MacIntyre, 177.

110. Ibid., 179.

111. Christopher Lasch, *The Culture of Narcissism: American Life in an Age of Diminishing Expectations.*

112. Thorstein Veblen, *The Theory of the Leisure Class*; Albert O. Hirschman, *Shifting Involvements: Private Interest and Public Action.*

CHAPTER FIVE

TOLERANCE AND TRADITION

1. Alexis de Tocqueville, *Democracy in America*, ed. J. P. Mayer and Max Lerner, 394.

2. I would like to register my thanks to S. N. Eisenstadt, with whom I discussed these issues and who convinced me of the critical importance of modernity's absolutizing tendencies to any understanding of the phenomena under discussion here. Some of these issues he touches on in his *Fundamentalism, Sectarianism and Revolution: The Jacobean Dimension of Modernity* as well as in his "Axial Age, Sectarianism and the Antinomies of Modernity," in *Order and History*, ed. Stephen McKnight and Geoffrey Price.

3. On this theme see David Martin, *Does Christianity Cause War?*

4. See David Levy, "Israel and Judah: Politics and Religion in the Two Hebrew Kingdoms," in his *The Measure of Man: Incursions in Philosophical and Political Anthropology*, 152–69.

5. David Levy, "The Good Religion: Reflections on the History and Fate of Zoroastrianism," in his *The Measure of Man*, 170–90.

6. Arnaldo Momigliano, "Some Preliminary Remarks on the 'Religious Opposition' to the Roman Empire," in his *On Pagans, Jews and Christians*, 120–41.

7. A recent example of such in the case of human rights can be found in Michael Perry, *The Idea of Human Rights*. See also my critique of these very assumptions in *Human Rights Review* (forthcoming).

8. Georg Jellinek, *The Declaration of the Rights of Man and of Citizens: A Contribution to Modern Constitutional History*, 48.

9. Ibid., 53.

10. Ibid., 80.

11. Ibid., 74–75.

12. Stephen Toulmin, *Cosmopolis: The Hidden Agenda of Modernity.*

13. Leo Strauss, *Spinoza's Critique of Religion*, 28.

14. Paul Ricoeur, *The Symbolism of Evil*, 150.

15. See Thomas O'Dea, "Sociological Dilemmas: Five Paradoxes of Institutionalization," in *Sociological Theory, Values and Sociocultural Change*, ed. Edward Tiryakian. The more macrohistorical aspects of this process are dealt with in Wolfgang Schluchter, *The Rise of Western Rationalism: Max Weber's Developmental History.*

16. Albert Jonsen and Stephen Toulmin, *The Abuse of Casuistry: A History of Moral Reasoning.*

17. Menachem Fisch, *Rational Rabbis.*

18. Toulmin, *Cosmopolis*, 45–87.

19. Michel de Montaigne, *The Essays of Michel de Montaigne*, trans. George Ives, 813.

20. Ibid., 589.

21. David Martin, *Tongues of Fire.*

22. Peter Berger, "Four Faces of Globalization," *National Interest* 49 (fall 1997):

23–29. On the new Confucianism see Robert Weller, "Divided Market Culture in China," in *Market Culture: Society and Morality in the New Asian Capitalisms*, ed. Robert Hefner, 78–103; Tu Wei Ming, "The Search for Roots in Industrial East Asia: The Case for Revival," in *Fundamentalisms Observed*, ed. Martin Marty and Scott Appleby, 740–81.

23. Robert Hefner, *Civil Islam: Muslims and Democratization in Indonesia.*

24. *Encyclical Letter, Fides et Ratio, of the Supreme Pontiff John Paul II: To the Bishops of the Catholic Church on the Relation between Faith and Reason.* Programs such as *Yesodot* in contemporary Israel, which seek to teach democratic norms to the heads of state religious schools, are a case in point.

25. John Horton, "Toleration as a Virtue," in *Toleration: An Elusive Virtue*, ed. David Heyd, 18–27.

26. On this see Jeremy Waldron, "Locke: Toleration and the Rationality of Persecution," in *Justifying Toleration: Conceptual and Historical Perspectives*, ed. Susan Mendus, 61–86.

27. On Hobbes's ideas of toleration see Alan Ryan, "A More Tolerant Hobbes," in *Justifying Toleration*, ed. Susan Mendus, 37–60.

28. See Richard Tuck, "Scepticism and Toleration in the Seventeenth Century," in *Justifying Toleration*, ed. Susan Mendus, 21–36.

29. Bernard Williams, "Toleration: An Impossible Virtue?" in *Toleration: An Elusive Virtue*, ed. David Heyd, 25.

30. Ernst Troeltsch, *The Social Teachings of the Christian Churches*, vol. 1; Max Weber, *The Protestant Ethic and the Spirit of Capitalism*; Jellinek, *The Declaration of the Rights of Man*; Luis Dumont, "A Modified View of Our Origins: Christian Beginnings of Modern Individualism," *Religion* 12 (1982): 1–27; Benjamin Nelson, *The Idea of Usury: From Tribal Brotherhood to Universal Otherhood*; Hans Blumenberg, *The Copernican Revolution*; Wolfgang Schluchter, *The Rise of Western Rationalism: Max Weber's Developmental History*; J.G.A. Pocock, *The Machiavellian Moment.*

31. On these processes in general see my *Innerworldly Individualism: Charismatic Community and Its Institutionalization*; on romantic nationalism see Ernest Tuveson, *Redeemer Nation: The Idea of America's Millennial Role.* See also his study of *The Imagination as a Means of Grace: Locke and the Aesthetics of Romanticism.*

32. Richard Popkin, *The History of Scepticism from Erasmus to Spinoza.*

33. Ibid., 8–18.

34. Thomas Weld, preface to *A Short History of the Rise, Reign and Ruine of the Antinomians, Familists and Libertines*, by John Winthrop, 74.

35. Peter Berger, *The Sacred Canopy: Elements of a Sociological Theory of Religion.*

36. Dzevad Karahasan, *Sarajevo: Exodus of a City*, 9.

37. Tractate Baba Mezia 59a, b, 352–53 (Sonchino translation).

38. Judah Goldin, *Studies in Midrash and Related Literature*; Menachem Fisch, *Rational Rabbis.*

39. John Clayton, "Common Ground and Defensible Difference," in *Religion, Politics and Peace*, ed. Leroy Rouner, 104–27.

# BIBLIOGRAPHY

Abercrombie, Nigel. *The Origins of Jansenism in France.* Oxford: Oxford University Press, 1936.

Abrams, Philip. *Historical Sociology.* Ithaca: Cornell University Press, 1982.

Agus, Ahron. *The Binding of Isaac and Messiah: Law, Martyrdom and Deliverance in Early Rabbinic Religiosity.* Albany: State University of New York Press, 1988.

Archer, Margaret. "Morphogenesis versus Structuration: On Combining Structure and Action." *The British Journal of Sociology* 33, no. 4 (December 1982): 455–79.

Arendt, Hannah. "Collective Responsibility." In *Amor Mundi: Explorations in the Faith and Thought of Hannah Arendt,* ed. James W. Bernauer, S.J., 43–50. Dordrecht: Martinus Nijhoff, 1987.

Arnold, Matthew. *Collected Prose Works.* Vol. 6, ed. R. H. Super. Ann Arbor: University of Michigan Press, 1968.

Arrow, Kenneth. *The Limits of Organization.* New York: Norton, 1974.

Assman, Jan. *Moses the Egyptian: The Memory of Egypt in Western Monotheism.* Cambridge: Harvard University Press, 1997.

Atiya, P. S. *The Rise and Fall of the Freedom of Contract.* Oxford: Clarendon Press, 1979.

Auden, W. H. "Notes on Music and Opera." In his *The Prolific and the Devourer.* Hopewell, N.J.: Ecco Press, 1987.

Babylonian Talmud. Sonchino Edition. London: Sonchino Press, 1936.

Barber, Benjamin. *Jihad vs. McWorld.* New York: Time Books, 1995.

Barry, Brian. *Sociologists, Economists and Democracy.* London: MacMillan Co., 1970.

Bellah, Robert. "Religious Evolution." *American Sociological Review* 29 (1964): 358–74.

Bendix, Reinhold. *Nation Building and Citizenship: Studies of Our Changing Social Order.* Garden City: Anchor Books, 1969.

———. *Kings or People: Power and the Mandate to Rule.* Berkeley: University of California Press, 1978.

Benton, John F. "Consciousness of Self and Perceptions of Individuality." In *Renaissance and Renewal in the Twelfth Century,* ed. R. Benson and G. Constable. Cambridge: Harvard University Press, 1982.

Berger, Peter. *The Sacred Canopy: Elements of a Sociological Theory of Religion.* New York: Anchor Books, 1969.

———. "On the Obsolescence of the Concept of Honor." In *Revision: Changing Perspectives in Moral Philosophy,* ed. Stanley Hauerwas and Alasdair MacIntyre. Notre Dame: University of Notre Dame Press, 1983.

———. "Four Faces of Globalization." *National Interest* 49 (fall 1997): 23–29.

Berman, Harold. *Law and Revolution: The Formation of the Western Legal Tradition.* Cambridge: Harvard University Press, 1983.

Betz, Otto. "The Essenes." In *The Cambridge History of Judaism*. Vol. 3, *The Early Roman Empire*, ed. W. Horbury, J. Sturdy, and W. D. Davies, 444–71. Cambridge: Cambridge University Press, 1998.

Birinbaum, Norman. "The Zwinglian Reformation in Zurich." *Archive Sociologie Religion* 4 (1959): 15–30.

Blau, Peter. "Justice in Social Exchange." *Sociological Inquiry* (spring 1964): 153–206.

Blumenberg, Hans. *The Genesis of the Copernican Revolution*. Cambridge: MIT Press, 1987.

Boyarin, Daniel. *A Radical Jew: Paul and the Politics of Identity*. Berkeley: University of California Press, 1994.

Briggs, Robin. "The Catholic Puritans: Jansenists and Rigorists in France." In *Puritans and Revolutionaries: Essays in Seventeenth Century History Presented to Christopher Hill*, ed. D. Pennington and K. Thomas. Oxford: Clarendon Press, 1978.

Brown, Peter. *The Making of Late Antiquity*. Cambridge: Harvard University Press, 1978.

———. *Society and the Holy in Late Antiquity*. Berkeley: University of California Press, 1982.

Brubaker, Rogers. *Citizenship and Nationhood in France and Germany*. Cambridge: Harvard University Press, 1992.

Buchler, Adolph. *Studies in Sin and Atonement in Rabbinic Literature of the First Century*. London: Oxford University Press, 1928.

Bynum, Caroline. "Did the Twelfth Century Discover the Individual?" *Journal of Ecclesiastical History* 31 (1980): 1–17.

———. *Jesus as Mother: Studies in the Spirituality of the High Middle Ages*. Berkeley: University of California Press, 1982.

Caillois, Roger. *Man and the Sacred*. New York: Free Press, 1959.

Calvin, Jean. *Commentary on the Epistle of Paul to Corinthians*. Vol. 2. Grand Rapids: W. B. Eerdman's, 1948.

Carleton-Paget, J. "Jewish Christianity." In *The Cambridge History of Judaism*. Vol. 3, *The Early Roman Empire*, ed. W. Horbury, J. Sturdy, and W. D. Davies, 731–75. Cambridge: Cambridge University Press, 1998.

Carrithers, Michael, Steven Collins, and Steven Lukes, eds. *The Category of the Person*. Cambridge: Cambridge University Press, 1985.

Chenu, Marie-Dominique. *Nature, Man and Society in the Twelfth Century*. Chicago: University of Chicago Press, 1968.

Clark, Francis. *Eucharist Sacrifice and the Reformation*. London: Darton, Longmans and Todd, 1960.

Clark, Jon, Celia Modgil, and Sohan Modgil, eds. *Anthony Giddens: Consensus and Controversy*. London: Falmer Press, 1990.

Clayton, John. "Common Ground and Defensible Difference." In *Religion, Politics and Peace*, ed. L. Rouner, 104–27. Notre Dame: University of Notre Dame Press, 1999.

Cohen, Charles. *God's Caress: The Psychology of Puritan Religious Experience*. Oxford: Oxford University Press, 1986.

Cohen, Hermann. *The Religion of Reason out of the Sources of Judaism*. Atlanta: Scholars Press, 1995.

Coleman, James. *Foundations of Social Theory.* Cambridge: Harvard University Press, 1990.

Collinson, Patrick. *The Elizabethan Puritan Movement.* Berkeley: University of California Press, 1967.

Cotton, John. *A Treatise on the Covenant of Grace.* London, 1652. In *Salvation in New England,* ed. Phyllis Jones and Nicholas R. Jones. Austin: University of Texas Press, 1977.

Dahrendorf, Ralf. *Class and Class Conflict in Industrial Society.* Stanford: Stanford University Press, 1959.

———. "Homo Sociologicus." In his *Essays in the Theory of Society.* Stanford: Stanford University Press, 1968.

Darwall, Stephen. *The British Moralists and the Internal 'Ought', 1640–1740.* Cambridge: Cambridge University Press, 1995.

Davies, W. D. "Paul from the Jewish Point of View." In *The Cambridge History of Judaism.* Vol. 3, *The Early Roman Empire,* ed. W. Horbury, J. Sturdy, and W. D. Davies, 678–730. Cambridge: Cambridge University Press, 1998.

Derrida, Jacques. *Given Time I: Counterfeit Money.* Chicago: University of Chicago Press, 1992.

Duby, George. *The Knight, the Lady and the Priest: The Making of Modern Marriage in Medieval France.* Chicago: University of Chicago Press, 1993.

Dumont, Louis. "A Modified View of Our Origins: Christian Beginnings of Modern Individualism." *Religion* 12 (1982): 1–27.

———. *Essays on Individualism: Modern Ideology in Anthropological Perspective.* Chicago: University of Chicago Press, 1986.

Durkheim, Emile. *Professional Ethics and Civic Morals.* Westport: Greenwood Press, 1983.

———. *Suicide.* New York: Free Press, 1958.

———. *Sociology and Philosophy.* New York: Free Press, 1974.

———. "Individualism and the Intellectuals." In *Emile Durkheim on Morality and Society,* ed. Robert Bellah. Chicago: University of Chicago Press, 1973.

Eisenstadt, S. N. *Revolution and the Transformation of Societies.* New York: Free Press, 1978.

———. "The Axial Age: The Emergence of Transcendental Visions and the Rise of Clerics." *European Journal of Sociology* 23 (1982): 294–314.

———. *Power, Trust and Meaning.* Chicago: University of Chicago Press, 1995.

———. "The Construction of Collective Identities." *European Journal of Social Theory* 1/2 (1998): 229–54.

———. "Axial Age, Sectarianism and the Antinomies of Modernity." In *Order and History,* ed. Stephen McKnight and Geoffrey Price. Sheffield: Sheffield University Press, forthcoming.

———. *Fundamentalism, Sectarianism and Revolution: The Jacobean Dimension of Modernity.* Cambridge: Cambridge University Press, forthcoming.

Eisenstadt, S. N., and Bernard Giesen. "The Construction of Collective Identity." *European Journal of Sociology* 36 (1995): 72–102.

Eisenstadt, S. N., ed. *Max Weber on Charisma and Institution Building.* Chicago: University of Chicago Press, 1968.

Eisenstadt, S. N., ed. *The Origins and Diversity of the Axial Age Civilizations.* Albany: State University of New York Press, 1986.

Ellemers, J. E. "The Revolt of the Netherlands: The Part Played by Religion in the Process of Nation Building." *Social Compass* 14 (1967): 93–103.

*Encyclical Letter, Fides et Ratio, of the Supreme Pontiff John Paul II: To the Bishops of the Catholic Church on the Relation between Faith and Reason.* Washington, D.C.: U.S. Catholic Conference, 1998.

Evans-Pritchard, E. E. *Theories of Primitive Religion.* Oxford: Clarendon Press, 1965.

Ferguson, Adam. *An Essay on the History of Civil Society.* 5th ed. London: T. Cadell, 1782.

Fisch, Menachem. *Rational Rabbis.* Indianapolis: Indiana University Press, 1997.

Fix, Andrew. *Prophecy and Reason: The Dutch Collegiants in the Early Enlightenment.* Princeton: Princeton University Press, 1991.

Fox, Marvin, ed. *Modern Jewish Ethics: Theory and Practice.* Columbus: Ohio State University Press, 1975.

Frankel, Yonah. *Iyunim b'olamo haRuchani shel Sipor haAggada* (Hebrew). Tel Aviv: Kibbutz Hameuchad, 1981.

Frankfurt, Harry. "Freedom of the Will and the Concept of the Person." *The Journal of Philosophy* 68, no. 1 (January 1971): 5–20.

Fredriksen, Paula. "Paul and Augustine: Conversion Narratives, Orthodox Traditions and the Retrospective Self." *Journal of Theological Studies*, n.s., 37, pt. 1 (April 1986).

———. "The Body/Soul Dichotomy in Augustine on Paul against the Manichees and the Pelagians." *Recherches Augustiennes* 23 (1988).

Fukuyama, Francis. *Trust: Social Virtues and the Creation of Prosperity.* New York: Free Press, 1995.

Garfinkel, H. *Studies in Ethnomethodology.* Englewood Cliffs: Prentice Hall, 1967.

Gay, Peter. *The Enlightenment: An Interpretation.* Vol. 1. New York: Knopf, 1966.

Gerth, G. H., and C. W. Mills. *From Max Weber.* New York: Free Press, 1958.

Gierke, Otto. *Natural Law and the Theory of Society 500–1800.* Cambridge: Cambridge University Press, 1934.

Goffman, Erving. *The Presentation of Self in Everyday Life.* New York: Doubleday Books, 1959.

Goldin, Judah. *Studies in Midrash and Related Literature.* Philadelphia: Jewish Publication Society, 1988.

Goldstone, Jack. *Revolution and Rebellion in the Early Modern World.* Berkeley: University of California Press, 1991.

Grief, Avner. "Reputations and Coalitions in Medieval Trade: Evidence of the Maghribi Traders." *The Journal of Economic History* 49, no. 4 (December 1989): 857–82.

———. "Historical Perspectives on the Economics of Trade: Institutions and International Trade: Lessons from the Commercial Revolution." *American Economic Review* 82, no. 1/2 (May 1992): 128–33.

———. "Contract Enforceability and Economic Institutions in Early Trade: The Maghribi Trader's Coalition." *American Economic Review* 83, no. 3 (June 1993): 525–48.

————. "On the Political Foundations of the Late Medieval Commercial Revolution: Genoa During the Twelfth and Thirteenth Centuries." *The Journal of Economic History* 54, no. 2 (June 1994): 271–87.

Groethuysen, Bernhard. *The Bourgeois: Catholicism vs. Capitalism in Eighteenth Century France.* London: Crescent Press, 1968.

Haakossen, Knud. *The Science of the Legislator: The Natural Jurisprudence of David Hume and Adam Smith.* Cambridge: Cambridge University Press, 1981.

Habermas, Jurgen, *The Structural Transformation of the Public Sphere.* Cambridge: MIT Press, 1989.

Halbertal, Moshe. *People of the Book: Canon, Meaning and Authority.* Cambridge: Harvard University Press, 1997.

Halbertal, Moshe, and Avishai Margolit. *Idolatry.* Cambridge: Harvard University Press, 1992.

Hall, David. *The Faithful Shepherd.* New York: Norton, 1972.

————, ed. *The Antinomian Controversy: A Documentary History.* Middletown: Wesleyan University Press, 1968.

Hall, John, ed. *Civil Society, Theory, History, Comparison.* Oxford: Polity Press, 1995.

Handel, Warren. "Normative Expectations and the Emergence of Meaning as Solutions to Problems: Convergence of Structural and Interactionist Perspectives." *American Journal of Sociology* 84, no. 4 (1979): 855–81.

Hart, H.L.A., and A. M. Honore. *Causation in the Law.* Oxford: Clarendon Press, 1959.

Hayek, Friedrich. *The Fatal Conceit.* Chicago: University of Chicago Press, 1989.

Hays, Sharon. "Structure and Agency and the Sticky Problem of Culture." *Sociological Theory* 12, no. 1 (March 1994): 52–72.

Hefner, Robert. *Civil Islam: Muslims and Democratization in Indonesia.* Princeton: Princeton University Press, forthcoming.

————, ed. *Market Culture: Society and Morality in the New Asian Capitalisms.* Boulder: Westview Press, 1998.

————, ed. *Civil Society and Democratic Civility.* New Brunswick, N.J.: Transaction Press, 1999.

Hegel, G.W.F. *The Philosophy of Right.* Trans. T. Knox. Oxford: Oxford University Press, 1952.

Heller, Agnes. *The Power of Shame: A Rationalist Perspective.* London: Routledge and Kegan Paul, 1985.

Heyd, David, ed. *Toleration: An Elusive Virtue.* Princeton: Princeton University Press, 1996.

Hilbert, Richard. "Towards an Improved Understanding of Role." *Theory and Society* 10, no. 2 (1981): 207–26.

Hirschman, Albert O. *Shifting Involvements: Private Interest and Public Action.* Princeton: Princeton University Press, 1982.

Holifield, E. Brooks. *The Covenant Sealed: The Development of Puritan Sacramental Theology in Old and New England 1570–1720.* New Haven: Yale University Press, 1974.

Hollis, Martin. *Reason in Action: Essays in the Philosophy of the Social Sciences.* Cambridge: Cambridge University Press, 1996.

Hopfl, Harvo. *The Christian Polity of John Calvin.* Cambridge: Cambridge University Press, 1982.

Horbury, W., J. Sturdy, and W. D. Davies, eds. *The Cambridge History of Judaism.* Vol. 3, *The Early Roman Empire.* Cambridge: Cambridge University Press, 1998.

Horton, John. "Toleration as a Virtue." In *Toleration: An Elusive Virtue,* ed. David Heyd, 18–27. Princeton: Princeton University Press, 1996.

Hume, David. *A Treatise on Human Nature.* Ed. L. A. Selby-Bigge. Oxford: Clarendon Press, 1955.

Huntington, Samuel. *Political Order in Changing Societies.* New Haven: Yale University Press, 1968.

———. *The Clash of Civilizations and the Remaking of World Order.* New York: Simon and Schuster, 1996.

Isser, Stanley. "The Samaritans and Their Sects." In *The Cambridge History of Judaism.* Vol. 3, *The Early Roman Empire,* ed. W. Horbury, J. Sturdy, and W. D. Davies, 569–95. Cambridge: Cambridge University Press, 1998.

Jacob, Margaret. "Private Beliefs in Public Temples: The New Religiosity of the 18th Century." *Social Research* 59 (1991): 59–84.

Jaspers, Karl. *The Question of German Guilt.* New York: Dial Press, 1947.

———. *The Origin and Goal of History.* New Haven: Yale University Press, 1953.

Jellinek, Georg. *The Declaration of the Rights of Man and of Citizens: A Contribution to Modern Constitutional History.* Westport: Hyperion Press, 1979.

Jones, Phyllis, and Nicholas R. Jones, eds. *Salvation in New England: Selections from the Sermons of the First Preachers.* Austin: University of Texas Press, 1977.

Jonsen, Albert and Stephen Toulmin. *The Abuse of Casuistry: A History of Moral Reasoning.* Berkeley: University of California Press, 1988.

Kant, Immanuel. *The Metaphysics of Morals.* Trans. Mary Gregor. Cambridge: Cambridge University Press, 1991.

Kantarowitz, Ernst. *The King's Two Bodies.* Princeton: Princeton University Press, 1957.

Karahasan, Dzevad. *Sarajevo: Exodus of a City.* New York: Kodansha International, 1993.

Klawans, Jonathan. "Notions of Gentile Impurity in Ancient Judaism." *American Jewish Studies Review* 20, no. 2 (1995): 285–312.

———. "Idolatry, Incest and Impurity: Moral Defilement in Ancient Judaism." *Journal for the Study of Judaism* 29, no. 4 (1998): 391–415.

Koren, Sharon. "Mystical Rationales for the Laws of Niddah." In *Woman and Water: Menstruation in Jewish Life and Law,* ed. R. Wassefall, 101–21. Hanover: University of New England Press, 1999.

Landa, Janet Tai. *Trust, Ethnicity and Identity: Beyond the New Institutional Economics of Ethnic Trading, Networks, Contract Law and Gift Exchange.* Ann Arbor: University of Michigan Press, 1994.

Lasch, Christopher. *The Culture of Narcissism: American Life in an Age of Diminishing Expectations.* New York: Norton Press, 1979.

Levinas, Emmanuel. *Totality and Infinity.* Pittsburgh: Duquesne University Press, 1969.

———. *Otherwise than Being.* Boston: M. Nijhoff, 1981.

Levy, David. "Israel and Judah: Politics and Religion in Two Hebrew Kingdoms." In his *The Measure of Man: Incursions in Philosophical and Political Anthropology.* Columbia: University of Missouri Press, 1993.

———. " 'The Good Religion': Reflections on the History and Fate of Zoroastrianism," In his *The Measure of Man: Incursions in Philosophical and Political Anthropology.* Columbia: University of Missouri Press, 1993.

Lewis, C. S. *The Lion, the Witch and the Wardrobe.* New York: Harper and Row, 1983.

Lichbach, Mark. *The Rebel's Dilemma.* Ann Arbor: University of Michigan Press, 1995.

Lichtenstein, Ahron. "Does Jewish Tradition Recognize an Ethic Independent of Halakha?" In *Modern Jewish Ethics: Theory and Practice,* ed. Marvin Fox, 62–87. Columbus: Ohio State University Press, 1975.

Lieberman, Shaul. *Hellenism in Jewish Palestine.* New York: Jewish Theological Seminary, 1962.

Lipset, Martin. *The First New Nation: The United States in Historical and Comparative Perspective.* New York: Basic Books, 1963.

Little, David. "Max Weber Revisited: The Protestant Ethic and the Puritan Experience of Order." *Harvard Theological Review* 59 (1966): 415–28.

———. *Religion, Order and Law: A Study of Pre-Revolutionary England.* New York: Harper and Row, 1969.

Locke, John. *Two Treatises on Government.* Part Two. Ed. Peter Laslett. Cambridge: Cambridge University Press, 1960.

Lottin, Odon D. *Psychologie et morale aux XIIe et XIIIe siècles.* Louvain: Abbaye du Mont César, 1948.

Lucas, Paul. *Valley of Discord: Church and Society along the Connecticut River, 1636–1725.* Middletown: Wesleyan University Press, 1968.

Lukács, George. *History and Class Consciousness.* Cambridge: MIT Press, 1971.

Lukes, Steven. *Emile Durkheim: His Life and Works.* Stanford: Stanford University Press, 1985.

Luther, Martin. *A Commentary on Saint Paul's Epistle to the Galatians.* London: Blake, 1833.

Maine, Henry. *Ancient Law.* New York: Henry Holt, 1887.

Mandeville, Bernard. *Fable of the Bees, or Private Vices, Public Benefits.* Vol. 2. Indianapolis: Liberty Classics, 1988.

Marshall, T. H. *Class, Citizenship and Social Development.* Westport, Conn.: Greenwood Press, 1973.

Martin, David. *Tongues of Fire.* Oxford: Basil Blackwell, 1990.

———. *Does Christianity Cause War?* Oxford: Oxford University Press, 1997.

Marx, Karl. *Grundrisse: Foundations for the Critique of Political Economy.* Harmondsworth: Penguin Press, 1975.

———. *The German Ideology.* New York: International Press, 1975.

Mauss, Marcel. "A Category of the Human Mind: The Notion of the Person, the Notion of the Self." In *The Category of the Person,* ed. Michael Carrithers, Steven Collins, and Steven Lukes. Cambridge: Cambridge University Press, 1985.

May, Larry. *Sharing Responsibility.* Chicago: University of Chicago Press, 1992.

May, Larry, and Stacey Hoffman, eds. *Collective Responsibility: Five Decades of Debate in Theoretical and Applied Ethics.* London: Rowman and Littlefield, 1991.

McNeill, John. "Natural Law and the Teachings of the Reformers." *Journal of Religion* 26 (1946): 168–82.

Meldon, A. I. *Rights and Persons.* Berkeley: University of California Press, 1980.

Mendus, Susan, ed. *Justifying Toleration: Conceptual and Historical Perspectives.* Cambridge: Cambridge University Press, 1988.

Merton, Robert. *Social Theory and Social Structure.* New York: Free Press, 1949.

Milbank, John. *Theology and Social Theory.* Oxford: Basil Blackwell, 1990.

Miller, Perry. *The New England Mind.* 2 vols. Cambridge: Belknap Press, 1953.

———. *Errand into the Wilderness.* Cambridge: Belknap Press, 1956.

———. *Orthodoxy in Massachusetts.* Boston: Beacon Press, 1959.

Momigliano, Arnaldo. "The Disadvantages of Monotheism for a Universal State." In his *On Pagans, Jews and Christians.* Hanover: Wesleyan University Press, 1987.

———. "Some Preliminary Remarks on the 'Religious Opposition' to the Roman Empire." In his *On Pagans, Jews and Christians.* Hanover: Wesleyan University Press, 1987.

Montaigne, Michel. *The Essays of Michel de Montaigne.* Trans. George Ives. New York: Limited Editions Club, 1946.

Moore, Barrington, Jr. *Social Origins of Dictatorship and Democracy: Lord and Peasant in the Making of the Modern World.* Boston: Beacon Press, 1971.

Moore, Sally, and Barbara Myerhoff, eds. *Secular Rituals.* Assen: Van Gorcum, 1977.

Morris, Colin. *The Discovery of the Individual, 1050–1200.* London: S.P.C.K. for the Church Historical Society, 1972.

Morris, Herbert. *On Guilt and Innocence: Essays in Legal Philosophy and Moral Psychology.* Berkeley: University of California Press, 1976.

Mullett, Michael. *Radical Religious Movements in Early Modern Europe.* London: George Allen and Unwin, 1980.

Nagel, Thomas. "Moral Luck." In his *Mortal Questions.* Cambridge: Cambridge University Press, 1979.

Nelson, Benjamin. "Self Images and the System of Spiritual Direction in the History of European Civilization." In *The Quest for Self Control: Classical Philosophies and Scientific Research,* ed. S. Klausner. New York: Free Press, 1965.

———. "Conscience and the Making of Early Modern Culture: The Protestant Ethic beyond Max Weber." *Social Research* 36 (1969): 16–17.

———. *The Idea of Usury: From Tribal Brotherhood to Universal Otherhood.* Chicago: University of Chicago Press, 1969.

———. "Self Images and Spiritual Directions in the History of European Civilization." In *On the Roads to Modernity: Conscience, Science and Civilizations,* ed. Toby Huff. Totowa, N.J.: Rowman and Littlefield, 1981.

Neusner, Jacob. *The Idea of Purity in Ancient Judaism.* Leiden: Brill, 1973.

Newman, Louis. *Past Imperatives: Studies in the History and Theory of Jewish Ethics.* Albany: State University of New York Press, 1998.

Nussbaum, Martha. *The Fragility of Goodness.* Cambridge: Cambridge University Press, 1986.

O'Dea, Thomas. "Sociological Dilemmas: Five Paradoxes of Institutionalization." In *Sociological Theory, Values and Sociocultural Change,* ed. Edward Tiryakian. New York: Harper and Row, 1963.

Olson, Mancur, Jr. *The Logic of Collective Action: Public Goods and the Theory of Groups.* Cambridge: Harvard University Press, 1971.

Otto, Rudolf. *The Idea of the Holy.* Oxford: Oxford University Press, 1950.

Ozment, Steven. *The Reformation in the Cities.* New Haven: Yale University Press, 1975.

Parsons, Talcott. "Christianity and Modern Industrial Society." In *Sociological Theory, Values and Sociocultural Change,* ed. Edward Tiryakian. New York: Harper and Row, 1967.

———. *The Structure of Social Action.* Vol. 1. New York: Free Press, 1968.

———. "Durkheim on Religion Revisited." In his *Action Theory and the Human Condition.* New York: Free Press, 1978.

Patrides, C. A. *The Cambridge Platonists.* London: Edward Arnold, 1969.

Perry, Michael. *The Idea of Human Rights.* Chicago: University of Chicago Press, 1999.

Pitkin, Hannah. *The Attack of the Blob: Hannah Arendt's Concept of the Social.* Chicago: University of Chicago Press, 1998.

Pocock, J.G.A. *The Machiavellian Moment.* Princeton: Princeton University Press, 1975.

Pollock, Frederick, and Frederic Maitland. *History of English Law before the Time of Edward I.* Vol. 2. Cambridge: Cambridge University Press, 1923.

Popkin, Richard. *The History of Scepticism from Erasmus to Spinoza.* Berkeley: University of California Press, 1979.

Putnam, Robert. *Making Democracy Work: Civic Traditions in Modern Italy.* Princeton: Princeton University Press, 1993.

Rescher, Nicholas. *Complexity: A Philosophical Overview.* New Brunswick, N.J.: Transaction Press, 1988.

Ricoeur, Paul. *The Symbolism of Evil.* Boston: Beacon Press, 1967.

Rieff, Philip. *The Feeling Intellect: Selected Writings.* Chicago: University of Chicago Press, 1990.

Riesman, David. *The Lonely Crowd: A Study of the Changing American Character.* New Haven: Yale University Press, 1950.

———. *Individualism Reconsidered.* Glencoe: Free Press, 1954.

Rivkin, Ellis. *A Hidden Revolution: The Pharisees' Search for the Kingdom Within.* Nashville: Abingdon Press, 1978.

Rosenzweig, Franz. *The Star of Redemption.* New York: Holt, Reinhart and Winston, 1971.

Roth, Guenther, and Wolfgang Schluchter, eds. *Max Weber's Vision of History: Ethics and Methods.* Berkeley: University of California Press, 1979.

Rudolph, Kurt. "The Baptist Sects." In *The Cambridge History of Judaism.* Vol. 3, *The Early Roman Empire,* ed. W. Horbury, J. Sturdy, and W. D. Davies, 571–600. Cambridge: Cambridge University Press, 1998.

Ryan, Alan. "A More Tolerant Hobbes." In *Justifying Toleration: Conceptual and Historical Perspectives,* ed. Susan Mendus, 37–60. Cambridge: Cambridge University Press, 1988.

Sahlins, Marshall. *Culture and Practical Reason.* Chicago: University of Chicago Press, 1979.

Sandel, Michael. *Liberalism and the Limits of Justice.* Cambridge: Cambridge University Press, 1982.

Sanders, E. P. *Paul, the Law and the Jewish People.* Minneapolis: Fortress Press, 1971.

———. *Jewish Law from Jesus to the Mishnah.* London: SCM Press, 1990.

Schama, Simon. *Citizens: A Chronicle of the French Revolution.* New York: Vintage Books, 1989.

Schaper, Joachim. "The Pharisees." In *The Cambridge History of Judaism.* Vol. 3, *The Early Roman Empire,* ed. W. Horbury, J. Sturdy, and W. D. Davies, 402–27. Cambridge: Cambridge University Press, 1998.

Schluchter, Wolfgang. "The Paradox of Rationalization: On the Relations of Ethics and the World." In *Max Weber's Vision of History: Ethics and Method,* ed. Guenther Roth and Wolfgang Schluchter. Berkeley: University of California Press, 1979.

———. *The Rise of Western Rationalism: Max Weber's Developmental History.* Berkeley: University of California Press, 1981.

Schmalenbach, Herman. "The Sociological Category of Communion." In *Theories of Society,* ed. T. Parsons, E. Shils, K. Naegele, and J. Pitts. New York: Free Press, 1961.

Segal, Paul. *Paul the Convert.* New Haven: Yale University Press, 1990.

Seligman, Adam B. "Innerworldly Individualism and the Institutionalization of Puritanism in Late 17th Century New England." *British Journal of Sociology* 41, no. 4 (December 1990): 537–58.

———. *Innerworldly Individualism: Charismatic Community and Its Institutionalization.* New Brunswick, N.J.: Transaction Press. 1994.

———. "Animadversions upon Civil Society and Civic Virtue in the Last Decade of the Twentieth Century." In *Civil Society, Theory, History, Comparison,* ed. J. Hall. Oxford: Polity Press, 1995.

———. *The Problem of Trust.* Princeton: Princeton University Press, 1997.

Sewell, William, Jr. "A Theory of Structure: Duality, Agency and Transformation." *American Journal of Sociology* 98, no. 1 (July 1992): 1–29.

Shepard, Thomas. *God's Plot: The Paradoxes of Puritan Piety, Being the Autobiography and Journal of Thomas Shepard.* Ed. M. McGiffert. Amherst: University of Massachusetts Press, 1972.

Shils, Edward. *Center and Periphery: Essays in MacroSociology.* Chicago: University of Chicago Press, 1975.

Siep, Ludwig. "Person and Law in Kant and Hegel." In *The Public Realm,* ed. R. Shurmann, 82–104. Albany: State University of New York Press, 1989.

Skinner, Quentin. *The Foundations of Modern Political Thought.* Vol. 1. Cambridge: Cambridge University Press, 1978.

Skocpol, Theda. *States and Social Revolutions: A Comparative Analysis of France, Russia and China.* Cambridge: Cambridge University Press, 1979.

Smith, Adam. *The Theory of Moral Sentiments.* Indianapolis: Liberty Classics, 1982.

Smith, Jonathan Z. *Imagining Religion.* Chicago: University of Chicago Press, 1982.

Smith, Morton. "The Troublemakers." In *The Cambridge History of Judaism.* Vol. 3, *The Early Roman Empire,* ed. W. Horbury, J. Sturdy, and W. D. Davies, 501–68. Cambridge: Cambridge University Press, 1998.

Southern, R. W. *The Making of the Middle Ages.* London: Hutchinson, 1953.

Stemberger, Gunter. "The Sadducees." In *The Cambridge History of Judaism.* Vol. 3, *The Early Roman Empire,* ed. W. Horbury, J. Sturdy, and W. D. Davies, 428–43. Cambridge: Cambridge University Press, 1998.

Stendhal, Krister. *Paul among Jews and Gentiles.* Minneapolis: Fortress Press, 1971.

Stinchcombe, Arthur. "Merton's Theory of Social Structure." In *The Idea of Social Structure,* ed. Lewis Coser, 11–33. New York: Harcourt Brace, 1975.

Stoever, William. *A Faire and Easie Way to Heaven: Covenant Theology and Antinomianism in Early Massachusetts.* Middletown: Wesleyan University Press, 1978.

Strauss, Leo. *Spinoza's Critique of Religion.* Chicago: University of Chicago Press, 1997.

Swartz, Benjamin. *Wisdom, Revelation and Doubt: Perspectives on the First Millennium. Daedalus* (spring 1975).

Sztompka, Piotr, ed. *Agency and Structure: Regrounding Social Theory.* Langhorne, Pa.: Gordon Breach, 1994.

Tawney, R. H. *The Acquisitive Society.* New York: Harcourt, Brace and World, 1920.

———. *Religion and the Rise of Capitalism.* Gloucester: Peter Smith, 1962.

———. *R. H. Tawney's Commonplace Book.* Ed. J. Winter and D. Josline. Cambridge: Cambridge University Press, 1972.

Taylor, Charles. *Human Agency and Language: Philosophical Papers.* Vol. 1. Cambridge: Cambridge University Press, 1985.

———. *Sources of the Self.* Cambridge: Harvard University Press, 1989.

Tilly, Charles. *From Mobilization to Revolutions.* Reading: Addison-Wesley, 1978.

———. *European Revolutions 1492–1992.* Oxford: Basil Blackwell, 1993.

Tiryakian, Edward, ed. *Sociological Theory, Values and Sociocultural Change.* New York: Harper and Row, 1967.

Tocqueville, Alexis de. *Democracy in America.* Ed. J. P. Mayer and Max Lerner. New York: Harper and Row, 1966.

Toulmin, Stephen. *Cosmopolis: The Hidden Agenda of Modernity.* Chicago: University of Chicago Press, 1990.

Trilling, Lionel. *Sincerity and Authenticity.* Cambridge: Harvard University Press, 1972.

Troeltsch, Ernst. *The Social Teachings of the Christian Churches.* Vol. 1. New York: Harper and Row, 1960. Vol. 2. Chicago: University of Chicago Press, 1975.

Tuck, Richard. *Natural Rights Theories: Their Origin and Development.* Cambridge: Cambridge University Press, 1979.

———. "Scepticism and Toleration in the Seventeenth Century." In *Justifying Toleration: Conceptual and Historical Perspectives,* ed. Susan Mendus, 21–36. Cambridge: Cambridge University Press, 1988.

Turner, Ralph. "Role Taking: Process Versus Conformity." In *Human Behavior and Social Processes,* ed. A. Rose. Boston: Houghton Mifflin, 1962.

———. "The Role and the Person." *American Journal of Sociology* 84, no. 1 (1978): 1–23.

Turner, Victor. *The Ritual Process.* Chicago: Aldine Press, 1969.

Tuveson, Ernest. *The Imagination as a Means of Grace: Locke and the Aesthetics of Romanticism.* Berkeley: University of California Press, 1960.

Tuveson, Ernest. *Redeemer Nation: The Idea of America's Millennial Role.* Chicago: University of Chicago Press, 1968.

Ullmann, Walter. *The Individual and Society in the Middle Ages.* Baltimore: John Hopkins University Press, 1966.

Van der Leeuw, G. "Primordial Time and Final Time." In *Man and Time: Papers from the Eranos Yearbook.* Princeton: Princeton University Press, 1973.

Veblen, Thorstein. *The Theory of the Leisure Class.* New York: Viking Books, 1967.

Voeglin, Eric. *The New Science of Politics.* Chicago: University of Chicago Press, 1952.

———. *Order and History.* Vols. 1–4. Baton Rouge: Louisiana State University Press, 1956.

Waldron, Jeremy. "Locke: Toleration and the Rationality of Persecution." In *Justifying Toleration: Conceptual and Historical Perspectives,* ed. Susan Mendus, 61–86. Cambridge: Cambridge University Press, 1988.

Waltzer, Michael. *The Revolution of Saints.* Cambridge: Harvard University Press, 1965.

Weber, Max. "Politics as a Vocation." In *From Max Weber: Essays on Sociology,* ed. G. H. Gerth and C. W. Mills. New York: Free Press. 1958.

———. *The Protestant Ethic and the Spirit of Capitalism.* New York: Scribner and Sons, 1958.

———. "The Social Psychology of World Religions." In *From Max Weber: Essays in Sociology,* ed. G. H. Gerth and C. W. Mills. New York: Free Press, 1958.

———. *Economy and Society.* Ed. Guenther Roth and Claus Wittich. Berkeley: University of California Press, 1978.

Wei Ming, Tu. "The Search for Roots in Industrial East Asia: The Case for Revival." In *Fundamentalisms Observed,* ed. Martin Marty and Scott Appleby, 740–81. Chicago: University of Chicago Press, 1991.

Weld, Thomas. Preface to *A Short History of the Rise, Reign and Ruine of the Antinomians, Familists and Libertines,* by John Winthrop. London, 1644. In *The Antinomian Controversy 1636–1638: A Documentary History,* ed. David Hall. Middletown, Conn.: Wesleyan University Press, 1968.

Wellemer, Albrecht. "Models of Freedom in the Modern World." In *Hermeneutics and Critical Theory in Ethics and Politics,* ed. M. Kelly, 227–52. Cambridge: MIT Press, 1990.

Weller, Robert. "Divided Market Culture in China." In *Market Culture: Society and Morality in the New Asian Capitalisms,* ed. R. Hefner, 78–103. Boulder: Westview Press, 1998.

Whichcote, Benjamin. "The Uses of Reason in Matters of Religion." In *The Cambridge Platonists,* ed. C. A. Patrides. Cambridge: Cambridge University Press, 1969.

Williams, Bernard. "Moral Luck." *Proceedings of the Aristotelian Society.* Supplementary vol. L (1976): 115–35.

———. *Ethics and the Limits of Philosophy.* Cambridge: Harvard University Press, 1985.

———. *Shame and Necessity.* Berkeley: University of California Press, 1993.

———. "Toleration: An Impossible Virtue?" In *Toleration: An Elusive Virtue,* ed. David Heyd. Princeton: Princeton University Press, 1996.

Williams, George. *The Radical Reformation*. Philadelphia: Westminster Press, 1962.

Williams, Patricia. *The Alchemy of Race and Rights*. Cambridge: Harvard University Press, 1991.

Wolheim, Richard. *The Thread of Life*. Cambridge: Harvard University Press, 1984.

Wolin, Sheldon. "Calvin and Reformation: The Political Education of Protestantism." *American Political Science Review* 51 (1957): 425–54.

Wrong, Dennis. "The Oversocialized Conception of Man in Sociology." *American Sociological Review* 26, no. 2 (April 1961): 183–93.

———. *The Problem of Order*. New York: Free Press, 1994.

Wuthnow, Robert. "A Reasonable Role for Religion? Moral Practices, Civil Participation and Market Behavior." In *Civil Society and Democratic Civility*, ed. R. Hefner. New Brunswick, N.J.: Transaction Press, 1999.

Yuval, Israel. "haPoschim al Shtei Hasi-ifim: HaHagada shel Pesach v'haPascha haNotzrit" (Hebrew). *Tarbitz* 55, no. 1 (1996): 1–28.

Ziff, Lazer. "The Literary Consequences of Puritanism." In *The American Puritan Imagination*, ed. S. Bercovitz. New York: Cambridge University Press, 1974.

# INDEX

Abelard, 103
Abraham, 65
Abrams, Philip, 16
action theories. *See* structure/action
  debate
*Agamemnon* (Aeschylus), 64–65
agency, human, 15, 30, 40, 78; and
  choices, 21–22; and power, 20–21, 24,
  75–76; and social role, 17, 31–32
Agus, Ahron, 65
Althusser, Luis, 19
Ames, William, 110
Amir, Yigal, 72
antinomianism, 106, 109–10, 118–19, 137
Archer, Margaret, 18
Arendt, Hannah, 49, 73, 76, 79
Arnold, Matthew, 10, 82, 86, 92
Arrow, Kenneth, 8, 44
Assman, Jan, 89
*ataraxia*, 135
Atiyah, P. S., 26–27
Auden, W. H., 58
Augustine, 12, 95, 101–2
authority: and community, 37, 38–39, 40–
  41, 47, 57; defined, 4; external nature
  of, 66, 86; legitimacy of, 24–26, 36, 125;
  in modernity, 3; moral, 35–38, 41–43;
  and power, 4–5, 125; and selfhood, 3–6,
  35–38, 54, 66, 119–23; sources of, 28–32,
  39–40, 47–52, 57–58; and transcendence, 29–33, 57–58, 125–26; and will,
  4–6, 36, 85
autonomy, 12, 72, 102, 114, 117–18, 124–
  27, 136–37; and authority, 125
Avodah Zarah, 45–46, 90. *See also* Talmud,
  Babylonian
Axial Age, 10, 29, 54–55, 64, 71–72, 89

baptism, 113
Barber, Benjamin, 7
Barry, Brian, 5
Bendix, Reinhold, 18
Benthamite understanding of society, 5–6
Berger, Peter, 36, 37, 121, 130, 138, 141
Bernard of Clairvaux, 103

Blau, Peter, 26
Bulkeley, Peter, 110
Burlamaqui, Jean Jacques, 117
Bynum, Caroline, 104, 105

Caillois, Roger, 113
Calvin, John, 12, 109, 137, 153–54n.66
Calvinism, 107
Cambridge Platonists, 116
Castellio, Sebastien, 137
casuistry, 103, 128, 140–41
causal chains, 77–79
chance. See *fortuna*
charisma, 120–22
Chavura, 95
Chrétien de Troyes, 103
Christianity, 61–62, 72; and community of
  saints, 107, 116; emergence of, 94–95;
  after the Protestant Reformation, 116–
  18. *See also* Protestantism
Clayton, John, 140
coercion, 25–26, 34, 35–36, 124
Cohen, Hermann, 88, 89, 92
Coleman, James, 44
collective identity, 10, 45; in Christianity,
  107; in Judaism, 93–94. *See also*
  community
collective responsibility, 6, 7, 14, 73–78
community, 3, 10, 30, 122–23; definitions
  of, 87–88, 98–99, 107; and moral authority, 35, 37, 38–39, 40–41, 47, 57; reason
  as basis for, 117–18; and the self, 107–8;
  and transcendence, 45, 87–89, 92
conscience, 62, 103, 105–6, 116, 118–19,
  128
conscience collective, 15, 20, 40–41, 67
contract law, 26–27
Cooley, Charles, 17
Cotton, John, 109, 110, 112

Dahrendorf, Ralf, 5, 16, 20, 31, 49
Darwall, Stephen, 114
Deuteronomy, 29
deviance, 41
Dumont, Louis, 12